Russia Business

Olga Medinskaya • Henk R. Randau •
Christian Altmann
Editors

Russia Business

Analyze the Economy, Understand the
Society, Manage Effectively

Editors
Olga Medinskaya
Cultural Connectors
Mannheim, Germany

Henk R. Randau
Weinheim, Germany

Christian Altmann
Dortmund, Germany

ISBN 978-3-030-64612-7   ISBN 978-3-030-64613-4 (eBook)
https://doi.org/10.1007/978-3-030-64613-4

© The Editor(s) (if applicable) and The Author(s), under exclusive license to Springer Nature Switzerland AG 2021
This work is subject to copyright. All rights are solely and exclusively licensed by the Publisher, whether the whole or part of the material is concerned, specifically the rights of translation, reprinting, reuse of illustrations, recitation, broadcasting, reproduction on microfilms or in any other physical way, and transmission or information storage and retrieval, electronic adaptation, computer software, or by similar or dissimilar methodology now known or hereafter developed.
The use of general descriptive names, registered names, trademarks, service marks, etc. in this publication does not imply, even in the absence of a specific statement, that such names are exempt from the relevant protective laws and regulations and therefore free for general use.
The publisher, the authors, and the editors are safe to assume that the advice and information in this book are believed to be true and accurate at the date of publication. Neither the publisher nor the authors or the editors give a warranty, expressed or implied, with respect to the material contained herein or for any errors or omissions that may have been made. The publisher remains neutral with regard to jurisdictional claims in published maps and institutional affiliations.

This Springer imprint is published by the registered company Springer Nature Switzerland AG.
The registered company address is: Gewerbestrasse 11, 6330 Cham, Switzerland

Acknowledgments

Of course, this book would never have been possible without the extraordinary help the authors received. It is hard to express the thanks and gratitude the authors have for:

- The tireless efforts of a few fantastic people who really strove to make this project a success: first and foremost Jens Salander, who helped us drive this project to completion, and Iryna Rivera Aedo, who worked on this project before it even became a book.
- The "insight" esxperts who have given our book invaluable knowledge and perspective.
- Family and friends giving us constant support and believing in us.

Finally, yet importantly, we thank Springer Publishing, especially Dr. Prashanth Mahagaonkar, who believed in the project from the start.

About the Book

30 years have passed since the Soviet Union was formally dissolved at the end of 1991. Since then, Russia's face has changed dramatically—and is yet still the same in some regards.

Politically, the union fell apart in 15 different countries. Several of the former Soviet republics have retained close links with the Russian Federation; others have drifted apart and joined NATO or the European Union. It seems as if Russia is still looking for its way in world politics and often cannot decide on who its allies or enemies are.

When looking at the economy, the picture is no different. Russia's rich commodities are both an opportunity and a burden at the same time. The country needs to wean itself off its dependence on oil, often referred to by Russians as "hanging on the oil needle." Russia also needs to develop its innovative power and high-tech commodities. Other challenges that undermine its competitiveness are the outdated infrastructure, high bureaucratic barriers, and corruption.

Russia has many assets it can rely on to succeed in this challenge: besides the rich energy resources, these are namely a low debt and high labor force participation. Unlocking this potential will require substantial structural and institutional reforms. Besides balancing the economy, it needs to fight corruption, increase its productivity and energy efficiency, foster stronger competition, modernize its infrastructure, and match human skills with the requirements of jobs in a digitalized world. It will need to cope with a declining workforce and improve its overall business climate. Finally yet critically, it will need a transition in leadership when Putin is gone.

This business environment makes it difficult for Western managers to lead effectively. Succeeding in Russia requires them to deeply understand the economic and societal development. *RUSSIA BUSINESS* is intended to assist managers in updating and deepening their knowledge in relevant business areas. The book covers **key issues on understanding Russia** from an executive's perspective. Each topic is presented in a **compact format** suitable for time-constrained business professionals and can be read independently from the remaining content.

We use a similar framework as in our previous Springer publication *China Business 2.0.* The first part of this book covers topics, which analyze the economic landscape. We then turn in the middle sections to topics that help to understand the Russian society and cover in the third section topics on how to manage effectively.

In addition, we have collected helpful, concise **"tips, opportunities and warnings"** in separate boxes and added **"suggestions for further reading"** at the end of several chapters. In order to give firsthand advice, we invited field experts to author the content for some chapters or so-called insight sections in which executives or academics share their opinions on the topic and future trends.

Contents

Part I Russia Today: Economy

1	**Russia: A Giant in Figures**	3
	Henk R. Randau	
2	**Political System and Administrative Structure**	7
	Christian Altmann and Henk R. Randau	
3	**Economic Structure**	25
	Henk R. Randau	
4	**Economic Clusters and Regional Policy**	37
	Florian Stache	
5	**Transport Infrastructure**	47
	Henk R. Randau	
6	**Competitiveness**	55
	Andreas Bitzi	
7	**Trading in Times of Sanctions and Protectionism**	61
	Alexander Hempfing	
8	**Russian Banking System**	71
	Aleksandr N. Dubianskii	
9	**The Russian Stock Market**	77
	Marina Sakovich	
10	**The Russian Ruble and Monetary System**	83
	Torsten Erdmann	
11	**Cryptocurrencies in Russia**	93
	Aleksandr N. Dubianskii	
12	**Russian Energy: Hanging on the Needle?**	95
	Christian Altmann	

13	**Import Substitution in Russia**	105
	Christian Altmann	
14	**The Russian Start-Up Ecosystem**	109
	Dmitrij Kononenko	

Part II Society

15	**Brief Overview over Russian History**	119
	Henk R. Randau	
16	**Geography**	125
	Olga Medinskaya	
17	**Population and Demography**	133
	Olga Medinskaya and Henk R. Randau	
18	**Ethnicity and Languages**	139
	Olga Medinskaya and Henk R. Randau	
19	**Migration**	147
	Olga Medinskaya and Henk R. Randau	
20	**Centralization and Urbanization**	157
	Olga Medinskaya and Henk R. Randau	
21	**Religion and Philosophy**	165
	Olga Medinskaya and Henk R. Randau	
22	**Festivals: Knowing the Roots**	171
	Olga Medinskaya and Henk R. Randau	
23	**Corruption and Fraud Risks**	181
	Henk R. Randau	
24	**Health and Healthcare**	187
	Olga Medinskaya and Henk R. Randau	
25	**Snapshot of Mass Media**	205
	Olga Medinskaya and Henk R. Randau	

Part III Doing the Business

26	**Legal Forms for Business Activity in Russia**	215
	Alex Stolarsky	
27	**The Russian Taxation System**	223
	Tanja Galander and Ekaterina Cherkasova	
28	**Tax Incentives and Tax Opportunities**	233
	Tanja Galander	

29	**Protection of Intellectual Property in Russia**	249
	Yulia Leonova and Christian Altmann	
30	**Etiquette: Do's and Don'ts**	255
	Olga Medinskaya and Henk R. Randau	
31	**Education: Quality and Quantity**	265
	Olga Medinskaya and Henk R. Randau	
32	**Working Culture and Effective Management Style**	275
	Sergey Frank	
33	**Negotiations: How to Deal in Russia**	283
	Henk R. Randau and Olga Medinskaya	

Index 285

Editors and Contributors

About the Editors

Olga Medinskaya is the founder of the training company Cultural Connectors. She is a lecturer on cross-cultural competence at several universities and a certified administrator of the Intercultural Development Inventory. Ms. Medinskaya is a Russian native, has previously worked in China and Germany, and holds a diploma degree in economics from the University Mainz, Germany.

Henk R. Randau is General Manager of the Healthcare Division within a subsidiary of US$ 10 bn. mixed industry conglomerate. In the past, he has worked in management positions in the USA and China. Dr. Randau studied business administration in Germany and the USA, received several scholarships, and coauthored business books. He holds a PhD in economics from the WHU Vallendar. Henk R. Randau and Olga Medinskaya are authors of *China Business 2.0*, a book published with Springer Publishing.

Christian Altmann is General Manager of the Investment Company "German House," St. Petersburg, Russia. He was the head of the German-Russian Chamber of Commerce in St. Petersburg and held several management positions of Lufthansa Group in Europe, the Middle East, and Asia. He studied political science at Ludwig Maximilians University Munich. Dr. Altmann is author of numerous books and publications on international political and economic subjects.

Contributors

Andreas Bitzi Quality Partners, St. Petersburg, Russia

Ekaterina Cherkasova PwC, Frankfurt, Germany

Aleksandr N. Dubianskii Saint Petersburg State University, St Petersburg, Russia

Torsten Erdmann Commerzbank, St. Petersburg, Russia

Sergey Frank Sergey Frank International, Leipzig, Germany

Tanja Galander PwC, Frankfurt, Germany

Alexander Hempfing Fraunhofer Center for Applied Research on Supply Chain Services, University of Bamberg, Bamberg, Germany

Dmitrij Kononenko Russian-German Chamber of Commerce, Moscow, Russia

Yulia Leonova Cliff Legal Service, Moscow, Russian Federation

Anna V. Pavlovskaya Moscow State University, Moscow, Russia

Marina Sakovich Grottbjorn, St. Petersburg, Russia

Florian Stache National Research University Higher School of Economics, Saint Petersburg, Russia
Freie Universität Berlin, Berlin, Germany

Alex Stolarsky Schneider Group, Moscow, Russia

Urs Unkauf Institut für Geschichtswissenschaften, Humboldt-Universität zu Berlin, Berlin, Germany

List of Abbreviations

a.k.a.	Also known as
ACCA	Association of Chartered Certified Accountants
Add.	Additional
ADZ	Advanced development zones
AHK	Auslandshandelskammer, German: Chamber of Commerce Abroad
AI	Artificial intelligence
AIDC	Acquired immunodeficiency syndrome
AO	Aktsionernoye Obshchestvo, Russian: "Joint Stock Company"
Approx.	Approximately
B.C.	Before Christ
B2B	Business-to-business
B2C	Business-to-consumer
BRICS	Brazil, Russia, India, China, and South Africa
CBR	Central Bank of the Russian Federation
CEO	Chief executive officer
CFC	Controlled foreign companies
cif	Cost, insurance, and freight
CIS	Commonwealth of Independent States
CIT	Corporate income tax
CMO	Cluster management organizations
CNPC	China National Petroleum Corporation
CPI	Consumer price index
CPRF	Communist Party of the Russian Federation
DIA	Deposit Insurance Agency
DTT	Double Tax Treaties
e.g.	exempli gratia, Latin: "for example"
E.O.	Executive order
EAEU	Eurasian Economic Union
etc.	et cetera, Latin: "and so forth"
ETF	Exchange traded funds
EXIAR	Russian Agency for Export Credit and Investment Insurance
EXW	Ex works
FASIE	Foundation for Assistance to Small Innovative Enterprises

FBK	Fond Borby s Korruptsiyey, Russian: "Anti-Corruption Foundation"
fob	Free on Board
FOMIF	Federal Obligatory Medical Insurance Fund
FTE	Full-time equivalent
FTS	Federal Tax Service of Russia
GDP	Gross domestic product
GFI	Global Financial Integrity
GNI	Gross national income
GTA	Global Trade Alert
HIV	Human immunodeficiency viruses
i.e.	id est, Latin: "that is"
ICO	Initial coin offering
ICPC	International Collegiate Programming Contest
IEA	International Energy Agency
IIDF	Internet Initiatives Development Fund
IMF	International Monetary Fund
IMOEX	Index Moscow Exchange MOEX Russia
IoT	Internet of Things
IP	Intellectual property
IPR	Intellectual property rights
IT	Information technology
JR	Just Russia (Political Party)
k, m, bn, tn	thousand, million, billion, trillion
LDPR	Liberal Democratic Party of Russia
LEB	Life expectancy at birth
LLC	Limited liability company
LNG	Liquefied natural gas
MAH	Moscow Aviation Hub
MICEX	Moscow Interbank Currency Exchange
MOEX	Moscow Exchange
Mtoe	Million tons of oil equivalent
NA	Not applicable
OECD	Organisation for Economic Co-operation and Development
OEZ	Osobye Ekonomičeskie Zony, Russian: "Special economic zones"
OOO	Obschtschestwo s Ogranitschennoi Otwetstwennostju, Russian: "Limited liability company"
OTC	Over-the-counter
P/BV	Price to book value
P/E	Price to earnings
PAO	Publichnoye Aktsionernoye Obshchestvo, Russian: "Public joint stock company"
PE	Permanent establishment
PIC	Pilot Innovative Cluster program
PIT	Personal income tax
PPP	Purchasing power parity

PSIG	Programme for the Study of International Governance
R&D	Research and development
REC	Russian Export Center
RF	Russian Federation
RF CCI	Chamber of Commerce and Industry of the Russian Federation
RNWF	Russian National Wealth Fund
RTS	Russian Trading System
RTSI	Russian Trading System Index
RVC	Russian Venture Company
RVI	Relative Volatility Index
RZD	Rossiyskie zheleznye dorogi, Russian: "Russian Railways"
SAR	Special administrative zones
SEZ	Special economic zones
SFSR	Soviet Federative Socialist Republic
SMEs	Small and medium-sized enterprises
SPIC	Special investment contract
SSR	Soviet Socialist Republics
TEP	Third Energy Package
TI	Transparency International
TPA	Third-party access
UN	United Nations
UNC	Unique numbers of contract
UR	United Russia (Political Party)
USSR	Union of Soviet Socialist Republics
VAT	Value-added tax
VC	Venture Capital
VR/AR	Virtual and Augmented Reality
VTB	Vneshtorg Bank
WHO	World Health Organization
WHT	Withholding tax
WTO	World Trade Organization

List of Figures

Fig. 2.1	The Federal structure according to the Constitution of RF	8
Fig. 2.2	Federal districts of Russian Federation	10
Fig. 2.3	Facts: Political structure	11
Fig. 2.4	Breakdown of the political system	12
Fig. 2.5	Separation of powers	13
Fig. 2.6	Factions in Duma 2020	16
Fig. 3.1	Russian GDP over time	27
Fig. 3.2	Growth of the Russian economy	28
Fig. 3.3	The dependency of the Russian economy on natural resources	29
Fig. 3.4	GDP (nominal) for regions	30
Fig. 3.5	General government gross debt	31
Fig. 3.6	Real net disposable income as a percentage of the 1991 level	32
Fig. 3.7	Income and pensions	33
Fig. 3.8	Poverty in Russia	33
Fig. 4.1	State of cluster development in comparison	39
Fig. 4.2	The Skolkovo ecosystem	40
Fig. 5.1	Breakdown of investment in transportation, 2014–2020	48
Fig. 6.1	Russia according to The Global Competitiveness Report 2019	57
Fig. 6.2	Real effective exchange rate of the Russian Ruble vs. labor productivity	58
Fig. 7.1	Indexed share in gross domestic product by selected activities	67
Fig. 10.1	Inflation and the ruble	87
Fig. 10.2	Russian per capita GDP (PPP) relative to EU average (His) and GDP share of the world (rhs), in percent	88
Fig. 12.1	Export share of Russian products	96
Fig. 12.2	Map of the major existing and proposed Russian natural gas transportation pipelines to Europe	97
Fig. 12.3	Split of EU and Russian energy consumption	98
Fig. 12.4	Growth of primary energy consumption worldwide from 2010 to 2040	101
Fig. 16.1	Geography in a nutshell	126
Fig. 16.2	Structure of the Russian mineral resource base	127
Fig. 16.3	Land used for agriculture	128

Fig. 16.4	Structure of planted crop area	129
Fig. 16.5	Wheat production and trade	129
Fig. 16.6	Traditional grain belt: production in percent of total wheat output	130
Fig. 16.7	Planted corps by farm type	131
Fig. 16.8	Livestock population	131
Fig. 17.1	Population and density	134
Fig. 17.2	Population and GDP	134
Fig. 17.3	Demographic crisis: Russian Cross	135
Fig. 17.4	Population by sex and age	137
Fig. 17.5	Russia missing men: Sex ratio	137
Fig. 18.1	Ethnic structure	140
Fig. 18.2	Language and religion diversity	142
Fig. 19.1	Waves of Russian migrations	149
Fig. 19.2	Emigration from Russia to major countries in 1983–2015	150
Fig. 19.3	Russian diaspora	151
Fig. 19.4	Total international migration: Inflow-outflow	152
Fig. 19.5	Russian emigrants of 2005–2015 by age	152
Fig. 19.6	Brain drain and muscle inflow	153
Fig. 20.1	Urbanization	159
Fig. 20.2	The number of Russian villages	160
Fig. 20.3	Dying village	161
Fig. 21.1	Upraise of religion in Russia	166
Fig. 22.1	Public holidays	172
Fig. 23.1	Corruption in major economies according to Transparency International	182
Fig. 23.2	Samples of fraud risks. Source: Based on an overview of fraud risks provided by Deloitte	185
Fig. 24.1	Health status	188
Fig. 24.2	Comparable life expectancy	188
Fig. 24.3	Change in life expectancy at birth	191
Fig. 24.4	Life expectancy at birth, male	192
Fig. 24.5	Everyone is at risk: new HIV diagnoses	193
Fig. 24.6	Estimated prevalence and incidence of HIV	195
Fig. 24.7	Cumulative number of registered HIV cases	196
Fig. 24.8	Health spending	197
Fig. 24.9	Health care: organizations and HR	198
Fig. 25.1	Internet penetration and use	208
Fig. 25.2	Active users by age of the most popular social networks	209
Fig. 28.1	Special economic zones	235
Fig. 29.1	Courts having exclusive authority to hear IP disputes or a particular kind of IP dispute	253
Fig. 31.1	Russian education system	268
Fig. 31.2	Facts on Russian education system in international comparison	273
Fig. 32.1	Retaining employees in Russia	281

List of Tables

Table 2.1	The Putin era	13
Table 3.1	Trade	34
Table 4.1	Distribution of Pilot Innovative Clusters in terms of industrial classification	42
Table 5.1	Length of transport networks, km, thousands	48
Table 5.2	Changes of Russia's position in the rating of quality of infrastructure	49
Table 7.1	Russian imports and exports with selected trading partners in bn USD (UN Comtrade, 2018)	65
Table 8.1	The largest 15 banks in Russia (as of June 1, 2018)[a]	74
Table 9.1	Equity trade at the stock exchanges (as of February 2020)	79
Table 18.1	Geographic distribution of ethnic minorities	141
Table 22.1	Professional days	176
Table 23.1	Transparency International Corruption Index: Major economies	182
Table 24.1	Russia's health in comparison	189
Table 28.1	The tax differences between business activities within and outside an SEZ	236
Table 28.2	Preferences in Special Economic Zones (SEZ)	237
Table 30.1	Titles and honorifics	257

Part I

Russia Today: Economy

Russia: A Giant in Figures

Henk R. Randau

The following data is compiled via the Pocket World in Figures 2020, published by The Economist (excluding other explicitly mentioned sources).

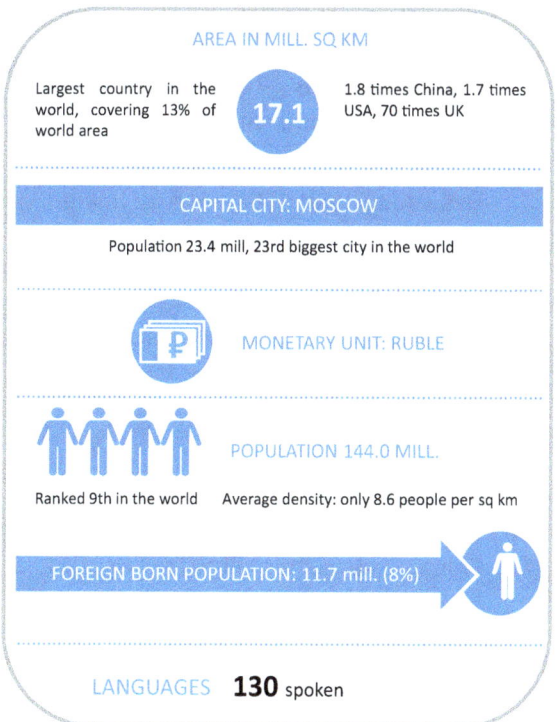

H. R. Randau (✉)
Weinheim, Germany
e-mail: hrandau@whu.edu

		World Rank
PER CAPITA	US$ 9,970 in 2020, estimate according to IMF	
NOMINAL	US$ 1.460 bn, 2020 estimate, according to IMF	11

INDUSTRIAL STRCUTURE

 **Industrial Output:** 474 bn US$, Russia's output is 9% of China's and 13% of the USA's 9

 **Agricultural Output:** 56 bn US$, Russia was the 4th biggest producer in the world of meat, the 4th of cereals, 6th of vegetables 9

 **Oil production*:** 507 mill. tons in 2020. The RF has 6.3% of proved total world oil reserves (which includes crude oil, shale oil, oil sands, natural gas liquids) 3

 **Gas production*:** 601 bn cubic meters in 2020 2

 **Coal production*:** 352 mill tons in 2020. Russia is also the 5th largest consumer of coal 6

Based on 2018 data, * Estimate, Russian Ministry of Economic Development

ENVIRONMENT

 **Emissions**:** Russia emits approx. 16% of CO2 of the world leading polluter China and is ranked 17th in CO2 emission per person 4

** Based on Moscow Times data 2019

SOCIETY

4.7 divorces per 1,000 population,

World Rank

Democracy Index
(most democratic = 10, year 2019)
USA: 8.0; China: 2.3; UK: 8.5; Germany: 8.7
Source: Economist Intelligence Unit

WEALTH DISTRIBUTION

Gini Coefficient
(the lower the value, the more equally household income is distributed)
USA: 0.45; China: 0.47; UK: 0.32; Germany: 0.27

No. of persons with net worth >US$ 1 million
USA: 18,614k (world rank no. 1),
UK: 2,460k, Germany: 2,187k
Source: Global Wealth Report 2019

INTERNET

Penetration in % of population: 76

* Percentage of the population who bought something online via any device in the past month [survey-based]. Source: Globalwebindex 2019

LITERACY RATE

99.7% of adult population 2019

EDUCATION

Enrollment as % of relevant age group: primary 102, secondary 105 tertiary 82 (world rank 15)

Political System and Administrative Structure

Christian Altmann and Henk R. Randau

Structure of State

Officially, Russia is a democratic federal republic governed by rule of law with a president acting as head of the government. The country consists of republics, territories, federal cities, autonomous regions, and autonomous areas. Legally they are equal subjects of the Russian Federation (RF) (Fig. 2.1).

Political, ideological, and ethnic plurality as well as a multi-party system are all recognized in the constitution of the RF. The constitution establishes a separation of powers, e.g., legislative, executive, and judicial branches. The RF is a secular state, e.g., no religion may be instituted as a mandatory religion. Religious associations are separated from the state and shall be equal before the law.

The state language of the RF throughout its territory has been the Russian language. However, each republic has the right to institute its own state language or languages, which can be used alongside Russian.

Although the legal framework of RF meets the superficial standards of a liberal Western democracy, many international organizations view human rights and democratic standards as not having been fully implemented. They categorize the RF as authoritarian or semi-authoritarian.[1]

---

[1]For example Freedom House: Freedom in the World 2020, https://freedomhouse.org, retrieved on October 21st, 2020.

C. Altmann (✉)
Dortmund, Germany

H. R. Randau
Weinheim, Germany

© The Author(s), under exclusive license to Springer Nature Switzerland AG 2021
O. Medinskaya et al. (eds.), *Russia Business*,
https://doi.org/10.1007/978-3-030-64613-4_2

85 Federal Subjects					
22 Republics*	46 Regions (Oblast)	1 Jewish autonomous region (Oblast)	9 Counties (Krai)	4 Autonomous Federal Districts (Okrug)	3 Cities of federal significance*

7 Federal Districts (for administrative reasons)
12 Economic Districts
5 Military Districts

*Includes Sevastopol and Republic of Krym

Fig. 2.1 The Federal structure according to the Constitution of RF

Administrative Structure

According to the Russian constitution in 2019, the country includes under the central government 85 subjects. Keeping in mind the immense geographical size of the country (17.1 mill. km^2, 144 mill. citizens) the quantity of citizens looks reasonable at first glance compared to the US (50 Federal States, 9.8 mill. km^2, 333 mill. citizens) or Germany (16 federal states, 0.357 mill. km^2, 83 mill. citizens). The structure of subjects in the RF considers historical borders, ethnic minorities, geographic borders, or political relevance of regions.[2]

The Russian Federation Consists of:

- Twenty-two Republics, which are states belonging to one or multiple ethnicities with their own constitution and legislature: Republic of Adygea, Republic of Altai, Republic of Bashkortostan, Republic of Buryatia, Republic of Dagestan, Ingush Republic, Kabardino-Balkarian Republic, Republic of Kalmykia, Karachay-Cherkessia Republic, Republic of Karelia, Republic of Komi, Republic of Mari El, Republic of Mordovia, Republic of Sakha (Yakutia), Republic of North Ossetia, Republic of Tatarstan, Republic of Tuva, Udmurt Republic, Republic of Khakassia, Chechen Republic, Chuvash Republic, the Republic of Crimea (Internationally recognized as part of Ukraine).

---

[2]Please note that most recently added subjects—Federal City of Sevastopol and Republic of Crimea—are seen as part of the Ukraine by United Nations.

- Forty-six regions that are called "oblast" in Russian and often surround big cities: Amur Region, Arkhangelsk Region, Astrakhan Region, Belgorod.
- d Region, Bryansk Region, Vladimir Region, Volgograd Region, Vologda Region, Voronezh Region, Ivanovo Region, Irkutsk Region, Kaliningrad Region, Kaluga Region, Kemerovo Region, Kirov Region, Kostroma Region, Kurgan Region, Kursk Region, Leningrad Region, Lipetsk Region, Magadan Region, Moscow Region, Murmansk Region, Nizhny Novgorod Region, Novgorod Region, Novosibirsk Region, Omsk Region, Orenburg Region, Oryol Region, Penza Region, Pskov Region, Rostov Region, Ryazan Region, Samara Region, Saratov Region, Sakhalin Region, Sverdlovsk Region, Smolensk Region, Tambov Region, Tver Region, Tomsk Region, Tula Region, Tyumen Region, Ulyanovsk Region, Chelyabinsk Region, Yaroslavl Region.
- Nine Territories or "Krai" which is a historical term and describes a "frontier region." Nowadays, it essentially means the same as oblast: Altai Territory, Kamchatka Territory, Khabarovsk Territory, Krasnodar Territory, Krasnoyarsk Territory, Perm Territory, Primorsky Territory, Zabaykalsky Territory, Stavropol Territory.
- Three federal cities which are a region of their own and have strategic importance are under federal control: Moscow, Saint-Petersburg, and Sewastopol.
- One Autonomous Region: Jewish Autonomous Region.
- Four Autonomous Areas are regions with predominant ethnic minorities: Nenets Autonomous Area, Khanty-Mansi Autonomous Area, Chukotka Autonomous Area, Yamal-Nenets Autonomous Area.

Beyond these 85 official subjects of the RF exists an informal structure of the country which breaks the country into seven federal districts. Federal districts are not provisioned by the Russian Constitution and are non-constituent units of the country, but purely exist for bureaucratic convenience of governing by federal government agencies and easy description of regions.[3] (Fig. 2.2).

> **TIPS, OPPORTUNITIES and WARNING**
> District Distinctions
>
> Besides dividing the country into federal districts for administrative reasons, the country is also divided into 5 military regions and 12 economic regions. One should be aware which region one is speaking about because it may depend on whether the context is in federal, military or economic terms.

---

[3]Recommendation for further reading: www.ribttes.com—Russian Government.

Fig. 2.2 Federal districts of Russian Federation

Political System: Main Structure

The Russian Federation was officially established on October 4, 1993, after the dismantling of the Soviet Union. For many former citizens of the Soviet Union, it is still difficult to imagine that Russia lost roughly 30% of its territory and almost 50% citizens compared to the former USSR. A new constitution was adopted after a national vote in December 1993. A democratic and federal constitutional state with a republican form of governance was formally established (Fig. 2.3).

The constitution of RF defines the fundamental rights for the Russian population, the administrative structure, foreign affairs, and the power of political institutions.

As in any federal system, power is shared between the national, and state (and local) governments. Accordingly, two levels of government (national and state) exercise a range of control over the same geographic area. It is fair to say that compared to other political systems, the RF is clearly more centrally driven as the most important political decisions are made in Moscow. The electoral system is based on a two-chamber legislature:[4]

---

[4]Constitution of Russian Federation at http://www.constitution.ru/10003000/10003000-7.htm, retrieved on October 22nd, 2020.

2 Political System and Administrative Structure

THE RUSSIAN FEDERATION

Form of State: Federal, with republican form of government. A new constitution was adopted after a national vote in Dec. 1993

Electoral System: Two-chamber legislature: State Duma (the lower house) has 450 deputies; the Federation Council (the upper house) has 178 deputies, two from each of the 89 republics and regions

THE NATIONAL GOVERNMENT

Head of State: President, elected for a six-year term. Currently, Vladimir Putin, elected in 2018

National Government: The government is appointed by the prime minister, who is appointed by the president

Main political parties: United Russia; the Communist Party of the Russian Federation (CPRF); Just Russia; and the Liberal Democratic Party of Russia (LDPR)

Fig. 2.3 Facts: Political structure

- State Duma (the lower house) has 450 deputies.[5]
- Federation Council (the upper house) has 178 deputies, 2 from each of the 85 republics and regions and 17 appointed by the president of the RF.[6]

Parliamentary elections take place every 5 years whereas presidential elections are held every 6 years (Fig. 2.4). The elections of 2016 showed following parties as the most important ones:

- *United Russia (UR)*
- *The Communist Party of the Russian Federation (CPRF)*
- *The Liberal Democratic Party of Russia (LDPR)*
- *Just Russia (JR)*

Main opposition parties as *Jabloko*, *Rodina*, or *The Greens* failed to reach the electoral threshold of 5%. In the past, most opposition parties, which were represented in the Duma, have been rather cooperative with the administration.

---

[5]State Duma at http://duma.gov.ru/duma/deputies/7/, accessed on October 22nd, 2020.

[6]Federation Council at http://council.gov.ru/structure/members/ retrieved on September 23rd, 2020.

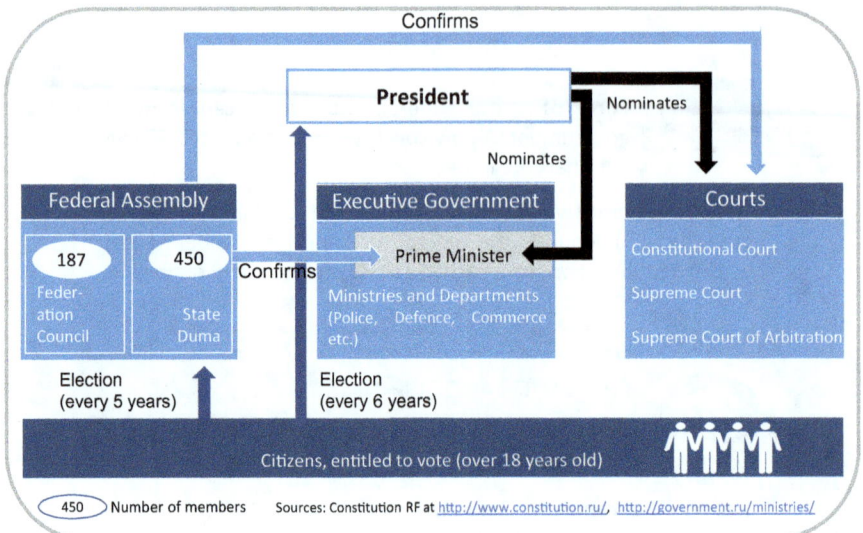

Fig. 2.4 Breakdown of the political system

Unlike opposition parties in western countries, they often supported the political initiatives of the incumbent administration.

In separate presidential elections, the president as head of state is elected for a 6-year term. Vladimir Putin was elected as the new head of state and president in September 2018. Although the president in Russia is not allowed to serve more than two terms consecutively, Putin managed to begin his fourth term as President of RF in 2018. He served as president two consecutive times from 2000 to 2004 and 2004 to 2008 before taking a break. Putin did not run as presidential candidate in March 2008 after his second term and rather became Prime Minister under President Medvedev from 2008 to 2012. However, Putin managed to be re-elected in 2012 and 2018 for a third and fourth time.[7] The new amendments to the constitution that came into force in July 2020 would allow him to run as president for another two terms and thus to stay into power until 2036 (Table 2.1).

Executive Power

Role of President in Russia

Russia's president wields strong power and determines the basic direction of Russia's domestic and foreign policy. The president also represents the RF within the country and in foreign affairs. He also appoints the Prime Minister and thereby

---

[7]Please note that the length of a presidential mandate was extended from 4 to 6 years in 2012.

2 Political System and Administrative Structure

Table 2.1 The Putin era

	Position of Mr. Putin	Means of Attaining Position
Aug. 1999–Dec. 1999	Prime Minister	Nominated by President Yeltsin
Jan. 2000–Mar. 2000	Acting President	After the resignation of President Yeltsin
Apr. 2000–Apr. 2004	President	After presidential elections
Apr. 2004–Mar. 2008	President	After presidential elections
Mar. 2008–Mar. 2012	Prime Minister	Nominated by President Medvedev
Mar. 2012–Mar. 2018	President	After presidential elections
Since Mar. 2018	President	After presidential elections

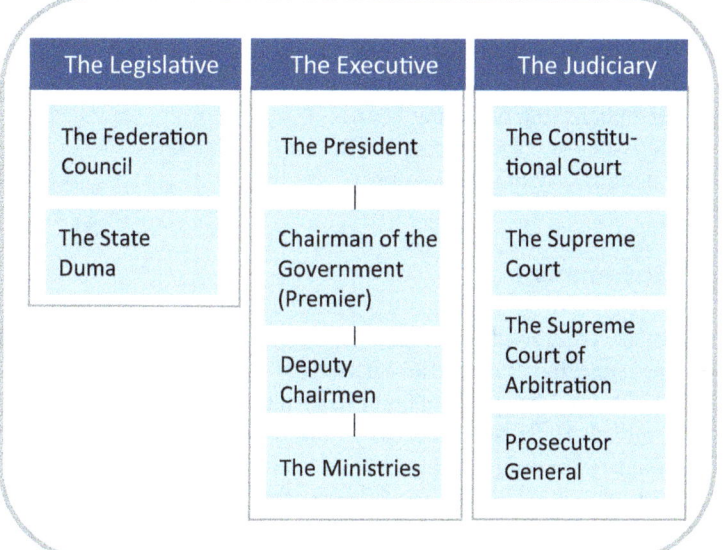

Fig. 2.5 Separation of powers

has an impact on the entire government and all ministries. The President is the head of a powerful presidential administration that initiates the majority of federal decision and guidelines (Fig. 2.5).

The President's power in practice is underlined by his power to make appointments of key officials. It is estimated that the size of the Presidential apparatus in Moscow and the localities is more than 75,000 people, most of them employees of state-owned enterprises directly under Presidential control (Schneider 2001).

The list of main powers and authorities of the President is impressive:

- "Appointment of the Chairman, Deputy Chairmen and other members of the Federal Government subject to consent of the State Duma and taking decision on their resignation.

- Submission to the Federation Council candidates for appointment to the office of judges of the Constitutional Court, the Supreme Court and the Supreme Arbitration Court of the Russian Federation as well as the candidate for Prosecutor-General of the Russian Federation, submission to the Federation Council the proposal on relieving the Prosecutor-General of the Russian Federation of his duties.
- Appointment of the judges of other federal courts.
- Appointment of and dismissal plenipotentiary representatives of the President Russian Federation.
- Formation and leadership of the Security Council of the Russian Federation.
- Endorsement of the military doctrine of the country.
- Appointment and dismissal of the Supreme Command of the Armed Forces of the Russian Federation as their Supreme Commander-in-Chief.
- Introduction of draft laws in the State Duma.
- Signing and publishing of federal laws.
- Resolution issues of citizenship of the Russian Federation.
- Granting political asylum and pardons."[8]

National Government

Executive power is exercised by the national government (Fig. 2.5). The members of the government are the Prime Minister, deputy prime minister, and the federal ministers. The Prime Minister is appointed by the President with the parliament's (Duma's) approval. He or she succeeds to the presidency if the current president dies, is incapacitated or resigns. It has its legal basis in the Constitution of the RF and the federal constitutional law "On the Government of the Russian Federation."

The government issues its acts in the way of decisions and orders. These must not contradict the constitution, constitutional laws, federal laws, and Presidential decrees, and are signed by the Prime Minister. It carries out administration in line with the constitution and laws and presidential decrees. It executes credit and monetary policies and defense, foreign policy, and state security functions, is responsible for ensuring the rule of law and respect for human and civil rights, protects property, and takes measures against crime. If the Government issues decrees and directives that are at odds with legislation or presidential decrees, the president may rescind them.

The government formulates the federal budget, submits it to the State Duma, and issues a report on its implementation. Compared to many other political systems in Europe, the Russian Federation has an extremely powerful and far-reaching executive.

---

[8]https://embrusscambodia.mid.ru/en_GB/web/cambodia-en/state-structure, retrieved July 28th, 2020.

Legislative Powers

Legislative powers in the RF are mainly with the Federal Assembly, which consists of two chambers: The Federal Council and the State Duma. They have the authority and obligation under the constitution to make laws and to alter or repeal them (Fig. 2.5).

Both chambers of the Federal Assembly possess different powers and responsibilities, with the State Duma being more powerful. Keeping in mind that Executive Powers are well organized and facilitated in the political system, the Legislative has to be very active and independent in order to balance the powerful Executive. Some analysts[9] point out that compared to western democracies, the Russian parliament and its political opposition parties seem to be politically less active and less vocal.[10]

The Federal Council of Russia

The Federation Council is the upper house composed of two representatives from every constituent entity of the Russian Federation (Fig. 2.5). It has 178 members that are called senators. The chairperson of the Federation Council has the third-highest official authorities after the President of Russia and Prime Minister of the RF.[11]

The Federation Council has lesser legislative power than the State Duma. In comparison to the Duma, it has more the character of a consultative and reviewing body than a law-making chamber. It deals primarily with issues of concern to the regional jurisdictions and has responsibilities in approving and removing all presidential appointments to the country's highest judicial bodies (Supreme Court and Constitutional Court) and the Attorney General. The Federation Council can declare elections of the president and has the final decision on an impeachment of the president. In addition, it reviews bills passed by the Duma dealing with the federal budget, taxes, and other fiscal measures, as well as issues dealing with war and peace and with international treaty ratification.[12]

---

[9]For example, Carnegie Moscow Center: Frozen Landscape: The Russian political system ahead of the 2018 presidential election, at https://carnegie.ru/2018/03/07/frozen-landscape-russian-political-system-ahead-of-2018-presidential-election-pub-75722, retrieved on May 22nd, 2020.

[10]For many years, the trust in the Duma and the political parties has been much lower than that in the president. See more by Russland Analysen Nr. 346, http://www.laender-analysen.de/russland, retrieved on May 22nd, 2019.

[11]http://council.gov.ru/en/structure/council/, retrieved October 25th, 2020.

[12]http://www.gov.ru/main/page7_en.html and http://worldheritage.org/article/WHEBN0000025704/Politics%20of%20Russia, retrieved September 25th, 2020.

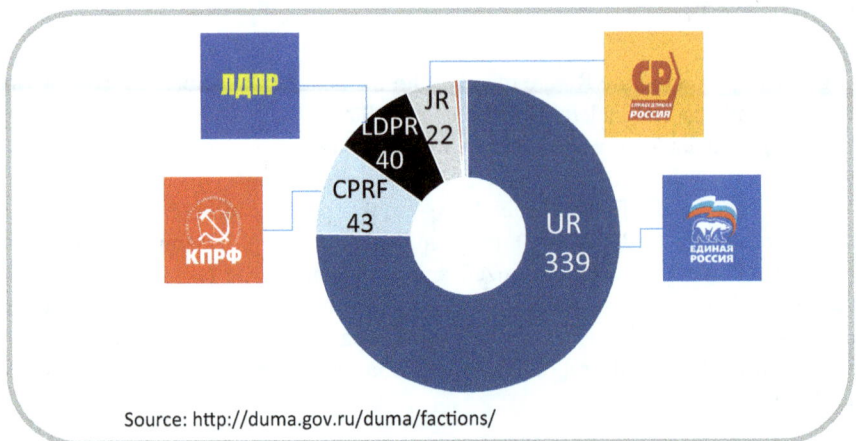

Fig. 2.6 Factions in Duma 2020

The State Duma

The lower house in the Russian Federal Assembly is the State Duma (Fig. 2.5). Its 450 members are known as deputies and work full-time on their legislative duties; they are elected by popular vote. The Duma is the more powerful house because all legislation must first pass it before being considered by the Federation Council. The Duma deputies are appointed in a hybrid system: half are elected by proportional representation according to the votes won by each party list, and half by single-member districts. The Duma is elected on a single day for a term of 5 years. In the elections of 2007, the threshold for seats by proportional representation was 7% percent, one of the highest in Europe, which made it extremely difficult for small parties to be elected to the Duma. In 2011, the electoral threshold was reduced to 5%. Like in other countries, chairmanships and memberships in committees are allocated among parties and factions in proportion to the size of their representation.[13]

Factions and Political Parties

A faction is an association of parliamentarians of the State Duma elected as part of the federal list of candidates that was admitted to the distribution of members' mandates in the State Duma (Fig. 2.6).

---

[13]https://www.britannica.com/place/Russia/Government-and-society#ref422449 and https://www.rexsresources.com/uploads/6/5/2/1/6521405/russian_political_system.pdf, retrieved on July 28th, 2020.

Political Parties

There are officially 61 political parties in Russia.[14] Only four of them are in the Duma. The main political party in the RF is called *United Russia*.[15] It was founded in April 2001 as a result of a merger between several political parties. It describes itself as centrist, but it is essentially a creation of Vladimir Putin and supports him in the Duma and the Federation Council. In the 2011 Duma election, even with the alleged voting irregularities, United Russia's share of the vote fell by 15% to just over 49%. However, in the election of 2016, the party won 54% of the votes and increased its number of seats to 339.[16]

The largest officially recognized opposition party is the *Communist Party of the Russian Federation* with 13% percent of votes and 43 seats. The other parties in the Duma are the ultra-nationalist *Liberal Democratic Party of Russia* and the opposition party *Just Russia*.

All these three political parties not in government are often called the "systemic opposition." Although they officially form the opposition, they tend to be Kremlin-loyal and thus in the eyes of most Russians not perceived as a viable alternative to the president. The *Communist Party* does not seem to be able to attract young voters and has difficulties to offer a realistic vision of the future. *Just Russia* is quite loyal to the president but follows more nationalistic and traditional values than *UR*. The *Liberal Democratic Party* is often seen as a reasonable supplement to the current system but not as a true alternative.

Judicial System

Russian judiciary consists of three branches: the Constitutional Court; courts of arbitration; courts of general jurisdiction (Fig. 2.5). The Constitutional Court and the Supreme Court represent the highest judicial bodies. The judges of these courts are nominated by the President and appointed by the Federation Council. The Constitutional Court interprets the Constitution and resolves cases of compliance with the Constitution while the Supreme Court is in charge to resolve economic disputes and civil, criminal, administrative, and other matters that are within the jurisdiction of courts established in accordance with federal constitutional law. Below the Supreme Court there are regional courts, which serve primarily as appellate courts, and district courts that are the primary criminal trial courts.[17]

Overall, the rule of law remains weak. Judges are often pressured when making decisions. Top-downs orders are given within the judiciary and/or decisions are

---

[14]Ministry of Justice at https://minjust.ru/ru/nko/gosreg/partii/spisok, retrieved on May 22nd, 2019.
[15]Party United Russia at https://er.ru/persons/3/, retrieved on May 22nd, 2020.
[16]Российская газета - Неделя № 214(7082) at https://rg.ru/2016/09/21/edinaia-rossiia-zajmet-bolee-75-mest-v-novoj-gosdume.html, retrieved on May 22nd, 2019.
[17]http://duma.gov.ru/en/news/28865/, retrieved September 29th, 2020.

influenced by the executive branch. Judges who attempt to remain independent and ignore these orders face a high risk of immediate dismissal.

Conclusion

The political system of the RF is subject to an increasing criticism from western countries and organizations. Some call the RF an authoritarian, semi-authoritarian state or even rate the country as not free because main human rights such as freedom of press or protection of minorities are perceived as violated.[18] Regularly powerful multinational organizations such as the Council of Europe or the European Parliament criticize the human rights situation in the RF.[19]

However, opinions about the evaluation of the political, social, and economic system are varying. Some institutions consider the short democratic history of the country and see the development of the RF as slightly more positive. They view Russia as a system in transition or as a fast-developing country with significant positive achievements.[20]

The Russian population is not completely unhappy with the given situation. Some evaluations show that more than 86% of the population call themselves "happy" and view family, kids' health and work as main sources of happiness.[21] Others show that the main parts of the population are not happy with the pace and direction of the political and economic development in the country.[22]

Main challenge in the future will be to build up the weak political and legal institutions in the RF. Institutions such as the Duma, the Federal Council, or the court system in the country have to be strengthened in order to play the central role, which actually gives them the constitution of the RF.

---

[18]Democracy Index compiled by Economist Intelligence Unit (EIU), http://www.eiu.com/topic/democracy-index, retrieved on October 22nd, 2020.

[19]Council of Europe at https://www.coe.int/en/web/portal/home and European Parliament at https://www.europarl.europa.eu/portal/en both retrieved on October 25th, 2020.

[20]Senior policy adviser to the President, Vladimir Surkov, went so far to call Russia's political system a model for others around the world. https://www.apnews.com, retrieved on February 11th, 2019; e-government Index of UN http://www.laender-analysen.de/russland/ retrieved on May 22nd, 2019.

[21]Russian Opinion Research Center, Счастье в России: мониторинг at https://wciom.ru/index.php?id=236&uid=9075, retrieved on May 22nd, 2019.

[22]Levada analytical center, Russian Public Opinion 2017, at https://www.levada.ru/cp/wp-content/uploads/2018/05/2017Eng.pdf and Levada Reports and Analyses in Russland Analysen, http://www.laender-analysen.de/russland/ both retrieved on May 22nd, 2019.

INSIGHT: What factors are influencing Russian politics?
Author: Urs Unkauf (B.A., License d'Histoire), Humboldt-Universität zu Berlin, Department of History, studied history and sociology with a focus on international relations at the Universities of Tübingen, Aix-en-Provence/Marseille and the Humboldt University of Berlin. Since August 2019, he is an advisor for diplomacy at the Federal Association for Economic Development and Foreign Trade (BWA)—Global Economic Network in Berlin.

Understanding the particularities and mechanisms of politics and the administrative system in Russia is important for outlining perspectives of cooperation, such as in economics and science. An appreciation of the function of these structures is only possible in the context of knowledge of their emergence. This chapter attempts to identify the main factors influencing the current political development in Russia.

1. Differences Between the Political and Administrative System in Russia Compared to Germany

In the 1990s, under Boris Yeltsin's presidency, Russia's political system gained its first political profile: experts in system comparison called it a "defective democracy." In fact, the regime included elements of democracy as well as authoritarianism and anarchy. Under the presidency of Vladimir Putin (2000–2008, 2012–2018, 2018–), Russia is often described by policy analysts as having been transformed into a strictly "controlled democracy" or "simulated democracy." What kind of influence is exercised by the stakeholders in Russia's current political landscape and which factors influence these decision-making processes? This chapter is going to provide a short, analytical overview on the political and administrative structure of the Russian Federation.

The President occupies the most powerful position in Russia's political system. Besides him, there are other positions of power: the prime minister, the national parliament (State Duma), business representatives, and regional officials. The fact that the parliamentary element of the constitutional order could not unfold in Russia was also due to the weakness of the political parties. After the first elections to the new Duma in December 1993 had resulted in the defeat of democratic forces, Yeltsin preferred to form a presidential cabinet of technocrats instead of a coalition government on a party basis. This process proved to be permanent. Even when President Putin had two-thirds constitutional majorities of the Kremlin parties, the government was still formed as a presidential cabinet. This expressed the Putin leadership's lack of confidence in the political parties it had created. They remained artificial entities with no profile of their own and no social roots. All previous Russian presidents indulged in the idea of a subordinate role for parliament in favor of a

(continued)

hegemonic presidency. Yeltsin and Putin justified this not least with the immaturity of the political parties. Putin went even further. He made the rise in national economic output a prerequisite for all democratic experiments.

As a result of the exchange between Putin and Medvedev, four governments emerged: a formal cabinet of technocrats of both economically liberal and conservatively authoritarian persuasions, a clearly conservative parallel government of hardliners in the administration, an informal cabinet of Putin's "friends" from large corporations, also geared to preserving the authoritarian system, and finally the institutional novelty of a so-called open government introduced by Medvedev. This advisory body of experts is linked to the cabinet by its own ministry led by an oligarch. Overall, the complexity of government institutions increased, while at the same time their political responsibility and social anchoring continued to dwindle.

2. Legislative and Executives Competencies on the Federative and Regional Level

The constitution adopted by referendum in December 1993 is modeled on the Fifth French Republic. It establishes a semi-presidential regime or a parliamentary-presidential mixed system. Both the parliament and the president have direct legitimacy from the electorate.

In Russia, there is a unified system of state power in which the regions are included. The constitution lists the responsibilities of the central power. The autonomy of the regions generally suffers from the lack of separation between federal and regional powers or the fact that the central state actually exercises "common powers." The tax autonomy of the regions is minimal. The federal level has about 700 areas of competence, while after the reforms under President Putin (2000–2008) only about 50 areas of competence remained with the regions. In 2004, the election of governors in the regions was abolished. The governors were appointed by the president from 2004 to 2012 until the ability to elect them was reinstated.

Most of Putin's reforms have aimed at centralizing state power once again. The reforms related to the implementation of federal law, especially through the annulment of regional legal acts and legal and technical supervision of governors and regional parliaments. The tasks of the presidential representatives in the federal districts include implementing government policy, including the president's personnel policy, coordinating federal bodies in the regions, participating in regional power bodies, enforcing presidential decrees and disciplinary reprimands. Putin also reformed the Federation Council: instead of the previously directly elected governors and presidents of the republics. The "senators" are now elected by the regional parliaments, with one representative each for the legislative and executive branches.

(continued)

There are huge discrepancies in income between the regions. In rich Moscow, one earns on average more than five times as much as in the poor Republic of Kalmykia. Unemployment is above average in many ethnic regions. The poorest regions include the republics of the North Caucasus, the republics of Kalmykia and Tuva, the Altai and Stavropol regions, and the Bryansk, Kirov, and Pskov regions. The Tyumen, Sakhalin, and Leningrad region, the cities of Moscow and Saint Petersburg and the republics of Komi, Tatarstan, and Chukotka are experiencing high-income growth. The least developed, however, are on average the ethnic republics and the southern Siberian periphery, the Far East of Russia, and the North Caucasus.

Public discourses on the need for a fundamental revision of the constitution have repeatedly emerged. This shows that awareness of the incompatibility of the formal and de facto constitutional order has grown, but has not pressured Putin enough to make any real change.

3. Decision-Making Processes and Lobbying in Russia

In Russia, the terms "lobbying" and "GR" (government relations) are typically treated as synonyms. In both cases, the words refer to people who act as intermediaries between businesses and the state, representing the interests of the former. Companies usually employ GR specialists as full-time staff. Often they also hire in addition outside lobbyists to support their work. It is sometimes assumed that Russian lobbyists work with all branches of the state, focusing their efforts on the parliament. In reality, lobbyists spend more time working with the executive branch and various federal agencies (especially the Anti-Monopoly Service and the ministries that oversee the real sector of the economy; such as the Industry and Trade Ministry and the Construction Ministry).

Finally, many businesses use informal channels between political and administrative structures, which makes it difficult to prove and trace the real influence of those structures. It is important to understand that there is an informal channel for each formal structure.

4. Conclusion: Working Principles of Political Influencing in Russia

In the conduct of President Putin's terms of office, a shift towards a preference for national interests can be observed. The structures of influence described above must not hide the fact that the position of the president is still decisive and that his political course guides the actions of the other political stakeholders.

In the wake of the Ukrainian crisis, and other geopolitical disruptions, such as the so-called Skripal affair or the activities of the world powers in Syria,

(continued)

Russia's political culture became more unified in opposition to external pressure. When considering Russia's political future, it seems necessary to assume that should Russian authorities and the aforementioned influential groups not agree on structural changes, they will not happen. Hence, unrealistic foreign strategies for rapid regime change need to be replaced with potential diplomatic solutions. While the political dynamics of the economic interests of Russia's energy sector, due to their continuing emphasis on natural gas and oil, seem to indicate unilateral policymaking, Russia's further participation in multilateral foreign policy will become apparent through the increasing implementation of Eurasian Economic Union policy and growing Russian participation in China's "One Belt One Road" project.

INSIGHT: Putin's 2020 Constitutional Amendments
Constitutional Plebiscite

The former states of the USSR have a long tradition of holding referendums and asking their citizens to support important governmental initiatives. The dissolution of the USSR and its separation into new independent states was accompanied by several referendums in Russia (1991, 1993), Ukraine (1991), Latvia (1991), Estonia (1991), or Georgia (1991) which confirmed the independence or structure of the newly established governmental system in the respective countries.

President Putin mentioned by the end of 2019 first time openly that he was considering changes to the constitution. He then proposed a draft of 14 main amendments to the state duma in January of 2020 as a preparation for a nationwide vote later in 2020.

Changes to Constitution

The amendments to the Constitution of 1993 received much international attention because they would allow President Putin to stay in power by extending his presidency by up to two more terms. The reason was that former presidencies would be nullified as soon as the amendments come into force. Other amendments ban same-sex marriages, prohibit senior officials to hold foreign passports, allow the president to fire federal judges, and contain a provision preventing Russia to surrender Russian territory. It was proposed that the new constitution should prevail over international law in case of legal disputes.

Result of Referendum

The referendum held on July 1, 2020 approved these amendments. The popular vote had a high turnout of voters (68%) from which 78% supported the amendments to the constitution and 21% voted against them. Only in the

(continued)

North-Western region of Nenezkij a majority of 55% of the population voted against the amendments. In particular, Southern regions like Chechnya, Dagestan, or Tuva heavily voted in favor of the amendments, and 68% of the Russians living abroad supported the referendum as well.

Consequences of Referendum

Shortly after the referendum on July 4, 2020, President Putin signed a presidential advice, which put the changes to the constitution into immediate power. Backed by the new constitution President Putin could stay in power, if he is re-elected, until 2036 when he turns 84. However, he did not comment on his intention to run for two more 6-year terms.

Suggestions for Further Reading

Freedom House: Nations in Transit 2018.	https://freedomhouse.org/report/nit-2018-table-country-scores
Information about Russian Government, Political System, etc.	www.ribttes.com
Eberhard Schneider: Das politische System der Russischen Föderation, 2. Auflage, 2001.	
Carnegie Moscow Center: Frozen Landscape: The Russian political system ahead of the 2018 presidential election	https://carnegie.ru/2018/03/07/frozen-landscape-russian-political-system-ahead-of-2018-presidential-election-pub-75722
Regular Reports about political and social developments in Russia	http://www.laender-analysen.de/russland/
Conceivable Surprises. Eleven Possible Turns in Russia's Foreign Policy. SWP (German Institute for International and Security Affairs) Research Paper, October 2016	https://www.swp-berlin.org/fileadmin/contents/products/research_papers/2016RP10_fhs_kle.pdf
Russia's geopolitical dilemmas. Valdai Discussion Club	http://valdaiclub.com/a/highlights/russia_s_geo_political_dilemmas/?sphrase_id=419068
Russia's invisible, ubiquitous lobbyists How armies of fixers and specialists negotiate the nation's dicey relationship between businesses and the state. Meduza	https://meduza.io/en/feature/2018/01/08/russia-s-invisible-ubiquitous-lobbyists

Reference

Schneider, E. (2001). *Das politische System der Russischen Föderation.*

Economic Structure

Henk R. Randau

There are not many countries that underwent as many deep economic changes as Russia in the twentieth century. At the beginning of the century, Russia was an agricultural and semi-feudal society. It was destroyed after the Russian Civil War (1918–1922) and saw full nationalization of certain parts of industries. As Lenin came into power he promoted his New Economic Policy (1921–1928), or "state capitalism." He saw the NEP as a necessary interim measure before socialism. He thought NEP was needed to quickly rebuild the destroyed economy. In this system, the state-controlled banks, foreign trade, and large industries of strategic importance. It also allowed some elements of free enterprise such as private individuals to own small enterprises and some foreign investment.

In its next stage of economic development (1928–1941), Russia saw Stalin abolished the NEP in favor of collectivization as he saw the need to quickly accumulate capital for his vast industrialization program. Collectivization meant that land was stripped of *kulaks* (wealthy farmers) and distributed among agricultural cooperatives (*kolhozes* and *sovhozes*). Under his leadership, the First Five Year Plan was introduced in 1928. After World War II (1939–1945), the Soviet Union continued to be an administrative command economy for many decades (1945–1991) with centralized, hierarchical decision-making until its collapse in 1991.

Since then, Russia has transitioned from a centrally planned economy to a market economy or capitalism. Over time, the wealth distribution of the economy developed a uniquely characteristic structure, in which a few billionaires controlled a large portion of the country's wealth. The hope many people had in the early 1990s that a Russia liberated from communist ideology would be enjoying a free market did not materialize. The reason is that Russia never managed to sufficiently separate political power and property. The sale of state assets in the mid 1990s saw control over

---

H. R. Randau (✉)
Weinheim, Germany
e-mail: hrandau@whu.edu

natural-resource firms and other valuable assets passed on to those who cultivated personal connections with the leaders in the government. This created a new class of powerful business tycoons, the *oligarchs* who still have privileged access to the country's most valuable assets today. Accordingly, Russia today displays huge wealth disparities. Nevertheless, new industries were born out of new practices of private ownership. These included restaurants, private banks, and mobile phone networks as well as many others. Now Russians have more freedom to earn money and travel as well as more access to information and the ability to experience different cultures.

GDP Development

In 2019, the Russian economy was the 6th largest in the world by PPP and 11th largest at market exchange rates (International Monetary Fund, 2020). The first decade after the fall of the iron curtain saw a dramatic economic contraction of the Russian economy: the nominal gross domestic product (GDP) fell to a low of USD196 bn in 1999, which represented a plunge of over 60% from USD versus 1990. The nation hit its lowest point and had to default on its debt and devaluated the Russian ruble in 1998 (also known as the "ruble crisis") (Fig. 3.1).

The following period from 1999 to 2008 saw a strong recovery and growth of the Russian economy. State finances and economic rules became stable, market reforms of the 1990s began to have an impact, and a continuous upward trend in oil prices supported the Russian economy that was and still is heavily reliant on its energy sector exports. This favorable economic environment stimulated further growth, mainly in the services and construction sectors, but also fueled imports, and the economy started to overheat.

Russia was then among the hardest-hit economies by the 2008 global financial crisis: the economy plunged 8% in 2009. Fortunately, the crisis did no long-term damage to the Russian economy, which began to grow again from 2010 to 2014. This time the recovery was driven by higher government spending that supported higher consumption. It also needs to be noted that even though the economy grew by 3% p.a., this was comparably low because revenues from oil exports were 70% higher than during the oil boom of 2004–2008 (The Economist, 2016).

In the second half of 2014 however, Russia's last crisis began, following western sanctions over the annexation of Crimea in conjunction with the decline of global oil prices. The impact of these twin shocks drove Russia's economy into a deep recession: the ruble lost about half its value, and in August 2015 hit its lowest point since the government default of 1998. Accordingly, Russia's GDP shrank in 2015 by almost 4%. Even more dramatic, the real disposable income went down by close to 10%. Investment in fixed assets declined by 37% over the past 4 years, with the steepest fall coming after Russia's attack on Ukraine in 2014 (World Bank, 2016). Russia was slowly recovering from this recession until the country was hit again in 2020 by the corona crisis and plunged again into a deep recession (Fig. 3.2).

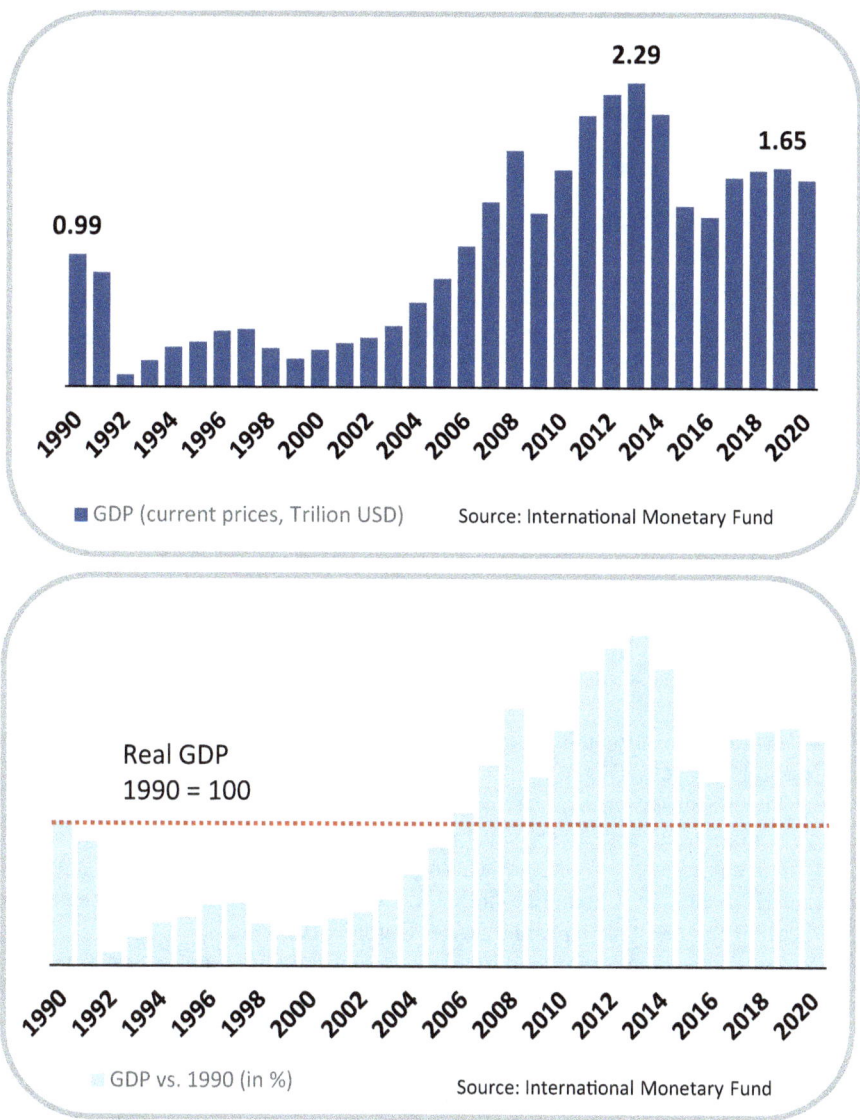

Fig. 3.1 Russian GDP over time

GDP Structure

The Russian government began to privatize many industries during the 1990s with the exceptions of the energy and defense sectors that are still state controlled. Today, the Russian Federation is currently the largest single producer of crude oil in the world. The GDP development is closely linked to the oil price. The high dependency

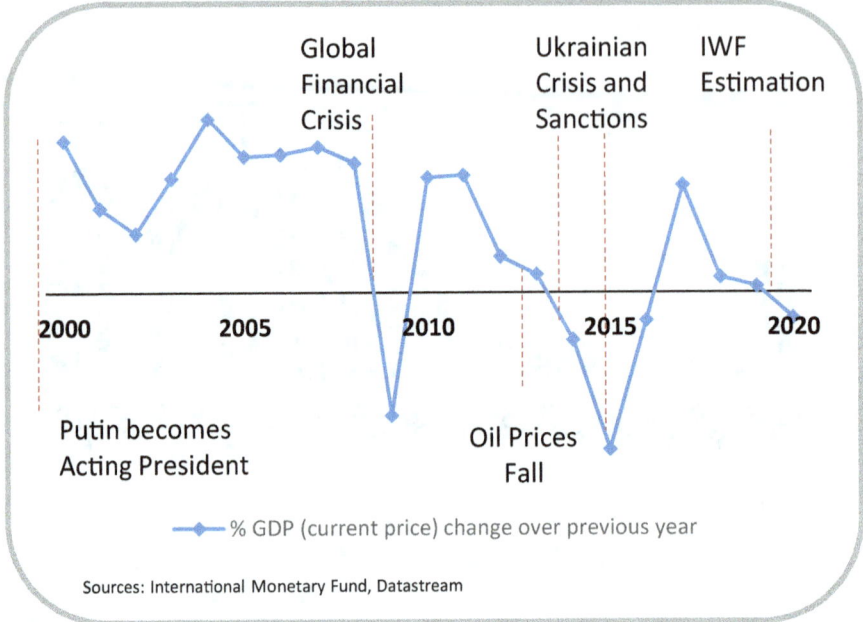

Fig. 3.2 Growth of the Russian economy

on the exploitation of natural resources makes the economy subject to commodity boom-and-bust cycles (Fig. 3.3).

Besides the strong oil and gas industry, Russia has a robust agricultural sector, which represents an important industrial pillar, generating 4.5% of the country's GDP and employing 7% of the working population[1] (section Agriculture and Animal Husbandry in Chap. 16). In 2017, it became the world's leading exporter of wheat for the first time since the Soviet Union collapsed.[2]

However, labor productivity in Russia is one of the lowest in Europe (Chap. 6). The only other industry that Russia is known for is its large and sophisticated arms industry that is capable of designing and manufacturing high-tech military equipment. The value of Russian arms exports is since 1999 second only to the USA.[3]

Another sector that is still comparably small but has further growth potential been the high-tech sector. According to a *Bloomberg Innovation Ranking 2020*, Russia is

---

[1] Russian Statistical Yearbook (www.gks.ru) retrieved on October 25th, 2020.

[2] https://www.world-grain.com/articles/13316-russia-forecast-to-remain-top-wheat-exporter, retrieved on October 27th, 2020.

[3] Borshchevskaya, A.: The Tactical Side of Russia's Arms Sales to the Middle East, The Jamestown Foundation at https://jamestown.org/program/tactical-side-russias-arms-sales-middle-east/#_edn1 and Woody, C: The US and Russia are dominating the global weapons trade, Business Insider Deutschland, at https://www.businessinsider.de/us-russia-global-arms-sales-2016-12?r=US&IR=T both retrieved on May 28th, 2019.

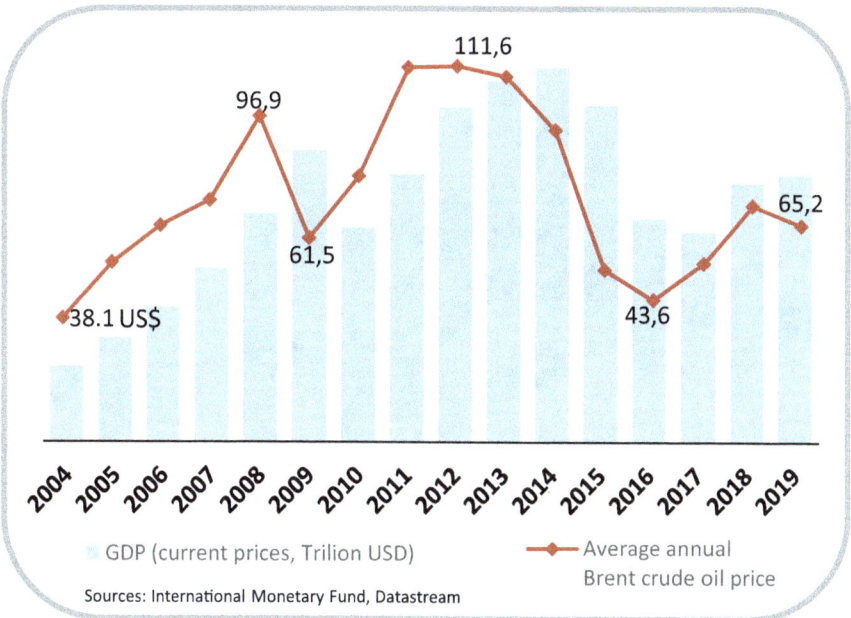

Fig. 3.3 The dependency of the Russian economy on natural resources

ranked 26th regarding the concentration of high-tech public companies, such as the internet, aerospace, or artificial intelligence. Russia has the third-best graduation rate of scientists and engineers and spending for research and development in Emerging Europe.[4]

Regional GDP Structure

Inequality in regional GDP distribution remains a key challenge for the country (Fig. 3.4). The economic development in the past has been uneven. The top 20 regions accounted for roughly 70% of GDP. These include metropolitan centers like the cities of Moscow and St. Petersburg. E.g., the Moscow region covers as little as 1.5% of the Russian territory but is home to about 10% of the Russian Federation's population and generates more than 20% of the country's GDP.[5]

---

[4]https://www.bloomberg.com, retrieved on May 28th, 2020.
[5]Rosstat (www.gks.ru) retrieved on October 25th, 2020.

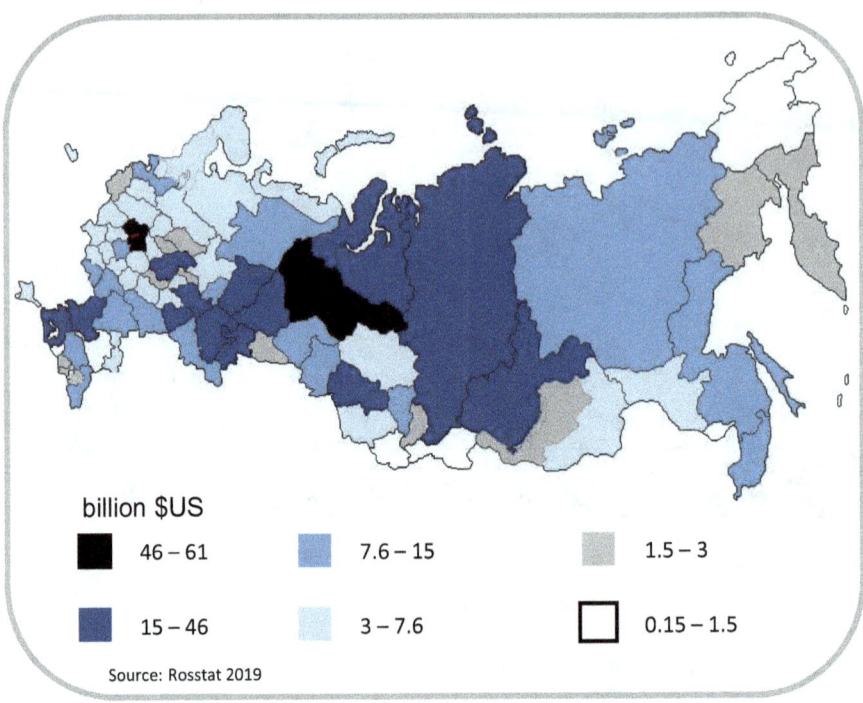

Fig. 3.4 GDP (nominal) for regions

Public Debt to GDP

Russia's central government gross debt as measured against GDP is slightly below 14% (International Monetary Fund, 2019). This is a low ratio, especially when compared to most OECD countries, which often exceed the Maastricht rules recommended maximum of 60%. The Russian government has a strong focus on maintaining a low level of debt to remain sanction-proof as more financial sanctions might be imposed on the country (Fig. 3.5). However, the public debt is projected to increase to around 20% of GDP until 2024 for investments in education, health care, and other structural reforms.[6] The outbreak of the COVID-19 pandemic has painfully shown again how urgently Russia needs to invest in infrastructure, especially the underfunded healthcare system.

---

[6]RIA news: Топливо роста. Россия готовится залезть в долги, at https://ria.ru/20180718/1524733371.html?referrer_block=index_daynews2_3 retrieved on May 28th, 2019.

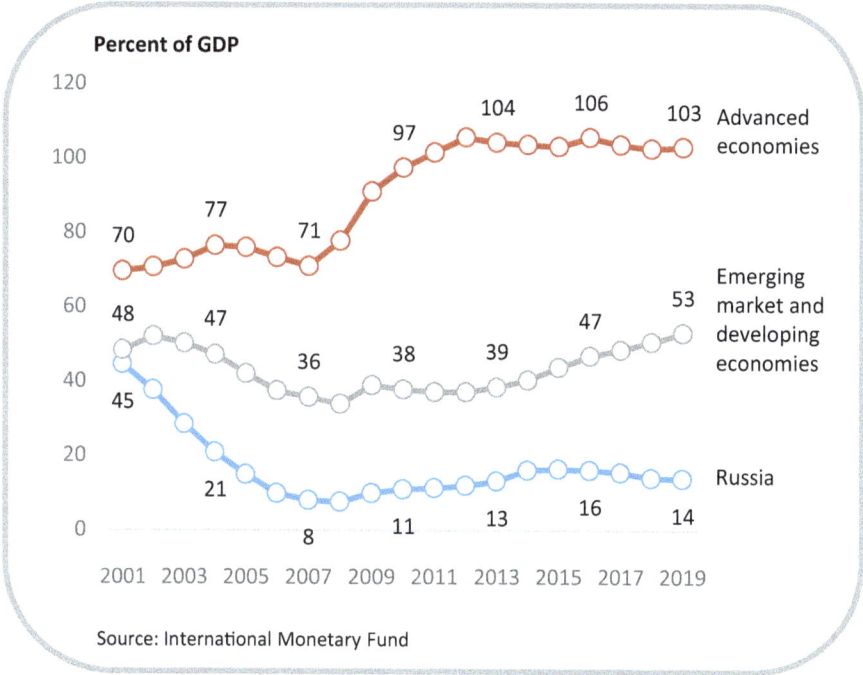

Fig. 3.5 General government gross debt

Wealth Distribution and Living Standards

The 1990s saw a rapid decline in disposable incomes (The money people have leftover after adjusting for inflation, utility payments, and essential services) in Russia. Since around 2000, living standards have rapidly improved. Today, Russia's living standards are still well below those of developed economies. The GDP per capita in 2019 was approx. USD11,335[7] while the household net adjusted disposable income was USD17.8 thousand (OECD average USD33.6 thousand)[8] but since 2008 the speed of convergence has slowed down and was even lower than in most BRIC countries. In recent years, the real disposable income has been falling and led to a slow deterioration in the quality of life for Russians (Fig. 3.6).

Russia today displays huge wealth disparities and inequality of household incomes and it is the biggest reason why Russians are unhappy with Putin. Half of the Russian workers earn salaries of less than 35,000 rubles (approx. USD550) a month, while the share of people who earn more than 1 mill. RUB (USD15,900) per

---

[7]www.imf.org, retrieved on June 29th 2020.
[8]OECD, at http://www.oecdbetterlifeindex.org/topics/income/, retrieved on June 29th, 2020.

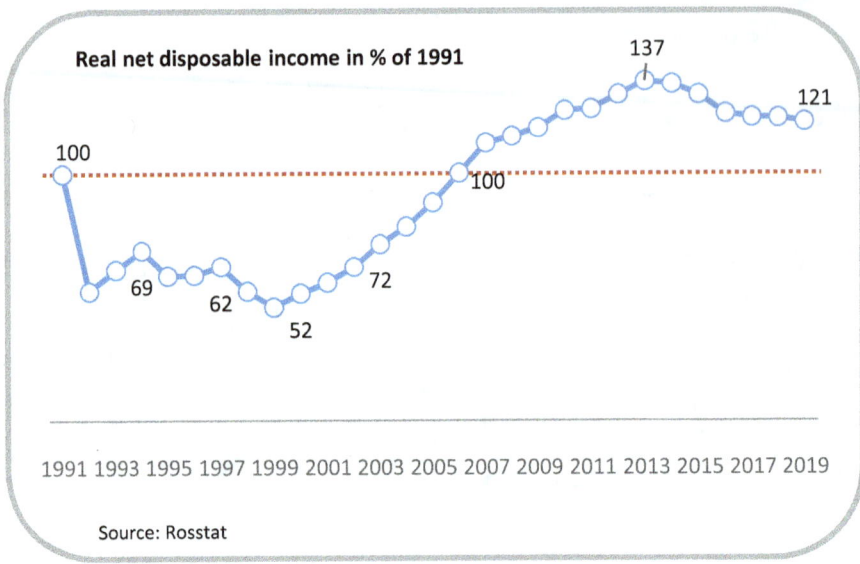

Fig. 3.6 Real net disposable income as a percentage of the 1991 level

month is as low as 0.1% of the working population[9] (Fig. 3.7). At the same time, the nation ranks globally fifth in number of billionaires in *Forbes Magazine* 2020 ranking.[10] According to *The Moscow Times*, the richest 3% of Russians hold almost 90% of the country's financial assets.[11] The Gini coefficient is high with 0.41 (Germany: 0.27; China: 0.47; USA: 0.45) and underscores this imbalance.[12]

In general, poverty has decreased significantly in past decades but the recent recession reverted the trend and lead again to an increase in poverty (Fig. 3.8). Currently approx. 13% of the population lives in extreme poverty by developed-world standards.[13] Already before the corona, crisis hit the country, the Russian government placed 36% of the population in the "consumer risk zone" with an income so low that it only allows them to buy decent food and clothes but little or even no disposable income.[14] The poverty rate was expected to decrease because of

---

[9]https://www.themoscowtimes.com/2019/07/19/half-working-russians-earn-less-than-550-usd-month-a66487, according to Rosstat data published in 2019, retrieved on October 25th, 2020.

[10]Annual assessment of wealth and assets compiled by Forbes magazine. www.forbes.com, retrieved on June 29th, 2020.

[11]The Moscow Times, April 2019, referring to a joint study by the Higher School of Economics and VEB Bank.

[12]CIA: The World Factbook, at https://www.cia.gov/library/publications/the-world-factbook/rankorder/rawdata_2172.txt retrieved on May 28th, 2020.

[13]World Bank and Russian Federal State Statistic Service, 2017.

[14]Report by the Russian Presidential Academy of the National Economy and Public Administration. www.ranepa.ru published October 2018.

3 Economic Structure

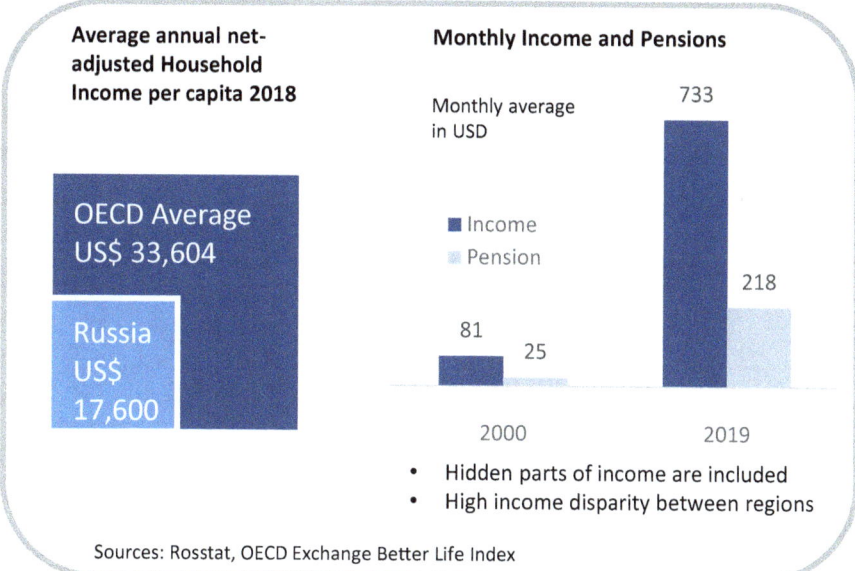

Fig. 3.7 Income and pensions

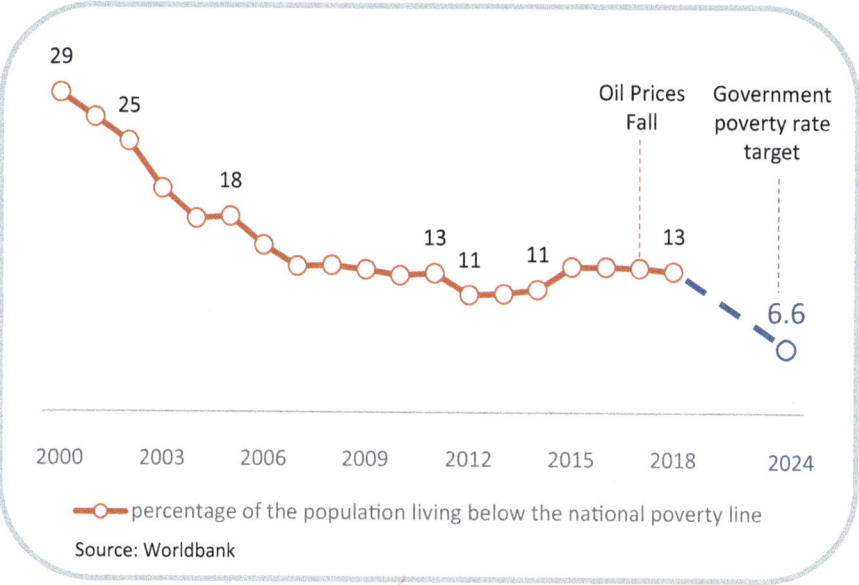

Fig. 3.8 Poverty in Russia

Table 3.1 Trade

Principal exports	bn USD fob	Principal imports	bn USD cif
Fuels	169.0	Machinery & equipment	86.3
Ores & Metals	38.0	Chemicals	33.8
Machinery & equipment	24.3	Food & Agricultural products	24.9
Chemicals	20.8	Metals	11.8
Total incl. others	285.8	Total incl. others	182.3
Main export destinations	Percent of total	Main origins of imports	Percent of total
Netherlands	10.2	China	20.9
China	9.8	Germany	10.6
Germany	7.4	United States	6.1
Belarus	4.9	Belarus	5.2
EU28	45.8	EU28	38.2

Source: The Economist. Pocket world in Figures. 2019

decelerated inflation and recoveries in private incomes and consumption until the corona virus hit the country (World Bank Group, 2017). It remains to be seen how quickly Russia can rebound after the crisis.

Trade

As an upper-middle-income country, Russia can only develop if its economy is integrated with the rest of the world. Russia enjoys traditionally trade agreements with its neighboring countries (Table 3.1). For the future, it should aim at extending them beyond immediate neighbors. This would open the door to new foreign markets and integrate the country into global commerce. If Russian prices get more competitive, exporting Russian companies would be able to benefit more.

Foreign Direct Investment

Since 2013, Russia has attracted far less Foreign Direct Investment (FDI) than other BRIC Economies. Over the last 10 years, it received a similar inflow like India, only a little more than half of Brazil's FDI and significantly less than China (approx. 15% of China's inflows). The average FDI inflow as share of GDP averaged from 2014 to 2018 only 1.5%. A significant drop versus the close to 2% average of the years 2009–2013. However, the average Five-Year FDI share of GDP is not too far behind China (1.9%) and India (1.7%).

Challenges

The Russian economy faces many challenges, especially because much of the past progress has been largely fueled by exploiting commodities rather than a structural transformation of the economy. Besides the unbalanced economy, other serious weaknesses that need to be tackled are the overall weak competition, outdated capital stock, and a declining workforce.

Thus, key in the long-term will be to increase productivity, improve energy efficiency, and to make the economy less dependent on volatile rents from natural-resource extraction. The main trigger to stipulate these developments would be a market-driven and fair competition. Russia also needs stronger investments in infrastructure and to find ways to better match education, skills, and jobs.

Finally, yet importantly, the government will have to improve the overall poor business climate (Chap. 6) which is mainly caused by corruption (Chap. 23) and continues to depress investment below the level needed to develop a higher growth trend. Accordingly, structural reforms will need to further strengthen macroeconomic policy settings and make substantial improvements in the business environment. Strengthening the rule of law and fighting corruption are the most crucial but also difficult to implement.

References

International Monetary Fund. (2019, April). *General government gross debt*. World Economic Outlook. Retrieved May 28, 2019, from https://www.imf.org/external/datamapper/GGXWDG_NGDP@WEO/OEMDC/ADVEC/WEOWORLD.
International Monetary Fund. (2020, April). World Economic Outlook. Retrieved June 29, 2020, from https://www.imf.org/external/datamapper/datasets/WEO.
The Economist. (2016, October 22). *Milk without the cow* (p. 6). Special Report Russia.
World Bank. (2016). *The long journey to recovery*. Russia Economic Report No. 35.
World Bank Group. (2017). *From recession to recovery*. Russia Economic Report No. 37.

Economic Clusters and Regional Policy

Florian Stache

Industrial policy in developed countries has shifted since the early 1990s away from supporting selective industry sectors to policies supporting so-called clusters. These can be defined as "geographic concentrations of interconnected companies, specialized suppliers, service providers, firms in related industries, training institutions, and support organizations linked around technologies or end products within a local area or region" (Porter, 1998). The trend towards cluster policy is supported by economic theory and academic research, e.g., publications by Noble Prize winner Paul Krugman (Krugman, 1993; Porter, 1998). Being embedded in a regional cluster is an important factor for competitive success as, e.g., Michael Porter found in his research, stating that "paradoxically, the enduring competitive advantages in a global economy lie increasingly in local things—knowledge, relationships, and motivation that distant rivals cannot match" (Porter, 1998). Today, cluster policies, with strong support by the *World Bank* or *OECD*, are also getting traction in emerging markets. The purpose is to strengthen a particular regional economy to make it a driver for the national economy by developing greater firm productivity and becoming an innovative hub. The most prominent example of a regional cluster is Silicon Valley (Saxenian, 1994). Today, states all over the world aim at supporting and creating more of these clusters. Whether or not it is possible to develop successful clusters through government support is uncertain, since clusters typically evolve naturally over time and without state intervention. Exactly this interesting aspect inspires a very interesting debate in economic and management research today. Much of it draws on the "Triple Helix" model of innovation (Etzkowitz & Leydesdorff, 2000), where business, entrepreneurial universities,

---

F. Stache (✉)
Management Department, National Research University Higher School of Economics Saint Petersburg, Saint Petersburg, Russia

Department of Management (Associated), School of Business and Economics, Freie Universität Berlin, Berlin, Germany
e-mail: fstache@hse.ru; florian.stache@fu-berlin.de

and the state play an equal role within a cluster. Today's state of research may be subsumed as following: intervention by the state may be fruitful through so-called cluster initiatives if relations between the three key actors are improved and the state supports, but does not take a leading role. In this chapter, the current state of clusters and cluster initiatives are explained looking at Russia, with a focus on its specific history and resulting opportunities and challenges; concluding, the relevant points for foreign investors are summed up.

Clusters and Cluster Initiatives in the Russian Federation: The Picture Today

In Russia, cluster policy was neglected in the immediate post-Soviet era since other more pressing issues in industrial policy, primarily relating to privatization of key industries, took precedence.[1] Currently, Russian economic policy seems to have caught up in this regard. Legislators are making active use of cluster initiatives to strengthen innovation.

The basic principles of Russia's cluster policy were established in 2008 as a central part of the long-term strategy for socioeconomic development up to 2020. The formation of clusters is now considered key for modernizing the economy and realizing the competitive potential of Russian regions. The focus is both on high-tech industries in priority sectors, as well as on modernizing the processing of raw materials and the production of energy. The Russian Ministry of Economic Development and the Ministry of Industry and Trade jointly formulated this policy within the frames of the "Strategy of Innovative Development of the Russian Federation until 2020" and the "Law on Industrial Policy in the Russian Federation" respectively.

Figure 4.1 shows Russia in comparison to other countries in terms of cluster development. The figure follows the current statistical macro data provided by the World Economic Forum Global Competitiveness Report. A comparison to the situation before Russian Cluster policies were put into action in 2012 shows positive dynamics: Russia's score already visibly increased, from 3 by then to 3.5 in the latest report (World Economic Forum, 2018).

Skolkovo: Government-Created Clusters Within a Centralized Innovation Center

Skolkovo Innovation City represents the most prominent initiative in Russia to develop clusters from scratch. The then President of the Russian Federation, Dmitry Medvedev, announced its construction in 2009. The city is financed primarily by the Russian federal budget and regulated directly by the president (Kremlin, 2010).

---

[1] For an overview of the changing priorities since 1990 see Simachev et al. (2014).

Fig. 4.1 State of cluster development in comparison

Located outside of central Moscow, it is intended to become one of the biggest tech innovation centers in the world. According to *Skolkovo Foundation*, it is planned to occupy roughly 400 ha of land and to have a permanent population of 21,000 employees upon full completion (Skolkovo Foundation, 2018).

The city will comprise an Innovation Center that offers resources for selected entrepreneurs, an Institute of Science and Technology, a research university as well as the Skolkovo Moscow School of Management. The Skolkovo Innovation City is a giant project including five so-called technology clusters, groups of companies specializing in different areas defined by the state. These include IT, Energy, Nuclear Technologies, Biomedicine, and Space Technologies. Initial start-up activities are already operational. It is aimed at creating an ecosystem that allows innovative companies to grow and connect to the international community (Fig. 4.2).

Skolkovo may offer potential, especially for large foreign companies; Siemens, SAP, Microsoft, Boeing, Nokia Solutions and Networks, as well as others, are already foreign partners (Skolkovo Foundation, 2018).

Taking Stock: The Russian Cluster Observatory

Apart from this endeavor of trying to set up entire clusters from scratch near Moscow, the as-is situation of economic agglomerations across the country has been assessed. To this end, the Russian Cluster Observatory was founded in 2012 by the Institute of Statistical Research as part of the National Research University Higher School of Economics. Instead of deciding top-down what does or does not

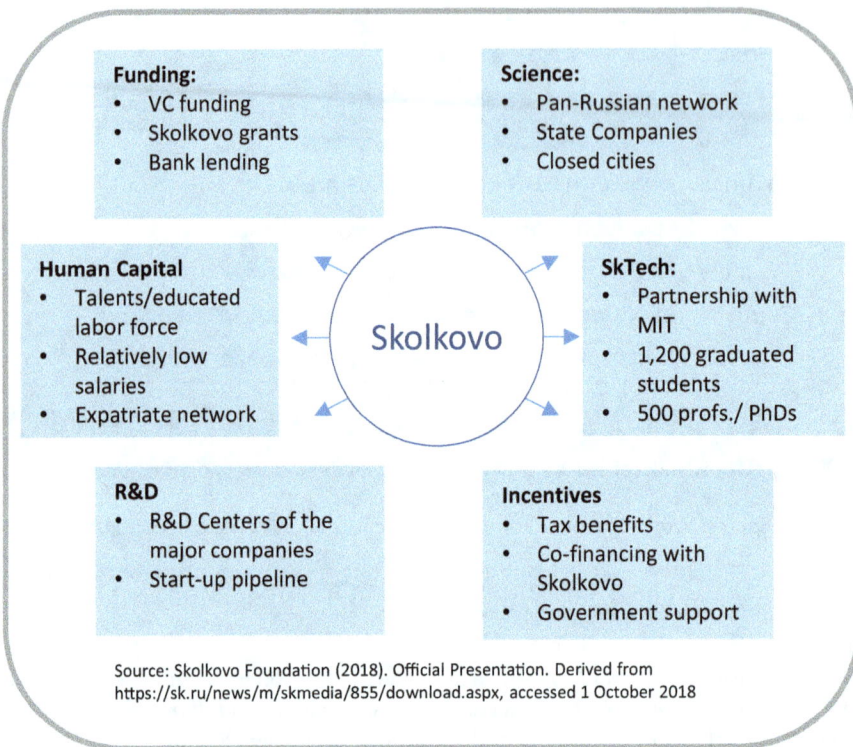

Fig. 4.2 The Skolkovo ecosystem

qualify as a cluster, the map functions as an interface where clusters can add and describe themselves in a grass-roots manner, subsequently forming part of an interactive cluster map (Higher School of Economics, 2018). The latter is designed to help interaction and exchange: the purpose is to give remote regional agglomerations of innovative industries an opportunity to become visible on an international level, and to stimulate mutual awareness and communication between clusters. Various dimensions of cluster development are described. The information is free and publicly available. Since 2008, more than 300 self-declared clusters across the Russian federation registered (Higher School of Economics, 2018).

The Pilot Innovative Cluster Program on Its Way to Internationalization

To better understand the potential influence of policy for decentralized cluster development building on existing agglomerations in the specific context of Russia and to generate local experience here, a Pilot Innovative Cluster program (PIC) was developed. The PIC took results from existing international programs into consideration, drawing on European, and specifically on German experience (BMBF, 2006). Thus, a competition for funding was organized first. In 2012, 94 clusters submitted documentation, which served as a basis for decision-making. Applications were screened by a board of representatives from government, academia, private sector firms, and innovation development institutions. An expert panel subsequently assessed quantitative and qualitative indicators derived from the applications towards the current cluster development status and prospects for future advancement. Some of the criteria included:

- Educational potential
- Industrial potential
- Quality of life and level of infrastructure (i.e., transport, energy, engineering, housing) in the cluster initiatives' home regions
- The organizational development level

Twenty-five clusters were selected to receive subsidies. The approved clusters were divided into two groups—group 1 were clusters with well-developed proposals and high potential, whereas group 2 were considered clusters in development.

The overall federal subsidy for PIC amounted to RUB 5.05 bn (at the time approx. EUR 90 mill.), and triggered private investments of approx. EUR 6 billion until 2016. Instead of direct state support for specific industries, this current Russian approach follows the very contemporary idea of improving collaboration within the clusters and supporting cluster member's ties with organizations abroad. Thus, cluster initiatives are facilitated by cluster management organizations (CMO) that support such interaction and are in charge of the strategic orientation of the whole cluster, spanning organizational borders. CMO's in Russia employ on average 4.5 FTE, comparable with the European average of 4 FTE. The latest policies show a strong turn towards the internationalization of cluster initiatives. It seems to be understood that clusters not integrated into the international competition can barely provide innovative solutions. Therefore, the currently ongoing program for cluster development launched by the Ministry of Economic Development in 2016 is specifically dedicated to support cluster initiatives with regard to attracting global investments (Islankina & Thurner, 2018) (Table 4.1).

Challenges and Opportunities Between Past and Future

The concept of geographic concentration of industries to foster innovation in key areas is certainly not new to Russia, having inherited its part of the Soviet industry structure. Soviet industrial policy was dominated by aggregated cost considerations (instead of individual profit considerations in Western countries), which led to concentrating productive forces in territorial-production complexes for efficiency gains mostly in terms of economies of scale (Islankina & Thurner, 2018). Innovation policy often directed funds towards concentrated "science cities" partly closed to the public. The state was the sole economic agent and responsible for economic

Table 4.1 Distribution of Pilot Innovative Clusters in terms of industrial classification

No.	Name of sectors	Name of clusters
1	Nuclear and radiation technologies	Nuclear and nanotechnology cluster (Dubna, Moscow region)
		Nuclear cluster (Sarov, Nizhniy Novgorod region)
		Nuclear and space technologies cluster (Zelenogorsk, Krasnoyarsk krai)
		Nuclear cluster (Dimitrovgrad, Ulyanovsk region)
2	Manufacture of aircraft and spacecraft, shipbuilding	Aerospace cluster (Samara region)
		Rocket engine building cluster (Khabarovsk krai)
		Aircraft and aviation cluster "Ulyanovsk-Avia" (Ulyanovsk region)
		Shipbuilding cluster (Arkhangelsk region)
3	Pharmaceutical, biotechnology, and medical industries	Pharmaceutical and medical devices' cluster (St. Petersburg)[a]
		Pharmaceutical and medical devices' cluster (Tomsk region)[b]
		Biopharmaceutical cluster (Novosibirsk region)[c]
		Pharmaceutical, biotechnology, and biomedical cluster (Obninsk, Kaluga region)
		Biotechnology cluster (Pishino, Moscow region)
		Biopharmaceutical cluster (Altai krai)
4	New Materials	Cluster of Moscow Institute of Physics and Technology ("Phystech 21") (Moscow region)
		New materials, laser, and radiation technologies (Troitsk, Moscow)
		Titanium cluster (Sverdlovsk region)
5	Chemicals and Petrochemicals	Automobile and petrochemical cluster (Nizhny Novgorod region)
		"Kamsk" cluster (Tatarstan republic)
		Petrochemical cluster (Bashkortostan Republic)
		Complex processing of coal and anthropogenic waste (Kemerovo region)
6	Information Technology and Electronics	"Zelenograd" cluster (Moscow region)
		Information technology cluster (Novosibirsk region)[c]
		Information technology and electronics cluster (Tomsk region)[b]
		Information technology cluster (St. Petersburg)[d]
		Radiation technologies cluster (St. Petersburg)[a]
		Energy-efficient lighting technology and intellectual lighting control systems (Mordovia Republic)

(continued)

Table 4.1 (continued)

No.	Name of sectors	Name of clusters
		Radio-electronics, instrument making and communication cluster (St. Petersburg)[d]

Source: Kutsenko, E., & Meissner, D. (2013). Key features of the first phase of the national cluster program in Russia. Basic Research Program Working Papers WP BRP 11/STI/2013. National Research University Higher School of Economics. Moscow
[a]These clusters were combined in the Medical, pharmaceutical, and radiology cluster (St. Petersburg)
[b]These clusters were combined in the Pharmaceutical, medical devices, and information technology cluster (Tomsk region)
[c]These clusters were combined in the Information technology and biopharmaceutical cluster (Novosibirsk Region)
[d]These clusters were combined in the Information technology, radio-electronics, instrument making, and communication cluster (St. Petersburg)

planning as well as for innovation in the Soviet era. Universities focused on teaching, without direct connection to research or even its application to marketable products. It is argued here, that the most important struggles of this emerging market, in terms of developing a viable industrial and innovation policy in general and clusters and cluster policy in particular, can be understood well through three elements of its specific past: centralization, state dominance and the specific status of universities.

Centralization

Traditionally, Moscow has been both the political and economic center of Russia (Chap. 20). This has given Moscow disproportionate economic significance. Centralist policies, which rely on Moscow's infrastructure or capital, are still reflected in initiatives like Skolkovo. Yet contemporary insights have built on the idea that innovation cannot be dictated centrally from above (Латов & Латова, 2015; Rowe, 2014). Continued support for structured centralization instead of supporting decentral grass-root initiatives can be seen everywhere today, even in Western Europe. An example of this would be Paris-Saclay near Paris in France. It is the promise of a state-planned "European Silicon Valley," currently under construction (Casassus, 2017). However, in a country like Russia, where economic activities have always been geographically centralized, it can be considered particularly difficult to establish a modern, decentralized cluster policy. Such policies require the close cooperation of different state bodies between the federal and the regional level to an extent not known before.

State Dominance

A large part of the country's painful transformation process concerns disentangling the state and economy. With all its constructive intent, cluster policy is in danger of becoming an instrument to finance existing state companies as the core of some of the clusters, which can be considered the same path-dependent pure state action support conserving of economic relations of the past instead of a contemporary cluster policy for the future. Modern concepts of innovating processes underlying such policy, like the "Triple Helix Model" (Etzkowitz & Leydesdorff, 2000), allocate a much more modest role to the state. They consider three key actors necessary for clusters to unleash their whole innovative potential: university, industry, and government—the "Triple Helix." Importantly, the state forms part of the triangle, but does not take over a leading role. Furthermore, instead of ordering pure geographic concentration, the relations between the involved organizations are understood as central, providing the tacit knowledge-sharing opportunities that generate new ideas. One viable way for development may be to give universities more responsibility within the triangle in order to push back state intervention and foster private sector initiatives. Even if universities are state-funded, they are more independent towards political interests, as it can be assumed that less direct relations with state companies exist than between state companies and local authorities. Furthermore, universities are the place where the most up to date knowledge circulates, and where a young generation with good education may find the environment to invent and innovate in a grass-roots manner.

Traditional Separation of University and Science-Based Innovation/Start-Ups

Further complicating such an approach, Russian universities themselves face problems to function according to the triple helix idea due to their specific past. This goes back to the fact that academic research was traditionally mostly concentrated within the Academy of Sciences and separated from universities and (state-owned) enterprises (Uvarov & Perevodchikov, 2012). Such universities defined as pure teaching institutions cannot take over the function attributed to them within a triple helix. Introducing National Research Universities, where research and teaching play an equal role, and the recent law allowing the creation of university spin-offs shows that this shortcoming has been realized and that institutional reforms to leverage synergies from innovation originating from research institutions and private companies are being targeted. Specific funding allowing universities to support their students setting up companies, drawing for example on the successful program *"EXIST"* (Freie Universität Berlin, 2020), can complement such an approach.

To sum up, learning from international experiences setting up cluster policies can be helpful. Still, some very specific challenges of the Russian context prevail, which could only be roughly touched upon here. In order to realize its potential, Russia is in strong need to find its own, Russia-specific innovation trajectory where adapted cluster policy may play an important role. Its definition must include first-hand ideas foremost from innovative entrepreneurs, and an understanding of their specific needs working in the Russian context. Such work can be accomplished with the help of qualitative network research and is well in line with the World Bank's (World Bank, 2009) recommendations to subsequently develop local funding mechanisms, markets, and management/digital skills.

Relevance for Foreign Investors and Outlook

There are strong signs for the political will in today's Russia to develop a modern approach to innovation and industrial policy in the form of cluster initiatives, and to use the latter as well as a means for internationalization of the respective industries. Within barely 10 years, international experts have been hired, foreign programs screened, pilot studies conducted, and serious amounts of money reserved for further development. Especially the initiatives to decentralize and form nuclei outside Moscow and St. Petersburg for local specialized growth are remarkable. The most recent programs show that collaboration with foreign companies is a priority for the distribution of future cluster subsidies. It is therefore advisable for foreign investors to make use of the developing cluster infrastructure to understand dynamics as well outside of the highly centralized urban metropolises of St. Petersburg or Moscow, and to profit from financial incentives here. Local contacts for this end have been developed in the form of regional cluster management centers.

The benefits of cluster economics are strongest in innovative industries, where instant knowledge transfer is key—the famous example of Silicon Valley is not accidentally situated in the fast-moving digital sphere. Here these initiatives may be particularly fruitful, as they meet an important strength of the Russian educational system: Russia ranks second worldwide in terms of IT developers,[2] and labor costs are comparably low. This aspect may today still be underestimated abroad, and cluster infrastructure can be helpful to support foreign companies in leveraging this comparative advantage by finding and approaching small, specialized innovative enterprises.

Future research can contribute to a better understanding of relevant output indicators of clusters and cluster development, for example, alternatives to dynamics of patents filed. Furthermore, it seems high time for a review of if and how clusters in Russia really function internally, and a better understanding of the related change processes. What are the social networks in and between clusters, and how can these be influenced by cluster initiatives, including the introduction of new, international ties? These questions are of a more qualitative nature, and currently on the research agenda internationally (Boari et al., 2016). Such research in Russia will be fruitful at this stage to receive input foremost from the perspective of the entrepreneurs—their

---

[2]For a recent study on the base of 1.5 million developers worldwide see Hacker Rank (2016).

view on how far relationships within the clusters really work, where the largest problems for (international) collaboration lie, and which part of past initiatives really supported such collaboration in their day-to-day activities. Results can be used for an improvement of policy in a more fine-grained manner towards adaptation to the specific reality of business in Russia today and can improve the attractiveness of Russian economic clusters for Russian and foreign firms alike.

References

BMBF. (2006). InnoRegio - Das Programm. Accessed September 30, 2018, from https://www.unternehmen-region.de/de/159.php.

Boari, C., Elfring, T., & Molina-Morales, X. F. (Eds.). (2016). *Entrepreneurship and cluster dynamics*. Routledge.

Casassus, B. (2017). French auditors criticize €5-billion science super-campus near Paris. *Nature, 2* (2017).

Etzkowitz, H., & Leydesdorff, L. (2000). The dynamics of innovation: From national systems and 'Mode 2' to a triple helix of University-Industry-Government relations. *Research Policy, 29*(2), 109–123.

Freie Universität Berlin. (2020). *EXIST Business Startup Grant*. Accessed October 1, 2020, from https://www.fu-berlin.de/en/sites/profund/gruendungsservice/exist_gruenderstipendium/index.html.

Hacker Rank. (2016). *Which country would win in the programming Olympics?* Accessed October 1, 2018, from https://blog.hackerrank.com/which-country-would-win-in-the-programming-olympics/.

Higher School of Economics. (2018). *Russian Cluster Observatory*. Accessed September 30, 2018, from https://cluster.hse.ru.

Islankina, E., & Thurner, T. W. (2018). Internationalization of cluster initiatives in Russia: Empirical evidence. *Entrepreneurship and Regional Development*, 1–24.

Kremlin. (2010). Official website. Accessed March 30, 2020, from http://www.kremlin.ru/events/president/news/9057.

Krugman, P. R. (1993). *Geography and trade*. MIT press.

Porter, M. E. (1998). Clusters and the new economics of competition. *Harvard Business Review, 76*(6), 77–90.

Rowe, E. W. (2014). The future, the foreign and the public–private divide: Socio-political discourses around Skolkovo. *Journal of Eurasian Studies, 5*(1), 39–47.

Saxenian, A. (1994). *Regional advantage: Culture and competition in Silicon Valley and Route 128*. Harvard University Press.

Simachev, Y., Kuzyk, M., Kuznetsov, B., & Pogrebnyak, E. (2014). Russia on the path towards a new technology industrial policy: Exciting prospects and fatal traps. *Форсайт, 8*(4).

Skolkovo Foundation. (2018). Skolkovo official website. Accessed September 30, 2018, from http://sk.ru/news/.

Uvarov, A., & Perevodchikov, E. (2012). The entrepreneurial university in Russia: From idea to reality. *Procedia-Social and Behavioral Sciences, 52*, 45–51.

World Bank. (2009). *Clusters for competitiveness*. Practical Guide & Policy Implications for Developing Cluster Initiatives.

World Economic Forum (Ed.). (2018). *The Global Competitiveness Report 2017–2018* (p. 249).

Латов, Ю. В., & Латова, Н. В. (2015). Сколково как инновационный центр: общее и особенное (историко-компаративистский подход). *Journal of Economic Regulation (Вопросы регулирования экономики), 6*(1), 37–45.

Transport Infrastructure

Henk R. Randau

Overall, Russia has a flawed transport infrastructure that in many regards does not come close to Western standards. Despite progress made in recent years, the quality of infrastructure remains poor. It represents a severe constrains in the connectivity of producers and consumers to global and regional markets. Obviously, the bad infrastructure has negative effects on the economic performance, competitiveness, and growth of regions. According to the latest ranking in *The Global Competitiveness Report 2019* Russia was only ranked 50 out of 141 in quality of overall infrastructure (the USA, China, and India are placed 13th, 36th, and 70th, respectively).[1]

One reason for the current situation is the type of economic infrastructure the Russian Federation inherited from the Soviet days. When Stalin came into power, he aimed for rapid industrialization of the economy, with an emphasis on heavy industry. He did so with much disregard for cost or human resources. Many factories and industrial centers were built in remote locations for geopolitical reason, using forced labor (section Internal Migration in Chap. 19). Often these factories were not efficient and were only allowed to continue existing because they employed millions of people, which helped prevent civil conflict.

The other reason for Russia's bad infrastructure is the lack of investment. The later decades of the Soviet era saw already massive problems due to investment shortages. The years immediately following the collapse of the Soviet Union did not resolve these issues. After a decline lasting until the early 2000s, physical capital stock began to increase in recent years—until it was hit heavily by the corona crisis

---

[1]World Economic Forum: The Global Competitiveness Report 2019, at http://www3.weforum.org/docs/GCR2019/05FullReport/TheGlobalCompetitivenessReport2019.pdf retrieved on October 2nd, 2020.

H. R. Randau (✉)
Weinheim, Germany
e-mail: hrandau@whu.edu

© The Author(s), under exclusive license to Springer Nature Switzerland AG 2021
O. Medinskaya et al. (eds.), *Russia Business*,
https://doi.org/10.1007/978-3-030-64613-4_5

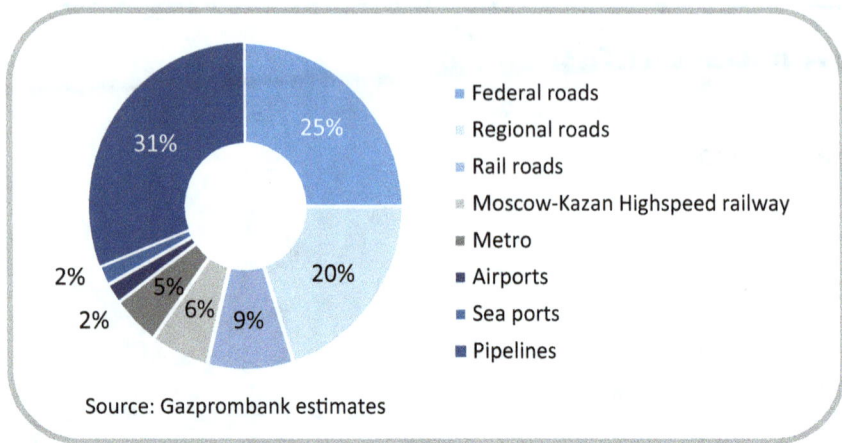

Fig. 5.1 Breakdown of investment in transportation, 2014–2020

Table 5.1 Length of transport networks, km, thousands

	1992 Russia	1990 USA	2017 Russia	2017 USA
Highways (paved and unpaved)	466	6187	1666	6672
Railroad	88	240	87	204
Navigable channels	98	42	101	41
Oil pipeline, total	66	336	70	347
Gas pipeline, total	140	2032	180	2597

Sources: Rosstat (Транспорт в России. 2018: Стат.сб./Росстат, М., 2018, at http://www.gks.ru/free_doc/doc_2018/transp18.pdf); US Department of Transportation (at https://www.bts.gov/topics/national-transportation-statistics)

in 2020.[2] Overall it can be said that infrastructure investments were simply not high enough to make a great leap forward (Fig. 5.1).

Density and Quality

Russia's transport network is vast but inadequate in terms of coverage, unevenly distributed across regions, and of overall poor quality (Table 5.1: Length of transport networks, km, thousands). When looking at the transport infrastructure in detail, only the quality of the railway system and Airport Connectivity is quite well developed. Accordingly, Russia ranks 17 by Efficiency of Train Services and 18 by Airport Connectivity in *The Global Competitiveness Report 2019.*[3] All

---

[2] Rosstat, 2019 at www.gks.ru/free_doc/new_site/effect/macr5-1.xlsx, retrieved on October 2, 2020.

[3] World Economic Forum: The Global Competitiveness Report 2019, at http://www3.weforum.org/docs/WEF_TheGlobalCompetitivenessReport2019.pdf
    Retrieved on October 2nd, 2020.

Table 5.2 Changes of Russia's position in the rating of quality of infrastructure

	Russia 2008	Russia 2018	China 2018	Brazil 2018	India 2018
Overall quality of infrastructure	78	51	29	81	63
Quality of roads	104	104	42	112	51
Efficiency of train services	32	15	25	97	26
Efficiency of air transport services	88	52	63	73	53
Efficiency of seaport services	76	45	48	105	40

Sources: World Economic Forum. The Global Competitiveness Report 2008–2009 (at http://www3.weforum.org/docs/WEF_GlobalCompetitivenessReport_2008-09.pdf) and The Global Competitiveness Report 2018 (at http://www3.weforum.org/docs/GCR2018/05FullReport/TheGlobalCompetitivenessReport2018.pdf) retrieved on June 2nd, 2019

other areas need significant improvement. It also needs to be noted that transport network accessibility is very uneven geographically.

Transport infrastructure is comprehensive in the European part of Russia, while some areas in Siberia and the Far East lack regular connections with the main transport network. Substantial gaps in the transport infrastructure create serious obstacles to economic development for these regions (Chap. 20).

On the positive side, it needs to be noted that the quality of infrastructure appears to have improved in recent years (Table 5.2: Changes of Russia's position in the rating of the quality of infrastructure). Persistent underinvestment had led to a steep decline in infrastructure quality since the collapse of the Soviet Union. Since 2007 however, quality is improving as indicated by a rise in perceived infrastructure quality (The World Bank in the Russian Federation, 2014).

Transport safety remains a serious problem. Road traffic mortality is comparably high like in China.[4] It is five times higher than in a several European Union countries like Netherlands or Germany, about twice higher than in the USA, and significantly higher than in other transition economies like Belarus or Ukraine.[5] A combination of factors is at work, including the bad state of the roads, a sharp decline in road police personnel, and drunk driving as well (section The Aging Population and High Death Rates in Chap. 17).

---

[4]WHO estimated death rate per 100 000 population (2016) after road traffic fatalities: Russia 18; China 18.2, Germany 4.1; Netherlands 3.8; Ukraine 13.7; Belarus 8.9; United States 12.4.

[5]WHO: Global status report on road safety 2018, at https://www.who.int/violence_injury_prevention/road_safety_status/2018/en/ retrieved on October 25th, 2020.

Railroads

Freight transport is dominated by railways. 85% of the total cargo output is carried along railroads. The railway system serves Russia's strong raw material industry in particular. Natural resources and construction materials are among the most frequently transported.

While the Russian Federation inherited an extensive railway system, repairs have not always been kept up while degradation and increasing freight demand have worn on the infrastructure.[6]

Since December 2009, high-speed trains on the upgraded infrastructure have connected regions such as Moscow, Tver, Novgorod, Leningrad, Vladimir, Sochi, and Nizhny Novgorod. For the next step, Russia aims to reduce bottlenecks in the system and is committed to altogether build 7000 km of high-speed railways by 2030.[7] In the past, many similar targets have been systematically missed. The main project of the six new High-Speed Rails (HSR) now is the 800 km long Moscow–Kazan line which should shorten the normally 14-h journey to just 3.5 h.[8] Originally, this was planned to be done by 2020 but after years of discussion and planning, it was decided that it should be postponed due to high costs and the uncertainty of the investment. Another reason why the project had been postponed is the fact that the express trains, which are already in use, for example, on the Moscow St. Petersburg line, can use the same upgraded infrastructure and could reach speeds around 200 km/h. This is not as fast as the proposed train, 350 km/h, but still functional.[9]

Roads and Highways

Road transport played only a secondary role during Soviet times. Even though Russia has increased investment in improving the road network, more than 1/3rd of the total investment in transportation infrastructure is used to develop and sustain roads.[10]

---

[6]OECD. Improving Transport Infrastructure in Russia. Economics Department Working Papers No. 1193, at http://www.oecd.org/officialdocuments/publicdisplaydocumentpdf/?cote=ECO/WKP (2015)11&docLanguage=En retrieved on June 5th, 2020.

[7]ОАО «РЖД»: Программа организации скоростного и высокоскоростного железнодорожного сообщения в Российской Федерации, at www.rzd.ru/dbmm/download?vp=1&load=y&col_id=121&id=85015 retrieved on June 5th, 2020.

[8]http://www.eng.hsrail.ru/hsrail-Moscow-Kazan/project-profile/.

[9]Путин не одобрил проект ВСМ Москва — Казань Когда в России появится первая скоростная железная дорога, at https://www.rbc.ru/business/28/03/2019/5c9cd0a49a7947366db46c69 retrieved on June 5th, 2020.

[10]Итоги реализации мероприятий федеральной целевой программы «Развитие транспортной системы России (2010–2021 годы)», интегрируемых в состав государственной программы «Развитие транспортной системы» at http://ppp-transport.ru/ru/o-fcp/itogi-realizacii-meroprijatij-federalnoj-celevoj/ retrieved on June 5th, 2019.

The Federation has made efforts to make road investments a more interesting business through public-private partnerships. This mainly includes projects under the jurisdiction of the state corporation *Avtodor*. It built new and upgraded existing highways, bridges, and other things all of which now impose tolls for transit.[11]

In spite of these improvements, the quality of the roads is relatively underdeveloped and fails to meet the needs of an increasingly motorized Russia. The consequence is many overloaded sections on the main federal roads—generally near big cities. Moscow, St. Petersburg, Rostov-on Don, Nizhny Novgorod, and Volgograd made it into the top 100 of INRIX 2018 Global Traffic Scorecard with Moscow holding first place for the last few years.[12] Most roads are not suited for heavy vehicles and up to a third of all rural cities and townships are not a part of the national paved road network.

Airports

Air travel is on the rise in Russia: the use of Russian airspace by aircraft has grown to be more than 50 times what it was in 2010 and reached more than 80 thousand flights in 2019.[13] Before the corona crisis struck, it was expected that within the next 20 years passenger traffic would continue to grow at a rate of 4% per year (Asia-Pacific more than 5%, Europe around 3%).[14] Moscow Aviation Hubs (MAH's) are growing especially fast because more than 50% of all flights (passenger and cargo) pass through Moscow due to the lack of direct connections to provincial cities and the natural higher demand in the capital city than in rural areas[15] (Chap. 20).

In spite of the increase in air passenger traffic, airport infrastructure remains underfinanced with the exception given to the largest airports. Smaller airports were often transferred to regions that lacked the money to properly invest in them and finance them and were therefore forced to close down or file bankruptcy. This is worrying for more remote areas as these regions often lack feasible alternatives to air travel. In response to this, new programs have been created to fund transport to regions deemed socially important. Improving the efficiency and reliability of already existing infrastructure is of equal importance to keeping it maintained and expanding it.[16] The current number of take-off and landing operations per runway

---

[11]The Russian Highways State Company (Avtodor). https://russianhighways.ru/en/about/mission/ retrieved on June 5th, 2020.

[12]INRIX 2018 Global Traffic Scorecard, at http://inrix.com/scorecard/ retrieved on June 5th, 2020.

[13]Federal Air Transport Agency, at https://m.favt.ru/novosti-novosti/?id=4832 at retrieved on June 5th, 2020.

[14]Airbus global market forecast 2019–2038, at https://www.airbus.com/aircraft/market/global-market-forecast.html, retrieved on September 5th, 2020.

[15]Federal Air Transport Agency http://www.favt.ru/dejatelnost-ajeroporty-i-ajerodromy-osnovnie-proizvodstvennie-pokazateli-aeroportov-obyom-perevoz/ retrieved on Feb. 2nd, 2020.

[16]Improving the business climate and transport infrastructure in Russia, Alexander Kolik, Artur Radziwill, Natalia Turdyeva, 2013 OECD Economic Survey of the Russian Federation.

for Moscow airports is only two thirds of some airports in China and half of airports in London. Ultimately, what Russia needs more than anything is more coordination between air traffic management and airport infrastructure development.

Seaports

Russia has 67 seaports in total. Recent years have seen massive investment in seaports and have increased total port capacity above the current and medium-term needs reaching the capacity more than 1 billion ton cargo volume p.a.[17] Proper usage of the ports is limited by bottlenecks in the inter-modal infrastructure. Sub-par access to roads and railways as well as an insufficient number of logistical facilities are problems that plague most Russian ports.

Pipelines

In order to exploit its vast energy resources, Russia needs to further develop and sustain a pipeline infrastructure. The Russian Federation owns the largest network for the transportation of oil and gas. The two giants, *Gazprom* and *Transneft*, are nationally the largest financiers of pipeline infrastructure.

Funding and State Monopolies

There are many strategies and programs dedicated to infrastructure development, modernization, and maintenance in Russia. Being a capital-intensive process, transport infrastructure improvements usually cannot be executed without state participation. Russia is using its National Wealth Fund (RNWF) to invest in different national infrastructure projects or other framework-related investments. However, this will not be enough to close the infrastructure gap to other emerging economies and improve the country's competitiveness.

It seems that by mobilizing private capital through public-private partnerships and opening up infrastructure subsectors to direct private investment many new infrastructure projects could be realized and additional pressure to the fiscal budget can be minimized.

This calls for more competition. Currently, the state-owned *Russian Railways (RZD)*, *Gazprom*, *Transneft*, and *Avtodor* are the most relevant companies investing in Russia's infrastructure. The four monopolies assist in financing the base by having a 40% total share from 2014 to 2020. Although they are ongoing negotiations in

---

[17]The Federal Agency for Maritime and River Transport, at http://www.morflot.ru/deyatelnost/napravleniya_deyatelnosti/portyi_rf.html retrieved on June 19th, 2020.

order to attract private investments with Russian and Chinese funds and banks.[18] For example, in order to increase competition in the transport sector, the country could open the railway market for independent operators. Today the railway system is legally closed for foreign operators. Lifting barriers to competition will be essential to intensify investments.

Reference

The World Bank in the Russian Federation. (2014, September). *Policy uncertainty clouds medium-term prospects* (p. 44). Russia Economic Report, No. 32.

---

[18]В России прогнозируется поток инвестиций в железнодорожную инфраструктуру at https://www.gudok.ru/infrastructure/?ID=1455394 retrieved on June 19th, 2020.

Competitiveness

Andreas Bitzi

A country's economic competitiveness can be determined by a set of microeconomic and macroeconomic factors. Prof. Klaus Schwab, who edits the annual competitiveness report[1] for the *World Economic Forum,* defines it as a set of institutions, policies, and factors that determine the level of productivity of an economy. The report uses 12 concrete factors, e.g., the quality of institutions, infrastructure, macroeconomic environment, education, labor market efficiency, financial market development, technological readiness, market size, etc.

According to the latest report, the main strengths of Russia are the higher education and market size. The weakest points are goods market efficiency, institutions, and financial market development.

If one were to ignore the market size factor, Russia would not be as highly rated but rather closer to rank 50. This also corresponds with the World Bank's *Doing Business Report 2019,* where Russia ranks 31st and has improved its rank constantly over the last years. The current reports see strengths in the ease of registering property, enforcing contracts and utilities. Main weaknesses are identified in cross-border trade and getting permits for construction. It is important to note that the report mainly focuses on Moscow and in part on St. Petersburg. It cannot necessarily be assumed that, for instance, utilities are as easily accessible anywhere else in the country. What can be said about the positive tendency, however, is that Russia's goal to become one of the top 20 countries within the next years is supported in practice

---

See more at https://www.q.partners, retrieved on October 19th, 2020.

---

[1]The Global Competitiveness Report 2019, Editor Klaus Schwab, www.weforum.org, retrieved on October 22nd, 2020.

A. Bitzi (✉)
Quality Partners, St. Petersburg, Russia
e-mail: ab@q.partners

by business friendly nominations of governors and many provinces, where there are clear steps taken to ease doing business and making investment easier. In comparison to their operations in other countries, some foreign investors view their Russian operations as less competitive. The main problems that weaken competitiveness are, in the opinion of respondents of foreign companies, bureaucracy, pressure from authorities, difficult regulations, lack of qualified labor, and a lack of supplier base that is able to deliver consistently and punctually. Many investors try to actively support potential suppliers to increase quality, some take part in programs for dual education, and others work closely with business associations, governments, and authorities to face bureaucracy and increase transparency. Such an active role of foreign businesses is an important factor to improve the business environment. Russia has never been an easy place to do business and there is a long way to go to get to the same level as the global leaders in competitiveness (Fig. 6.1).

The Ruble's Influence on Competitiveness

One of the main reasons for the collapse of the Soviet Union was the economic inefficiency. What had to be produced would be decided centrally to fulfill state plans. Delivering high-quality products or finding ways for more efficient production were not high on the agenda of the huge conglomerates that were created at the time. The mentality of a planned economy was lasting. An economic depression would plague the country in the immediate aftermath of the fall of Communism.

Since then, Russia has become a force to be reckoned with once again. Following the financial crisis of 1998, the economy grew rapidly due to a stable political environment and driven by the ever-increasing prices of oil and other commodities.

The tremendous increase in commodities prices led to massive trade balance surpluses and, consequently, capital inflows. In theory, inflows of capital lead to an appreciation of the domestic currency, and that was exactly what could be observed in Russia.

At first sight, the foreign exchange rate of the Russian ruble remained stable from 1999 through 2008. This stability coincided with the goal of the Central Bank of Russia to keep the Russian ruble within a certain corridor against a basket of Euro and US dollar. It is important to understand that these are the published nominal exchange rates that represent the number of units of the domestic currency that can purchase a unit of a certain foreign currency. The real exchange rate means something different. It focuses on the ratio of the price level abroad and the domestic price level. The foreign price level is converted into domestic currency units via the current nominal exchange rate and hereby shows a different picture than the published exchange rate.

An immense appreciation is not necessarily a bad thing. Russians love to travel and they enjoyed the increased purchasing power they had abroad. For manufacturers though, the competition from imported goods got stronger. The same effect is applied to imported components used in the industry, which get cheaper. To counter the increasing pressure from cheaper imports, manufacturers

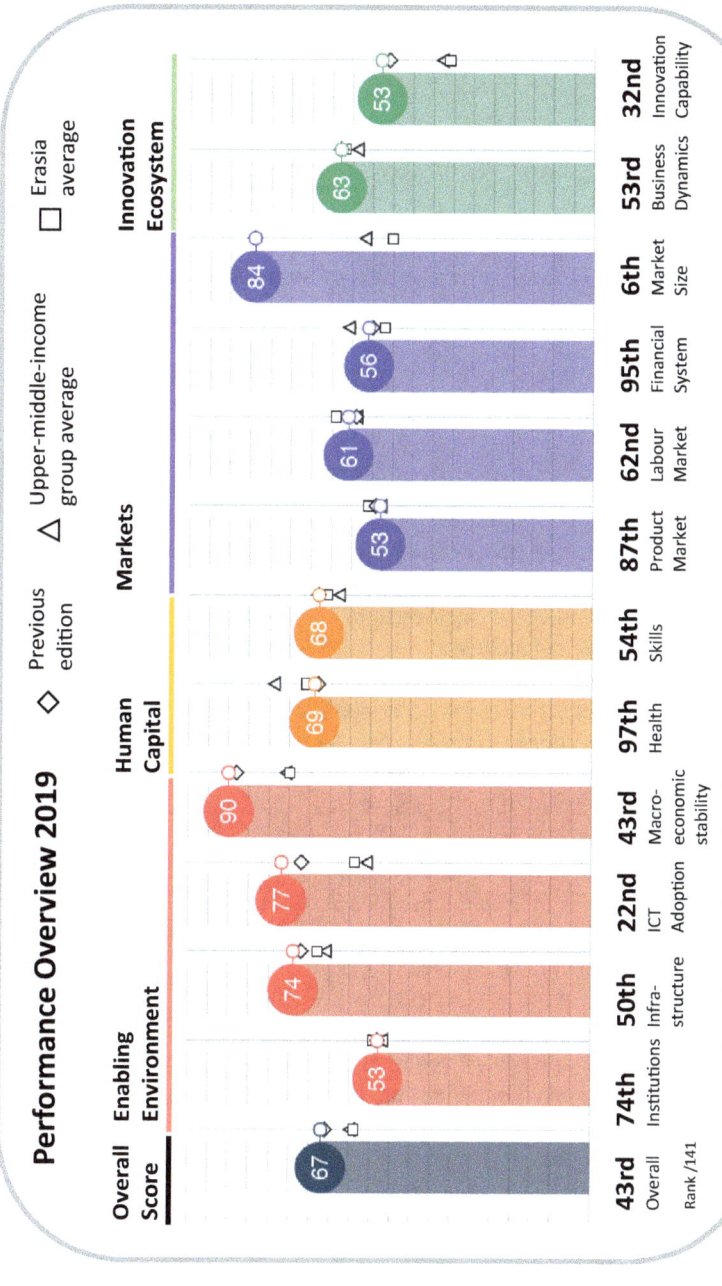

Fig. 6.1 Russia according to The Global Competitiveness Report 2019

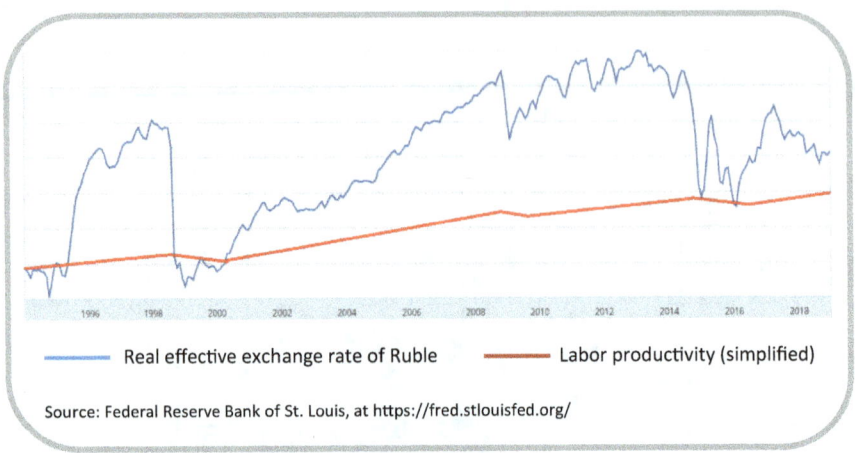

Fig. 6.2 Real effective exchange rate of the Russian Ruble vs. labor productivity

are forced to become more efficient. If not, they would lose market share. The same applies on the macroeconomic level: The economy must increase its efficiency to counterbalance the effects of the expensive ruble. There are countries that have, historically, constantly been faced with appreciating currencies, such as Switzerland (with a much lesser but more constant increase) and were successful in increasing their efficiency to remain competitive.

In Russia, however, the much-needed rapid increase in efficiency could not be observed. Labor productivity has grown at comparatively low rates (showed in a simplified way by the red line put into Fig. 6.2) for many years and was weaker than in other emerging market economies, such as Turkey, or neighboring European countries, such as Poland or the Baltic states. As a result, the Russian economy got less competitive, in parallel to the appreciation of the ruble. Consequently, domestic manufacturing became less attractive; it was simply cheaper to import goods from abroad using the strong ruble. The consequence of this was a lack of appetite for investments in production capacity in most industries (except for commodities, as a matter of course), although the manufacturing base and infrastructure were outdated and desperately needed huge investments to keep the industrial base in healthy shape. The result of the underinvestment was an even further increased dependency of Russia from the developments of commodities prices (Fig. 6.2).

The high dependence on commodities prices is fine so long as prices increase. As soon as prices start to decrease or even collapse, an economy will almost immediately face trouble. This was clearly demonstrated in 2008/2009, in the face of the global financial crisis, when commodities prices would drop dramatically. The economy shrank by almost 8%, the ruble devaluated by some 30% against the dollar and the euro. The Russian Central Bank could no longer keep the exchange rate within the target bandwidth.

The devaluation of the ruble was widely considered a disaster in Russia. Actually, it was not. The devaluation was needed to recover the competitiveness of the Russian economy in a short period. After the crisis, the economy made a rapid recovery and so did the prices of commodities. With the recovery, the ruble regained strength. In real terms, the ruble was able to return to pre-2008 crisis levels after a few years. The increased competitiveness that came from the decline in the ruble exchange rate was gone.

In 2014, the country faced another crisis caused by collapsing oil prices, Western sanctions and countersanctions, coupled with increased structural issues. These effects forced the Central Bank of Russia to give up its exchange rate regime. The ruble was announced to float freely. This proved to be a wise decision, as a floating ruble would stabilize the economy. The ruble devaluated massively, at times more than 60% until it stabilized. It is now about 40–45% lower than before the crisis. In real terms, the devaluation was not as high, as the inflation rates skyrocketed in 2015 and got lower afterwards to levels of around 3% for 2018. The competitiveness of the Russian economy got a massive boost through its weaker currency and the government displays a high interest in keeping the ruble exchange rate low. It has taken several measures to do so. Even though commodity prices have increased strongly since their lows in 2015, the almost parallel movement of oil prices and the ruble exchange rate no longer hold. The ruble exchange rate remains relatively independent of commodities' prices. Should current political factors persist, the competitiveness of the Russian economy is not likely to be undermined by a strong ruble again.

The New Industrial Policy

The lack of investment, the high dependence on commodities, and the increased tensions with the West forced the Russian government to introduce an industrial policy in 2014 in an effort to restore its decayed manufacturing base. The Law on "Industrial Policy" defines key areas of industrial activity. The legislation aims to stimulate investments in manufacturing and technology transfer. It authorizes the government to strengthen the industrial base, support research, and to build a competitive national economy. Under the law, there have been many government decrees that limit the import of industrial goods to tenders of the state, municipalities, and state-owned companies for about 20 industries. The exclusion or significant price discrimination of imported goods for any tender of the state or state-owned entity has certainly had an impact on the economy because the state's share in the Russian economy is high (up to 50%).

The idea of an industrial policy being used to revive manufacturing is certainly a positive one overall. Russia needs to diversify the economy and move away from commodities, yet commodities will always play an important role.

The method to enforce import substitution by local production has so far led to mixed results. On the one hand, significant investments, which strengthen the economy and the industrial base. On the other hand, there are examples where the strict exclusion rules lead to closed markets without increased competitiveness that in the long-term will weaken the economy.

Even though the new industrial policy has already had a certain impact on the industrial base the productivity remains weak. The Russian government is well aware of this challenge and has made considerable increases in productivity a major goal for 2024. The Minister for Economic for Industry and Trade of Russia, Denis Manturov, mentioned at an event of the AEB in March 2019 that the Russian economy cannot compete with the EU economies in many areas. According to the minister in case if the current sanctions/countersanctions regime and protective measures would be lifted, it would be a blow to the Russian economy. These statements show that the competitiveness has to improve considerably.

The laws on industrial policy and localization have in certain cases led already to new investments, new production capacities, and the use of new technologies while in other industries it has not helped to establish efficient structures. The success of localization is highly dependent on the industry it is applied. E.g., deeply globalized industries, such as big pharma or medical technology demand high investments and economies of scale. Investments meant just to serve the Russian market may not have the necessary size to be efficient. This can be the case where factories for certain drugs are produced in just one or two places worldwide. It is not economically reasonable to build local factories in each market; economies of scale matter, and purely national thinking will lead to higher production costs.

Outlook

The competitiveness of the Russian economy has generally improved within the past few years. The government has taken a number of measures to push investments, to produce locally, in some cases also to export. There are initiatives to improve infrastructure and education. The industrial strategy as it is now, with the aim of producing everything domestically, may not remain the same in the future. What would be more desirable is for more industries that are integrated into global supply chains, capable of being market leaders, hidden champions, with innovative products that are in demand worldwide, which do not hide behind market-entry barriers but are able to compete globally. Apart from that, bureaucracy, government pressure on business and corruption have to be fought to lead Russia to more competitiveness and prosperity. The challenges from the currency's appreciation are currently well under control. However, challenges as the corona crisis show that modern economies need not only a clear strategy for growth; they need to also strengthen their resilience, e.g., their ability to quickly recover after a crisis that can hit them anytime.

Trading in Times of Sanctions and Protectionism

Alexander Hempfing

Introduction

For centuries, countries have used economic sanctions to achieve international policy objectives. From the Embargo Act of 1807 to sanctions during both world wars, the dispute following the nationalization of the Suez Canal in 1956, the conflict about Cyprus in the 1970s, or the measures against the Islamic Republic of Iran in recent years, sanctions are a frequently used tool to pressure governments. Therefore, not only bi- or trilateral but also internationally coordinated sanctions have been put in place. Examples, therefore, are the UN Security Council resolution S/RES/216 against Southern Rhodesia (Zimbabwe) in 1965 or resolution S/RES/660 condemning the Iraqi invasion of Kuwait in August 1990 (United Nations, 2017). Between 1914 and 1990 alone, *Hufbauer, Schott, and Elliot* identified 115 cases (Hufbauer et al., 1990). Nevertheless, the success of economic sanctions is widely disputed as researchers cast doubt on the claim that economic sanctions can achieve primary foreign policy goals (Pape, 1997). Following the crisis in Ukraine in 2014, several governments have imposed sanctions against the Russian Federation. This chapter intends to give an overview of the sanctions imposed on both sides, elucidate the economic effects the measures have as well as to point out possible ways out of the deadlock.

A. Hempfing (✉)
University of Bamberg, Bamberg, Germany

Department Analytics, Fraunhofer Center for Applied Research on Supply Chain Services SCS, Nuremberg, Germany
e-mail: alexander.hempfing@iis.fraunhofer.de

© The Author(s), under exclusive license to Springer Nature Switzerland AG 2021
O. Medinskaya et al. (eds.), *Russia Business*,
https://doi.org/10.1007/978-3-030-64613-4_7

The Crisis in Ukraine and Its Aftermath

The 2014 crisis in Ukraine involving the territory of Crimea has been characterized as a case of the annexation of a part of Ukraine's territory by Russia, and as one of rightful secession by the Crimean people's legitimate expression of self-determination. While this dispute is a matter of international law, Western governments did not hesitate to react to the situation in Ukraine by introducing various sanctions against Russia. The Russian government responded accordingly. This section gives a short overview of the sanctions against Russia, especially from the United States (US) and the European Union (EU), as well as the countermeasures by the Russian Federation.

Sanctions Against Russia

Sanctions against Russia have been introduced on several levels. In March 2014, the Council of the European Union presented the first set of restrictive measures against 21 Russian and Ukrainian officials. With a similar purpose, the USA began its Ukraine/Russia-related sanctions program triggered by the Executive Order (E.O.) 13660 of President Barack Obama. In June, an import ban on goods from Crimea was imposed following the EU's policy of non-recognition of the illegal annexation. In July 2014, the Council of the European Union adopted a package of targeted economic sanctions prohibiting the purchase or sales of new bonds, equity or similar financial instruments, the import and export of arms and arm-related materials from and to Russia, the export of dual-use goods and technology for military use as well as specific energy-related equipment and technology. These sanctions have been enlarged to specific economic sectors reinforcing the measures taken 2 months earlier. In the following year, the EU and the USA extended the sanctions to Crimea and Sevastopol by introducing a measure that includes prohibitions on the import of products, investment, tourism, transport, and infrastructure services as well as exports of certain goods and technologies. With the E.O. 13661, 13662, and 13685, the USA took similar measures against individuals, entities, and sectors identified by the US Secretary of the Treasury. In total 207 individuals, 447 enterprises, banks, and (governmental) organizations as well as two vessels. Since then the measures have been extended several times. Furthermore, it seems that they will not be lifted until substantial progress in the dispute is made.[1,2] Moreover, in July 2017, the US House of Representatives passed a legislative

---

[1] General Secretariat of the Council: Timeline – EU restrictive measures in response to the crisis in Ukraine – Consilium. Edited by Council of the European Union. Available online at http://www.consilium.europa.eu/en/policies/sanctions/ukraine-crisis/history-ukraine-crisis/, retrieved on October 23rd, 2020.

[2] Office of Foreign Assets Control: Ukraine-/Russia-related Sanctions Program. Available online at https://www.treasury.gov/resource-center/sanctions/Programs/Documents/ukraine.pdf, retrieved on October 22nd, 2020.

package calling for stricter sanctions against Russia, primarily targeting the energy sector, as well as measures targeting the Islamic Republic of Iran and North Korea. Different to the E.O.'s mentioned above, the "Countering America's Adversaries Through Sanctions Act" can only be lifted involving the lower house of the US Congress.

Reaction and Countersanctions of Russia

As countermeasures, the Russian president stipulated by Executive Order No. 560 of August 2014 a ban and restrictions on foreign economic operations involving imports of certain kinds of agricultural produce, raw materials, and foodstuffs originating from certain countries.[3] Russian countersanctions targeted specifically countries that had imposed economic sanctions on Russian entities, products, or individuals. However, after an analysis of the Ministry of Agriculture, this list has been adjusted to exclude, e.g., seed grains or biologically active additives. Later on, the government of the Russian Federation extended the scope of the embargo to live pigs and to fat and offal of individual animals (European Commission, 2016). Similar to the Western governments, the Russian president extended the special economic measures to protect Russia's security in the following years with the four subsequent E.O.'s which will be in force at least until the end of 2020.[4] Also, following the "Countering America's Adversaries Through Sanctions Act" of July 2017, the Russian president demanded that the US reduces its diplomatic and technical personnel in the Moscow embassy and its consulates in Saint Petersburg, Yekaterinburg, and Vladivostok to 455 persons—the same as the number of Russian diplomats posted in the USA. However, it seems to be more interesting to understand how these somewhat technical decisions and resolutions are translated into practical economic effects and how the sanctions gained momentum in doing business in Russia and beyond.

Sanction and Protectionism Effects

Global Effects

It would be too far-fetched to say that the recent economic downswing in Russia was triggered and caused solely by the sanctions imposed by Western governments. With oil prices tremendously declining in the second half of 2014, falling from over $100 to less than $60 by the end of the year, the Russian ruble (RUB) collapsed. This

---

[3]US, EU, Canada, Australia, Norway, Ukraine, Albania, Montenegro, Iceland and Lichtenstein.

[4]Presidential Executive Office: Executive Order on special economic measures to protect Russia's security. Decree of the President of the Russian Federation of June 24, 2019, No. 293, available under https://apps.fas.usda.gov/, retrieved October 25th, 2020.

caused a weakening of confidence in the Russian economy as investors started to sell off their assets while the country itself was and is heavily dependent on the revenues from oil and gas exports. Suffering from Dutch disease (The Economist, 1977) the sanctions imposed on several financial instruments and goods accelerated the economic recession. From a macroeconomic perspective, the combination of financial and fiscal instability as well as sanctions had a massive effect on the Russian economy as well as its imports and exports (Table 7.1).

Russian imports from the USA and the European Union dropped around 40% from 2014 to 2015 while exports, especially to the EU, plunged 30% within the same time span and again roughly 20% 1 year later. Nevertheless, it is interesting to notice that from 2016 to 2017 imports as well as exports gained pace again despite persisting sanctions.

Specific Economic Effects for the EU and the USA

Still, as explained in the previous section, macroeconomic down- and upswings may have various reasons. Thus, it is necessary to pin down the sanction effects more precisely. In general, it can be said that the EU was and will be the most affected partner among all those targeted by the counter-sanction measures of Russia, as 73% of imports that are banned come from the EU. The European Commission reacted fast and announced, already 3 days after the EO of President Putin, first measures supporting EU producers of perishable fruits and vegetables, emergency market support for milk as well as dairy and livestock producers. Moreover, promotion funds have been established in order to help boost exports to alternative markets outside the EU (European Parliamentary Research Service, 2014; European Commission, 2018). However, the support measures did not hinder the exports to tumble, even though economic effects are heterogeneous across EU countries. The Directorate-General for External Policies of the EU Parliament estimated that sanction-related export losses across the EU were at USD7.9 bn in 2014, USD12.9 bn in 2015, and USD13.9 bn in 2016. In absolute terms, German exports to Russia decreased by around USD13 bn, a decrease of 13% vis-à-vis predicted exports, between 2014 and 2016. In relative terms, other countries such as Cyprus (−35%), Greece (−25%), and Croatia (−21%) are primarily more affected due to the decrease in exports of agricultural products (Directorate-General for External Policies, 2017). Despite subsidies, several EU companies and fruit growers were affected. Not only Greek farmers, who exported more than 60% of their peaches and nearly 90% of their strawberries to Russia, were existentially threatened, but also German mechanical engineering companies went bankrupt (The Guardian, 2014; Deutsche Mittelstands Nachrichten, 2018; Mitteldeutsche Zeitung, 2017).

However, the economic effects from sanctions have been substantially more significant for the EU than for the USA. Ranking 22nd among the US' main trade partners, the trade volume in goods and services with Russia represented less than 1% of total US world trade in 2014. Therefore, a report from the *Graduate Institute's Program for the Study of International Governance (PSIG)* concluded in 2017 "the

Table 7.1 Russian imports and exports with selected trading partners in bn USD (UN Comtrade, 2018)

	United States		European Union		China		World	
	Imports	Exports	Imports	Exports	Imports	Exports	Imports	Exports
2013	16,717	11,177	158,985	274,191	53,173	35,625	314,945	527,265
2014	18,594	9553	136,267	220,906	50,853	37,414	286,648	497,833
2015	11,489	8393	81,727	151,314	35,199	28,334	182,781	343,907
2016	11,065	9425	79,311	118,744	38,086	28,021	182,257	285,491
2017	12,589	9884	96,671	148,253	48,373	37,524	228,212	359,151

US economy has been fundamentally indifferent to the Russia-Ukraine crisis in general and the sanctions in particular" (The Graduate Institute Geneva, 2017).

Winners and Losers of Sanctions in Russia

The Russian government used the sanctions as a protectionist measure for domestic producers opening an excellent window of opportunity for the Russian agricultural sector. To cope with the embargo the Government of the Russian Federation increased its public support, increasing the federal budget aid by 27%, from 190 bn in 2014 to 242 bn RUB in 2017. Moreover, from 2015 onwards the state reimbursed 20–35% of the costs of construction and modernization of dairy and greenhouse facilities and expanded the state support for partial reimbursement of the costs of laying and maintenance of perennial fruits and berry plantations. This might also be a reason why several wealthy and influential investors started to set up companies specialized in vegetable farming (Russia Beyond, 2016, 2017). Billions of RUB have also been invested in meat as well as livestock farms and cooperatives. This led the imports to decline three times for pork, 2.5 times for poultry, and vegetable imports twofold within 3 years. Especially livestock producers like *Rusagro* were able to capitalize on the situation by more than doubling its share price (Rusagro Group, 2018). Also, within the strategic development policy "International Cooperation and Export" of the Russian Federation, small businesses and cooperative exporters of agricultural products will be substantially supported through lending and consulting programs in the upcoming years. This is aiming to upturn the agricultural export of Russia by 27% to USD21 bn by 2020 (Ministry of Agriculture of the Russian Federation, 2017) (Fig. 7.1).

That the agricultural sector and neighboring industries like the fishing industry could grow proportionally more than other industries during the economic downturn and the imposed sanctions. Figure 7.1 shows the indexed share in the gross domestic product by selected activities during 2010 and 2016. While activities like electricity, gas, and water supply as well as wholesale and retail trade were not able to recover to their 2010 level by 2016, especially from 2014 onwards the agriculture and fishing industry could profit from a less intense competitive environment and attract investors.

Losers of the sanctions are undoubtedly the Russian consumers. According to the World Bank's Russia Monthly Economic Development Report, the Consumer Price Index (CPI) saw tremendous upheavals during 2015 and 2016, letting food inflation hit a record high of 23.3% in February 2015. With the RUB on a record low, buying abroad was getting more and more expensive. Furthermore, household consumption plummeted given negative real income growth and higher consumer credit costs. The wholesale and retail trade industry was the only sector that was not able to recover from 2014 onwards, holding the lowest share in the gross domestic product by 2016. Before the corona crisis hit, the Russian economy recovered visibly, with a decreasing unemployment rate and lending activities continuing to recover, Russian consumers might have already left the worst behind them (World Bank, 2018).

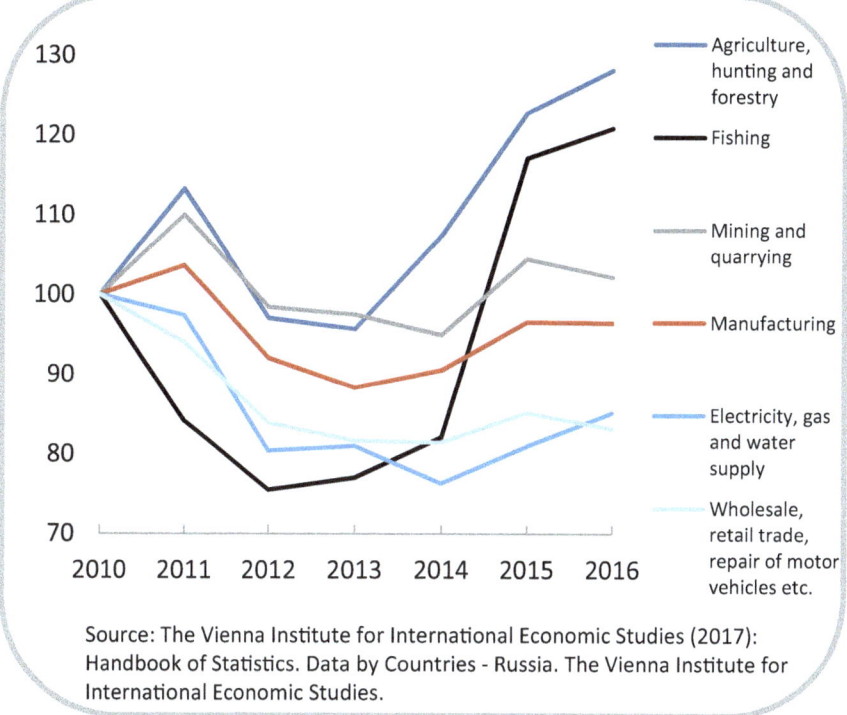

Fig. 7.1 Indexed share in gross domestic product by selected activities

However, the unilaterally introduced US sanctions in 2017 may also bring forth new losers, as there are not only Russian but also European enterprises engaged in Russia. With the provision "Countering Russian Influence in Europe and Eurasia Act of 2017" of the "Countering America's Adversaries Through Sanctions Act" mentioned above, the USA is targeting the Russian energy sector and in particular the gas market. Thereby, the sanctions package also allows measures against European companies if they are involved in specific projects, such as the construction, repair, modernization, or expansion of Russian export pipelines. In concrete terms, the law calls the Euro-Russian "North Stream II" project, for example. This led Germany and Austria to issue a joint statement that said that the proposed bill heralded a "new and very negative quality in European-American relations" and that the provision mentioned above was an illegal threat to the EU energy security (German Federal Foreign Office, 2017). The president of the *German-Russian Chamber of Commerce* also shares this view that the US sanctions can have an extraterritorial impact on European companies (German-Russian Chamber of Commerce, 2017). Though, while the challenging problems continue to persist, it is indispensable to look ahead.

Ways Out of the Deadlock

Ways out of the deadlock are hard to find. This is not only the case since political frontiers seem to be hardened, but also specific economic interests might hinder an amicable agreement. Politically, there are two highly unlikely scenarios. First, the Western countries will accept the secession of Crimea and lift their sanctions. Second, Russia will stick to the Minsk protocol, give in to the wrongful annexation of Crimea, and restore the status quo ante. Hence, it is more likely that there will be a process in between. If Russia loosens its grip on the Donbass-Region, Europe might be willing to ease its sanction measures (TASS, 2017). Moreover, if countries hit hard by the Russian embargo will veto further European sanctions, this could also pave the way for leaving the impasse, as decisions in the EU council must be taken unanimously. Nevertheless, when it comes to agricultural imports to Russia, the new strong domestic agricultural investors will have an influence upon political decisions lifting sanctions on European fruits, vegetables, and livestock products, as it seems likely that they are willing to protect their new flourishing businesses.

Hence, the question could arise whether turning towards China or intensifying the cooperation with the Eurasian Economic Union (EAEU) could be a valuable solution eluding the current deadlock? The Yakutia–Khabarovsk–Vladivostok pipeline, the most extensive gas transmission system in Russia's east and the biggest and most ambitious energy project since the Soviet Union may be a first sign. Therefore, in May 2014, *Gazprom* and the *China National Petroleum Corporation (CNPC)* signed a 30-year gas deal opening up a market worth as much as USD400 bn. The pipeline with an export capacity of 38 bn. cubic meters per year is operational since December 2019 (Gazprom, 2020). Thus, intensifying trade with China may be a strategy to cushion the blow of Western sanctions. However, not only China could be a piece to the solution of the puzzle. Developing its Southern, Eastern, and Far-East regions would enable Russia to become more independent from Western trading partners and at the same time to increase its access to (Central) Asian markets. Coming to life at the beginning of 2015, the EAEU is an international organization for regional economic integration of Armenia, Belarus, Kazakhstan, Kyrgyzstan, and Russia. With a combined GDP of about USD1.98 trillion in 2018 (estimated) and a population of more than 180 mill., the EEAU could represent a geopolitical success that supports both its ambitious political agenda and the Union's economic potential. However, to promote a stable development and raise the competitiveness of and cooperation between the national economies, notably the Russian Federation with its longstanding role within the region needs to act cautiously looking for balanced prospects for all EEAU partners. If this can be achieved, Russia could unlock new economic opportunities to the south and in the east while facing a deadlock to the west.

Conclusion

This chapter gave an overview of the current trading situation between Russia, Europe, and the United States in times of sanctions and protectionism. As the politically stagnant situation prevails, casting doubt on the claim that the imposed economic sanctions can achieve primary foreign policy goals may be adequate. Nevertheless, the economic effects from sanctions have been substantially more significant for the EU and Russia than for the USA. Therefore, it seems likely that the EU will also be more willing to strive for a solution. It will also be interesting to see if European producers can regain market shares in the Russian retail market, as several domestic suppliers have successfully taken their place. In addition, Russia needs to adapt to the new situation but may be able to capitalize on its new trading relations to the south and in the east. Still, in response to the alleged poisoning of a former Russian–British double agent and the reputed Russian government interference in the 2016 Presidential elections, a fresh batch of sanctions released in Mid-August 2018 added to mounting concerns that the USA is about to start retching up the severity of its restrictions against Russia (Bloomberg, 2018).

On top of the thread that sanctions could be extended, the Russian economy was heavily hit by the coronavirus pandemic in the first half of 2020. The resulting drop in oil demand has caused oil prices to collapse and put significant pressure on the Russian currency. However, it might prove an advantage that the Russian economy—forced by sanctions—had focused previously on keeping debt low and stimulated its agricultural sector. It will remain interesting to see whether the Russian economy can master the current situation and how the Russian government will react to new additional challenges in times of sanctions and protectionism.

References

Bloomberg. (2018). *Russia Blasts New U.S. Sanctions Plan as Ruble Slides. With assistance of Wadhams, Nick and Kravchenko, Stepan*. Retrieved October 25, 2020, from https://www.bloomberg.com/news/articles/2018-08-08/u-s-sanctions-russia-over-nerve-agent-attack-on-sex-spy-in-u-k.

Deutsche Mittelstands Nachrichten. (2018). *Russland-Sanktionen: Maschinenbauer SHW ist insolvent*. Retrieved August 26, 2018, from https://www.deutsche-mittelstands-nachrichten.de/2018/06/93800/.

Directorate-General for External Policies. (2017). *Russia's and the EU's sanctions: Economic and trade effects, compliance and the way forward*. Retrieved August 26, 2018, from http://www.europarl.europa.eu/RegData/etudes/STUD/2017/603847/EXPO_STU(2017)6038 47_EN.pdf.

European Commission. (2016). *Russian import ban on EU products*. Retrieved October 22, 2020, from https://ec.europa.eu/food/safety/international_affairs/eu_russia/russian_import_ban_eu_produ cts_en.

European Commission. (2018). *Russian import ban on agricultural products – Agriculture and rural development – European Commission*. Retrieved August 26, 2018, from https://ec.europa.eu/agriculture/russian-import-ban_en.

European Parliamentary Research Service. (2014). *Russian measures against European Union agricultural products. With assistance of Ana Martinez Juan*. Retrieved August 26, 2018, from https://epthinktank.eu/2014/10/03/russian-measures-against-european-union-agricultural-products/.

Gazprom. (2020). *Power of Siberia*. Retrieved October 27, 2020, from http://www.gazprom.com/projects/power-of-siberia/.

German Federal Foreign Office. (2017). *Foreign Minister Gabriel and Austrian Federal Chancellor Kern on the imposition of Russia sanctions by the US Senate*. Retrieved September 28, 2018, from https://www.auswaertiges-amt.de/de/newsroom/170615-kern-russland/290664.

German-Russian Chamber of Commerce. (2017). *Neue US-Sanktionen gefährden die deutsche Wirtschaft in Russland*. Retrieved September 28, 2018, from https://russland.ahk.de/infothek/news/detail/neue-us-sanktionen-gefaehrden-die-deutsche-wirtschaft-in-russland/.

Hufbauer, G. C., Schott, J. J., & Elliott, K. A. (1990). *Economic sanctions reconsidered. History and current policy*. Peterson Institute.

Ministry of Agriculture of the Russian Federation. (2017). *The Ministry of Agriculture of Russia has just summarized the implementation results of the imports phase-out program for 3 years*. Retrieved August 26, 2018, from http://mcx.ru/en/news/imports-phase-out-program/.

Mitteldeutsche Zeitung. (2017). *Wegen Russland-Sanktionen?: Leipziger Stahlbauunternehmen IMO insolvent*. Retrieved August 26, 2018, from https://www.mz-web.de/wirtschaft/wegen-russland-sanktionen%2D%2Dleipziger-stahlbauunternehmen-imo-insolvent-28074774.

Pape, R. A. (1997). Why economic sanctions do not work. *International Security, 22*(2), 90–136.

Rusagro Group. (2018). *Stock Chart*. Retrieved August 26, 2018, from https://www.rusagrogroup.ru/en/investors/shares/stock-chart/.

Russia Beyond. (2016). *Why has Roman Abramovich's son become a cucumber farmer? With assistance of Anna Kuchma*. Retrieved August 26, 2018, from https://www.rbth.com/business/2016/05/17/why-has-roman-abramovichs-son-become-a-cucumber-farmer_593753.

Russia Beyond. (2017). *3 years of embargo in Russia: The winners and losers. With assistance of Kira Kalinina*. Retrieved August 26, 2018, from https://www.rbth.com/business/2017/08/06/3-years-of-embargo-in-russia-the-winners-and-losers_816898.

TASS. (2017). *German top diplomat comments on initiative to deploy UN mission in Donbass*. Retrieved August 26, 2018, from http://tass.com/world/963797.

The Economist. (1977). The Dutch disease. *The Economist* (p. 82).

The Graduate Institute Geneva. (2017). *Sanctions on Russia: Impacts and economic costs on the United States*. Retrieved June 26, 2018, from http://graduateinstitute.ch/files/live/sites/iheid/files/sites/internationalgovernance/shared/Russian-Sanctions-Report.pdf.

The Guardian. (2014). *Greek farmers hit hard by Russian sanctions against EU produce. With assistance of Helena Smith*. Retrieved August 26, 2018, from https://www.theguardian.com/world/2014/aug/13/greece-farmers-russian-sanctions-rotten-fruit.

UN Comtrade. (2018). *International Trade Statistics*. Retrieved August 24, 2018, from https://comtrade.un.org/data/.

United Nations. (2017). *Consolidated United Nations Security Council Sanctions List | United Nations Security Council Subsidiary Organs*. Retrieved October 23, 2020, from https://www.un.org/sc/suborg/en/sanctions/un-sc-consolidated-list.

World Bank. (2018). *Russia Monthly Economic Development. With assistance of Apurva Sanghi*. Retrieved August 26, 2018, from http://pubdocs.worldbank.org/en/643291531922098819/June26-MAY-RMED-eng-final.pdf.

Russian Banking System

Aleksandr N. Dubianskii

The Russian banking system is relatively young compared to other countries because the RF inherited the banking system of the Soviet Union. Michail Gorbatchev's perestroika program, under which the first commercial banks were formed, marked the beginning of a modern banking system in Russia. Since then, the financial system has undergone several reforms structured in the following periods.

1988–1996 Initial Privatization

This initial stage was characterized by an explosive increase in the number of commercial banks. Russia's first commercial bank under the symbolic name Union was registered by the state Bank of the USSR on August 24, 1988, in Chimkent (Kazakh SSR). Just 2 days later in Leningrad (now St. Petersburg), the Patent bank was registered (now called Viking). By 1991, there were 869 banks in the banking system. At the end of 1992, more than 2000 credit institutions had already been registered in the country. The maximum number of banks in Russia was observed in 1994, with 2439 banking organizations.

1997–1998 Reformation and Maturity

The young Russian banking sector faced its first crisis in 1997, which pushed many newly established banks that lacked qualified specialists and basic experience in the banking sector out of business. A year later, the Russian economy was hit even harder by the global financial crisis of 1998. The Russian government and the

A. N. Dubianskii (✉)
Department of Economic History and Economic Thoughts, Saint Petersburg State University, Saint Petersburg, Russia
e-mail: a.dubianskii@spbu.ru

Russian Central Bank devalued the ruble, set a 90-day memorandum on external commercial debt payments, and eventually defaulted on its debt. The crisis had severe impacts on the entire Russian economy and is remembered as a major turning point in the country's recent history. Even though the crisis sparked further reforms, which in the following years led to rapid economic growth, the crisis had a negative impact on the still young banking system. Banks with weak management, insufficient assets, and large volumes of government bonds went bankrupt. Many of them were comparably large banks, such as *Menatep*, *SBS-Agro*, and *Incombank*. A bank restructuring strategy was implemented which eventually led to a more oligopolistic structure with less strong players in the market.

1999–2009 Formation of Monopolistic Structures

Russia bounced back quickly from the financial collapse and the economy grew fast in the following decade. The Russian banking system continued to form oligopolistic, if not even monopolistic, structures. During this period, dozens of the largest private monopoly banks were formed, in the hands of which a significant part of the country's banking assets is concentrated.

2009–2015 Strengthening of State Banks

This period saw the strengthening of state banks, primarily *PAO Sberbank of Russia (Sberbank)*, *Vneshtorg Bank (VTB)*, and *Vnesheconombank*. The growing importance of state-owned banks was due to the patronage of the state that became an important competitive advantage for them during the crisis. Clients preferred the reliability of state-owned banks to potentially volatile private commercial banks.

2016 Until Today: Further Consolidation

Recent years have seen a further consolidation of the banking sector through mergers, acquisitions, or liquidations of credit institutions. All these processes have has happened as the requirements from the Central Bank of the Russian Federation to banks have simultaneously toughened. The result of which has been a massive withdrawal of licenses from banks that do not comply with prudential requirements and standards from the regulator. Every year several dozen banks lose their licenses. As of March 2020, there are only 396 banks with valid licenses in Russia.

The Banking System Today

The banking system is not large enough in relation to the size of the Russian economy because the total assets of the banking system amounted to only 92% of GDP. From the structural point of view, the Russian banking system is two-tiered, as in most countries of the world. The first tier is a set of commercial banks and above them on the second tier is the Central Bank of the Russian Federation (CBR). The CBR is the main regulator of banking activity. The Central Bank enjoys powers beyond those typically found in other Western countries. In a way, a mega-regulator that performs a supervisory function over Russian credit institutions and in addition regulates foreign exchange markets, financial markets, and securities markets.

Another level of the banking system can be unofficially distinguished in Russia, which is formed by two state banks with a special status, namely *Sberbank* and VTB. In addition, another sub-level of banks can be considered as systemically important which means their stability ensures the stability of the entire banking system. These banks are *Alfa-bank, Gazprombank, Credit Bank of Moscow, Russian Agricultural Bank, Promsvyazbank, Bank Otkritie,* and the Russian subsidiaries of *Unicredit, Rosbank (Societe Generale),* and *Raiffeisen* bank. Among the above listed, five banks are under the direct control of the Russian state. These are namely: *Sberbank, VTB, Russian Agricultural Bank, Otkritie Bank,* and indirectly *Gazprombank* because it is controlled by the state-owned enterprise *Gazprom*. Only three banks (*Alfa-bank, Credit Bank of Moscow, Promsvyazbank*) are under private ownership while the three remaining banks are subsidiaries of large international financial groups (*Unicredit, ROSBANK Societe Generale, and Raiffeisen*). Banks that are considered as being of systemic importance are under greater control and need to fulfill higher mandatory standards than non-systemic institutions (Table 8.1).

A Strongly Nationalized System

Since 2004, Russia has installed a deposit insurance system that guarantees depositors a license from a commercial bank, the return of the deposit up to 1,400,000 rubles, in the event of revocation. This insurance is carried out through a specially created institute—*Deposit Insurance Agency (DIA)*, which accumulates the insurance premiums of banks and makes payments to depositors of affected banks. For individuals, one cannot be afraid to open deposits within the insurance amount. For business, it is better to focus on banks with state participation, which seem more reliable in comparison with private banks.

In the Russian banking system, there is another feature that distinguishes local banks from foreign credit institutions. This is the lack of the practice of irrevocability of deposits in Russia. The Civil code of the Russian Federation allows citizens at any time to cancel the contract on bank deposits and withdraw money from the bank. It is important to note that the lack of irrevocability of deposits creates a competitive advantage for state banks and branches of foreign banks, as well as banks whose owners own large raw material assets.

Table 8.1 The largest 15 banks in Russia (as of June 1, 2018)[a]

Place	Banks	Assets (mill. rubles)	Credits of citizens (mill. rubles)	Deposits citizen (mill. rubles)
1	Sberbank (Moscow)	23,761	5213	9055
2	VTB (Saint Petersburg)	11,691	2093	2599
3	Gazprombank (Moscow)	5753	409	639
4	Russian Agricultural Bank (Moscow)	3211	377	816
5	AO "Alfa-bank" (Moscow)	2631	291	352
6	Credit Bank of Moscow (Moscow)	1791	84	293
7	Otkritie Bank (Moscow)	1191	75	341
8	Unicredit Bank (Moscow)	1159	128	125
9	Promsvyazbank (Moscow)	1025	78	344
10	Raiffeisen Bank (Moscow)	908	242	96
11	Russia Bank (Saint Petersburg)	903	14	82
12	Rosbank (Moscow)	860	117	82
13	B&N Bank (Moscow)	780	28	450
14	Sovcombank (Kostroma)	724	135	304
15	Russian Regional Development Bank (Moscow)	617	17	66

[a]https://www.kommersant.ru/, retrieved on October 25th, 2020

The banking system in Russia is clearly nationalized. This is confirmed by the dominance of state and quasi-state banks as they account for up to 75% of all banking assets. Such a large share of state-owned banks corresponds to the ownership structure and the degree of concentration in the real sector of the Russian economy, in which state-owned enterprises occupy leading positions (Ivanter, 2017). When comparing Russian banks with firms in the real sector of the economy in terms of production, it turns out that these banks are too small in relation to enterprises in financial capabilities, and therefore cannot provide them with credit resources in the required amounts. The share of bank loans in total investments of Russian organizations in fixed assets for the period 2011–2015 varied between 8.4 and 10%. Currently, this share has remained practically unchanged (Mandron & Gutorova, 2016).

Recent Reforms and Trends

In 2018, the CBR introduced changes to the banking system that divided banks into two levels. The first level includes banks whose capital will be above 1 billion rubles. These banks operate under a universal license, i.e., they are allowed all types of banking operations. The second level comprises those banks whose owners are not able to produce 1 billion rubles of capital. Such banks are required to have a minimum capital of 300 mill. rubles and need to operate under a basic license, which implies restrictions on certain banking operations.

Currently, there is a change in the model of the banking business, which is moving to the so-called new reality. The latter term implies a stable, low inflation and further reduction of the key rate by the CBR. As a result, relatively low interest rates on loans and deposits will become the norm with the prospect of further reduction of the spread, i.e., the difference between the rates on deposits and loans (Dolzhenkov, 2017).

Tough measures on the part of the CBR are imposed on most banks that do not meet modern standards. Most commercial banks in Russia are captive banks, which were established by large corporations to lend to their own business. Accordingly, these banks have a narrow focus and are dealing only with a limited number of private or corporate clients. Under today's conditions with increasing regulation by the CBR, many owners prefer to get rid of bank assets.

Outlook

What is troubling about the Russian banking system is the fact that it was established in a non-market economy. As a result, all banks in Russia are universal and can only be organized as joint-stock companies. The banking act does not authorize the creation of specialized, co-operative, or regional banks. That restriction deeply impoverishes the Russian banking system and limits its capability to structurally reflect the real sectors of the economy.

To sum up, the Russian banking system is still in a transitional phase. The main challenge is that it needs to resolve the double role of the Central Bank and the inherit problems that come with it. The Central Bank is the majority owner and supervisor of the largest Russian banks. It is difficult to imagine that it can fulfill both tasks without avoiding potential conflict of interests. In addition, further fundamental structural reforms are necessary with the objective to make the system more efficient and to have a more significant impact on stimulating the growth of the Russian economy.

References

Ivanter, A. (2017). The abolition of the syndrome. *Expert, 40*, 19. [Ivanter A. Sindrom otmeny. // EHkspert. 2017. №40. S.19.].

Dolzhenkov, A. (2017). Survive the "new normality". *Expert, 51*, 44. [Dolzhenkov A. Perezhit' «novuyu normal'nost'» // EHkspert 2017. №51. S.44.].

Mandron, V. V., & Gutorova, A. A. (2016). Investment activity of Russian banks and problems of its implementation. *The Young Scientist, 28*, 486–491. Retrieved September 4, 2018, from https://moluch.ru/archive/132/37020/ [Mandron V. V., Gutorova A. A. Investitsionnaya deyatel'nost' rossijskikh bankov i problemy ee osushhestvleniya // Molodoj uchenyj. — 2016. — №28. — S. 486-491. — URL https://moluch.ru/archive/132/37020/ (data obrashheniya: 04.09.2018).]

The Russian Stock Market

Marina Sakovich

The Russian economy is still undergoing profound social and political change and displays many characteristics of an emerging market. Like the other BRIC[1] countries, it offers an enormous growth potential that attracts international investors to the Russian stock market. Due to the high dependency of the economy on natural resources and the generally low productivity, the Russian stock market and the oil price have been often tightly correlated in past periods. Not for the faint-hearted, the investment risk in Russia is higher in comparison with markets of developed countries and thus offers higher yields for most financial instruments.

The current structure of the stock market began to evolve in the early 1990s. Today it displays similar structures to developed countries with a well-developed exchange infrastructure and the presence of a central counterparty to ensure the reliability of operations with securities.

The *Moscow Exchange (MOEX)* dominates the Russian securities market and is the biggest exchange of Eastern Europe. It was created in 2011 when the two major Russian stock exchanges, the *Moscow Interbank Currency Exchange* (*MICEX*, established in 1992) and the *Russian Trading System* (*RTS*, founded in 1995) were merged. There are six more exchanges, some of these operate with securities but most focus on commodity trading.

MOEX currently operates trading markets for equities (stock market), bonds, derivatives, currencies, money market instruments, and commodities. The *MOEX* includes the central depository and the central counterparty. The stock market of *MOEX* includes corporate shares, sovereign, regional and corporate bonds,

---

[1]The four largest merging economies Brazil, Russia, India, and China, are known collectively as BRIC an acronym coined by Jim O'Neill. All have huge populations, are rich in natural resources, and have enormous growth potential.

M. Sakovich (✉)
Université Grenoble Alpes, Grenoble, France

Grottbjorn, St. Petersburg, Russia

sovereign and corporate Eurobonds, depositary receipts, investment funds shares, exchange-traded funds (ETF), and mortgage securities. Futures contracts for indices (MOEX, RTS index, RVI volatility index), futures on shares, government bonds, and Eurobonds, currency pairs, interest rates, contracts for precious metals, futures for oil and sugar, option contracts for some of these futures are traded. The Moscow Exchange provides repurchase agreement services (repo), including repo with the central counterparty.

The infrastructure of the exchange market in Russia includes also brokerage organizations, dealers, asset managers, depositories, registrars, and clearing organizations. Securities in Russia can be traded on the exchange and the Over-The-Counter (OTC) market. Regulation of the securities market is carried out by the *Central Bank of Russia (CBR)*, which regulates and supervises all participants in the financial sector. There are also self-regulating organizations of stock market participants; the biggest is the National Association of Stock Market Participants.

Statistics of the Stock Market

Equities

At the Moscow Exchange, more than 200 issuers of shares are registered in 2020.[2] This represents a little more than 1% of the total number of registered open joint-stock companies in the country. The Russian market capitalization was with 35% of the country's GDP (in 2018)[3] low for global standards with a high concentration on the ten most capitalized Russian issuers. They alone account for about more than 60% of the total market capitalization of the Moscow Exchange.[4] Mostly these companies represent the oil and gas industry, mining, metallurgy, and finance sectors of the economy. The market is accordingly very cyclical.

Equities of domestic issuers dominate the Moscow Exchange market. The share of foreign equities and depositary receipts in total amounted to less than 1% in 2019.[5] The average Price to Earnings (P/E) ratio and Price to Book Value (P/BV) has been low by international standards in recent years. The dividend yield of the Russian stock market mainly demonstrated an upward trend and by the end of 2019 was at the level of 7%[6] (Table 9.1).

---

[2]Russian National Association of Securities Market Participants (www.naufor.ru) retrieved June 30th, 2020.
[3]Russian National Association of Securities Market Participants (www.naufor.ru) retrieved June 30th, 2020.
[4]World Federation of Exchanges (www.world-exchanges.org/) retrieved June 30th 2020.
[5]Russian National Association of Securities Market Participants (www.naufor.ru) retrieved June 30th, 2020.
[6]Russian National Association of Securities Market Participants (www.naufor.ru) retrieved June 30th, 2020.

Table 9.1 Equity trade at the stock exchanges (as of February 2020)

	Moscow Exchange	Deutsche Boerse	ICE & NYSE
Market capitalization (USD bn./global rank)	4.1/14	31.5/5	51.7/2
Equity: no. of issuers (2019)	217	515	2.143
Market concentration[a] (%)	63	40	NA

Source: World Federation of Exchanges, www.moex.com retrieved June 30, 2020
[a]Top 10 most capitalized and most traded domestic companies in 2017

The market of the Moscow Stock Exchange provides three levels of listing for shares issuers. Russian joint-stock companies may issue common stocks or preferred shares. The number of preferred shares issued cannot exceed 25% of the total number of shares or preferred shares may not be issued. Preferred shares give their owners greater certainty in receiving dividends. Common stocks give their owners the right to vote at the general meeting of shareholders. Preferred shares receive the right to vote if dividends are not paid. Equities are issued only in a non-documentary form in Russia.

Bonds

The corporate debt market has boomed since 2014 because sanctions have limited the possibility for Russian companies to raise new finance on global markets. Thus, it has become a key platform for Russian enterprises to raise capital. In 2017, Russian debt capital markets grew by more than 21% versus the previous year[7] and saw 251 new issues of corporate bonds with a volume totalling 2880 billion rubles. The share of credit institutions is 18.2% of the total issue volume.[8] 95% of the secondary market of corporate bonds accounted for organized exchange trades.

Reforms were implemented to simplify the procedure of issuance corporate bonds have and also fueled the issuance of bonds and attracted debut entrants to the bond market. Bonds can be issued in the form of coupons or discount bonds. In addition, Eurobonds and some types of government bonds are also traded on the Moscow Exchange.

---

[7]Russian National Association of Securities Market Participants (www.naufor.ru) retrieved June 30th, 2020.

[8]Report on the Development of the Banking Sector and Banking Supervision in 2017. The Central Bank of the Russian Federation.

Other Instruments of the Market

The repo (repurchase agreements) market demonstrated strong growth in recent years.[9] The number of exchange-traded funds (ETFs) rose in 2019 on MOEX to 35. MOEX includes shares of 145 funds[10] and 48 types of derivatives are traded here (24 futures and 24 options).[11] E.g., the Moscow Exchange is one of the global leaders by Brent Oil futures trading.

Indices

There are two main indices of Moscow Exchange: *MOEX Russia Index (IMOEX)* and *RTS Index (RTSI)*. The Moscow Exchange indices are capitalization-weighted composite indices calculated based on prices of the most liquid Russian equities of the largest Russian issuers with economic activities related to the main sectors of the Russian economy presented on the Exchange. The *IMOEX* is denominated in rubles and the *RTS Index* denominated in US Dollars. The *MOEX* also calculates sectoral indices for specific industries, namely oil and gas, electric utilities, telecoms, metals and mining, financials, consumer goods and services, chemicals, transport; and a number of other instruments indices.

Investors

Participants of the Russian stock market are both individuals and legal entities, residents, and non-residents. The number of unique individual clients has grown in recent years, also in connection with the application of special taxation incentives for individuals. By the end of 2019, the Moscow Exchange the number of unique individual clients had 3.8 mill. private investors with brokerage accounts (97% more compared to the previous year) which still represents only a small portion of the nation's working-age population.[12]

Non-resident individual or legal entity can be a client of any brokerage company registered in Russia allowing access to instruments of the Russian stock market. It is important to note that for non-residents higher tax rates are applied for income received from operations with securities. In accordance with Russian law, a broker acts as a tax agent that calculates, retains, and pays taxes associated with operations in the stock market.

---

[9]Russian National Association of Securities Market Participants (www.naufor.ru) retrieved June 30th, 2020.
[10]Russian National Association of Securities Market Participants (www.naufor.ru) retrieved June 30th, 2020.
[11]www.moex.com, retrieved June 30th, 2020.
[12]www.moex.com, retrieved June 30th, 2020.

To stimulate the development of the stock market, a number of tax incentives are applied, for example, part of the income from operations with bonds, including corporate ones, is exempt from taxation.

The category of qualified investors is singled out, for which a wider range of securities is available. In addition to institutional investors, such status can be assigned to a legal entity or an individual subject to certain criteria.

Suggestions for Further Reading

Report on the Development of the Banking Sector and Banking Supervision in 2017. The Central Bank of the Russian Federation.	http://www.cbr.ru/publ/bsr/bsr_2017.pdf
The Russian Stock Market 2017. Events and Facts. National Association of Stock Market Participants	http://www.naufor.org/download/pdf/factbook/ru/RFR2017.pdf
WFE Annual Statistics Guide 2017. World Federation of Exchanges	https://www.world-exchanges.org/home/index.php/statistics/annual-statistics
Moscow Exchange	https://www.moex.com/

The Russian Ruble and Monetary System

Torsten Erdmann

The Russian financial system went through various phases after the breakdown of the Soviet Union, closely linked to the economic situation and geopolitical situation in the country. Today Russia's currency is within the top 20 traded currencies by value worldwide.[1] The ruble is freely convertible and while currency control regulation is maybe still a bureaucratic burden, it is not a real obstacle for international and cross-border payments. The volatility of the currency remains a real burden and usually requires additional attention and/or hedging instruments.

The ruble is the oldest national currency after the Pound sterling and is the world's first decimal currency.[2] It accounts for approx. 1.1% of the global foreign exchange market turnover ahead of the Indian rupee, the Brazilian real, and the South African rand. It is the only national currency used for transactions between Russian residents (including Russian legal entities with taxpayer status in Russia) because the use of other currencies is a punishable offense.[3] This makes local transplants of foreign companies that are usually engaged in cross-border trades particularly vulnerable as they are exposed to foreign currency risks. Often these companies purchase goods from their head office or other group companies, which are dominated, by the Euro or US Dollar but the further distribution takes place against Russian rubles. It is possible to minimize this risk by indexation clauses ("price of the good is Euro XXX,xx payable in Russian rubles at the official

---

[1]Triennial Central Bank Survey. Basel, Switzerland: Bank for International Settlements. 11 December 2016.

[2]The history of Russian ruble and kopeck, 19 August 2011 at the Wayback Machine at the law-theory.ru (in Russian).

[3]Federal law 173, at https://normativ.kontur.ru/document?moduleId=1&documentId=206129#h418, retrieved April 29th, 2019.

T. Erdmann (✉)
Commerzbank (Eurasija), Saint Petersburg, Russia
e-mail: torsten.erdmann@commerzbank.com

Exchange rate of the Central Bank of Russia at the date of payment/date of delivery/date of erection etc.").

Russia has attempted on several occasions to make the Ruble more relevant in international trade. In 2010, Russia and China agreed to use their national currencies for bilateral trade. The political objective of the agreement was to improve and deepen relations between both countries. The economical rational of the arrangement was to protect their domestic economies against foreign exchange fluctuation. Consequently, the trading of the Chinese Yuan against the Ruble was introduced in both, the Chinese interbank market and the Russian foreign exchange market by the end of the year.[4]

Currency Control Regulations

In order to protect the national economy against capital outflow and illegal transfers, currency controls and regulations were introduced as a separate field of federal law.[5] Subject under this law is only operations between residents and non-residents of Russia. It establishes rules on performing currency operations in the territory of Russia, as well as rights and duties in respect of possession, usage, and disposal of currency values, of the Russian currency and securities. According to this law, the currency control bodies are the Government of Russia, the Central Bank of Russia (CBR), and the Federal Agency of Financial and Budget Supervision. Currency control agents are defined as tax agencies, customs bodies, and banks. Banks are imbued with control over currency operations and the right to observe transactions between residents and non-residents to ensure they meet currency legislation stipulations. Realizing this power, banks must request and receive documents regarding currency operations from residents and non-residents, namely documents (draft documents) necessary for making currency operations, including

- Agreements (contracts), as well as addenda and/or amendments to them, letters of attorney, extracts from the minutes of a general meeting.
- Documents confirming the fact of goods delivery (performance of work, rendering of services), information and results of intellectual activities, including exclusive rights, and acts of government bodies.
- Documents issued by credit organizations, including bank statements.
- Customs declarations, documents confirming import or export of goods to or from Russia, currency of the Russian Federation, foreign currency, and foreign and domestic certified securities.[6]

---

[4]China, Russia quit dollar, Su Qiang and Li Xiaokun in China Daily, at http://www.chinadaily.com.cn/china/2010-11/24/content_11599087.htm, retrieved on April 29th, 2019.

[5]The federal law on currency regulation and currency control. Federal law No. 173 adopted 10.12.2003.

[6]Commerzbank AG, Information for clients on Currency Control in Russia, February 2018.

For the purpose of regulation, any operation or loan agreement for an amount in excess of RUB 3 mill. (for export contracts the limit is RUB 6 mill.) or equivalent in another currency, which fall under this law a resident shall register an agreement with a "Unique Number of Contract" (UNC). The UNC is used for customs and bank control to test the validity of import of prepaid goods transactions into Russia and over the repatriation of currency proceeds from goods/services exports out of Russia. The UNC contains some of the basic requisites of the contract to be transferred from banks to customs bodies for customs clearance purposes.

If a resident customer intends to make a payment for the import of goods (or services) to a non-resident, the customer has to present a payment order, supporting documents, and a certificate on the payment purpose to the bank. The bank checks if the presented documents correspond to the specified purpose of payment, contractual terms of payment, and to the UNC. If everything is correct, the bank makes the payment. Usually banks refuse to process the payment in case the customer did not present supporting documents or documents were suspicious in nature. Banks also refuse to process the payment in the case where the customer did not present a certificate on currency operation. The certificate shows the type of operation and contains the specific code of operation (VO-code). A specific VO-code is assigned depending on the purpose of the operation. The total list of VO-codes includes more than 200 different codes.

The bank delivers information about the UNC payments to CBR and customs bodies on a bi-weekly basis.[7] Settlements under loan agreements between residents and non-residents are not limited in any aspect by the loan amount, interest rate, or maturity. However, non-residents will have to open a ruble account with a Russian bank for settlements. These settlements can also be made through a ruble account of a non-resident bank opened with a Russian bank.

Income from investments into Russian companies (Investments made into the charter capital of a Russian limited liability or joint-stock company) can be freely transferred in a foreign currency as dividends in favor of a foreign shareholder (or a foreign parent company). There is no requirement for non-residents to open an account with a Russian bank for these purposes.

In general, if a foreign company acts just as an exporter (cross-border), it will never be confronted directly by currency controls, because only importers (resident companies) are obliged to fulfill the requirements mentioned above. The picture changes completely if the foreign company has set up its own subsidiary/trading house in the country. In this case, the importer (subsidiary) is responsible but all further transactions with Russian counterparts are not subject to currency control.

---

[7]Instruction of the Central Bank of Russia No. 181 dated 16.08.201, at https://normativ.kontur.ru/document?moduleId=1&documentId=305536&cwi=5501, retrieved on Apr. 29th, 2019.

The New Foreign Exchange Regime Since 2014

For many years, the monetary policy of the Central Bank of Russia was mainly focused on the exchange rate of the Russian ruble. A good example was the financial crisis 2008/2009, when a big part of foreign currency reserves (USD210 billion) was used to support the Russian Ruble (Maternowskiy, 2009). At that time, it was the right decision to support the national currency and to avoid a banking run. However, in the following years, it became clear, that the less controlled the Russian national currency is, the more efficient it is, making the economy react more effectively and timely.

The financial crisis hit Russia with full force when the Ruble started to collapse and devaluate in the second half of 2014. After the Crimean crisis, initial sanctions were introduced, causing a deep decline in confidence in the Russian economy. The effect of the sanctions on the economy was difficult to assess at this point and led to a great uncertainty amidst investors. Consequently, investors began to sell off their Russian assets resulting in a deep decline in the value of the Russian Ruble. The lack of confidence in the Russian economy had at least two major roots. The first reason was the fall in oil prices in 2014. Crude oil, one of Russia's major exports, declined in price by nearly 50% in the second half of 2014. The second reason was the effect of international economic sanctions against Russia imposed by the EU and the USA (Chap. 7) (Kitroeff & Weisenthal, 2014). However, it must be said, that the Russian economy had already lost its momentum years before.

The crisis affected the whole Russian economy: consumers, companies, and regional financial markets alike. From July 2014 to February 2015 the ruble fell dramatically against the USD. The interest rate shot up from 6.5% to 17%. However, even this maneuver did not protect the Ruble hitting record lows in the first quarter of 2015 (Tanas & Andrianova, 2014). In this situation, the free float of the Russian ruble was the only way to stabilize the economy (Fig. 10.1).

From 2015 to late 2018, the Central Bank decreased interest rates numerous times. Surprisingly, the long-term target of the Central bank to reduce core inflation to 4% was reached in 2017 but in late 2018 and early 2019 inflation increased above 4% before the trend to reduction continued. The low inflation rate opened the door to another decrease of the key interest rate and has opened the option space of the Central Bank to react more efficient to other upcoming external and internal shocks and partly absorb them to defend the local economy.

The Russian Gamble

In order to understand the volatility of the Russian ruble, two fundamental questions must be answered:

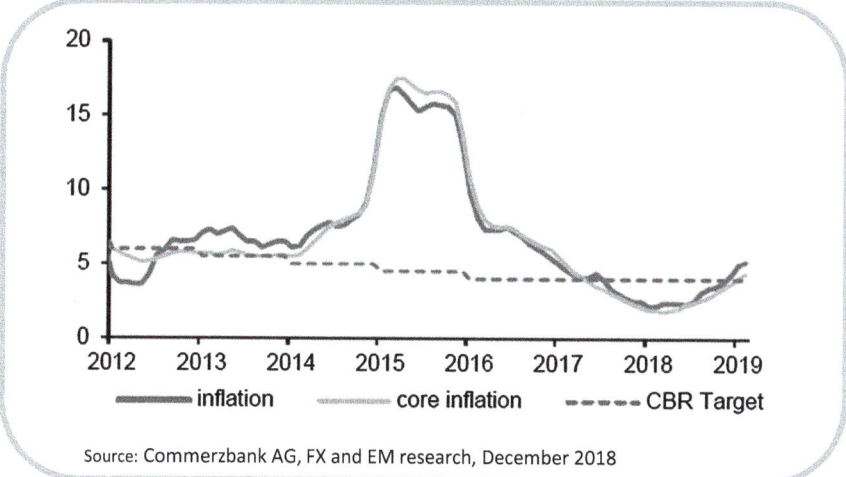

Fig. 10.1 Inflation and the ruble

1. Have Western sanctions had much impact or have they had inadvertently positive effect as some claim?
2. Has Russia's dependence on the price of oil decreased at all since a decade ago?[8]

Are Sanctions Effective?

The impact of western sanctions on Russia since 2014 has been a controversial topic: several commentators, including Russian officials, claim that sanctions have been futile—that life goes on much the same in Russia. These commentators point to the healthy capital adequacy of financial institutions whose access to capital markets was barred or the increased profitability of systemic oil and gas and other exporters, which received a windfall from the weaker ruble. Because so many opposing forces act on individual sectors and institutions, the net impact can be confusing, especially because this period also happened to coincide with an abrupt downward shift in the oil price.

Still, it may be useful to lay out a baseline. Let us compare Russia's economic performance relative to GDP and regional benchmarks, Russia's per capita GDP relative to the euro zone average. Russia's economic performance experienced a discrete turning point around 2014. Until the Crimean crisis struck, Russia's GDP per capita was outperforming the world average and the neighboring euro zone. After the sanctions, however, performance has steadily fallen (Fig. 10.2).

---

[8]Commerzbank AG, FX and EM research, December 2018.

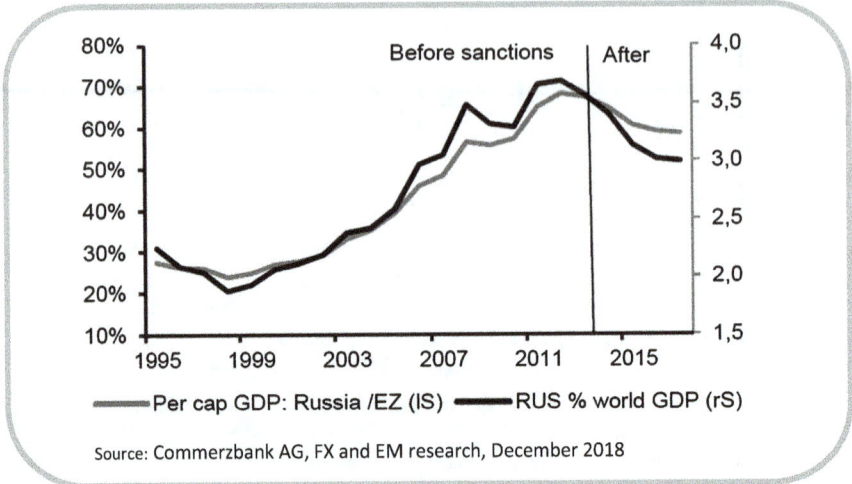

Fig. 10.2 Russian per capita GDP (PPP) relative to EU average (His) and GDP share of the world (rhs), in percent

Entangled with Oil Price Impact

The real share of oil and gas exports in the Russian economy is difficult to estimate. The Federal Service for State Statistics (*Rosstat*) does not provide the value-added of oil and gas within the sectoral breakdown of GDP. Yet, even if it had, the estimate would be misleading. If one were looking for the significance of the sector for the economy, its influence is spread over many variables. These range from fiscal revenue, rental on fixed assets of the sector, and the operation of monetary and fiscal policy as well as the wealth fund, which are all functions of the oil price.

If one were to take just a simple measure—such as export revenue from oil and gas as percentage of GDP—one notices a longer-term downward trend. Within the downtrend, the collapse of the oil price in 2015 made a noticeable impact, but it did not start the trend itself. The Russian economy's good days prior to 2014 occurred against a background of gradual decline in the share of oil and gas exports. One is tempted to conclude that the sanctions made the bigger dent in changing the trend of Russia's relative performance post-2014.

While the influence of oil and gas on the economy may be difficult to evaluate, it is probably more meaningful to look at the relationship between the sensitivity of the ruble exchange rate and oil prices. This is easier to tackle, since elasticity increased noticeably (became more negative) beginning around 2009–2010. It reached a high sensitivity of around −0.7 (meaning a 10% rise/fall in the oil price would result in 7% cumulative appreciation/depreciation of the RUB within a few months). Crucially, this elasticity began to reduce gradually post-2016 and was trending around −0.4 in 2018. Why should the sensitivity to the oil price decline after increasing?

Because Russia failed to diversify the economy. The elasticity was almost non-existent (zero) in prior years. This is because the ruble was at a controlled exchange rate at the time. The volatility clearly increased after the exchange rate began to be gradually freed up beginning in 2009. Ultimately, from 2015 onwards, the exchange rate became a free float and its soft peg to the USD and EUR.[9]

Nevertheless, after reaching a peak around that time, why did the elasticity decline? It represents the increasing credibility of the CBR, which readily offsets pressure on the currency by hiking or cutting rates. In the early days of exchange rate liberalization, CBR's credibility was not yet established—in fact, CBR struggled visibly and unsuccessfully to maintain the corridor. The Central Bank even worked with interim, temporarily elevated inflation targets, which are bad for credibility. Nevertheless, CBR's credibility and its readiness to hike rates whenever necessary were established later. It was crucial that President Putin did not interfere with monetary policy despite the tough recession. CBR's reaction function is now discounted by the market, which no longer anticipates large, volatile exchange rate moves that would move around the inflation rate. Instead, the market assumes that CBR's rate will move.

While Russia's long-term goal of diversifying away from hydrocarbons may not have really taken off, CBR's strict inflation targeting has eliminated part of the Ruble volatility and risk that would otherwise arise because of fluctuations in the oil price.

How Should One Deal with the Situation?

Despite the decrease in volatility, the ruble remains vulnerable due to geopolitical tensions and overall investor behavior towards emerging markets. Companies active in Russian with substantial exposure to foreign exchange risk should consider the use of hedging instruments like forwards or options. In light of the expected decrease of the rates difference between the Euro zone and Russia, such instruments will become less expensive. As always, a 100% hedge is difficult to achieve and may not be desired but at least part of it. Especially the cash flow with mid- or long-term exposure should be secured.

Overall, the undervalued ruble helps the Russian economy to reach at least a small growth rate and to be competitive in some international export markets and in comparison to (more expensive) imports. It is also attractive for foreign companies to locate production in Russia due to the comparably low labor and overall production costs. Despite the generally high level of inflation, it must be assumed that the Central Bank will gain further creditability and will succeed in lowering inflation, which will help to stabilize and improve the social situation in Russia.

---

[9]Commerzbank Currency Research, December 2018.

Tips, Opportunities, and Warning

History of the Ruble

The ruble has been used in the Russian territories since the thirteenth century. It remains unclear where the word "ruble" comes from. According to one vers-ion, the word "ruble" is derived from the Russian verb *рубить* (*rubit*), "to cut, to chop, to hack," as a ruble was considered a cutout piece of a silver gri-vna. Rubles were parts of the grivna or pieces of silver with notches indicat-ing their weight. Usually, each grivna was divided into four parts. Another version is that the ruble was never part of a grivna but a synonym for it. This is given credence from a thirteenth century Novgorod birch bark manuscript, where both ruble and grivna referred to 204 g (6.6 troy ounces) of silver. The casting of these pieces included some sort of cutting (the exact technology is unknown), hence the name from рубить (rubit). (The Museum of money at http://muzeydeneg.ru/research/700-let-istoriya-rublya/ retrieved on Apr. 29th, 2019.)

A third version is that the word's origin is the Russian noun рубец (rubets), the seam that is left around silver bullions after casting: silver was added to the cast in two steps. Therefore, the word ruble means "a cast with a seam." (Sergey Khalatov, National Currency: Russian Ruble, at http://statesymbol.ru/currency/20050421/39595617.html retrieved on April 29th, 2019.) The ruble was the Russian equivalent of the mark, a measurement of weight for silver and gold used in medieval Western Europe.

Ruble coins as such did not exist until Peter the Great, when in 1704 he reformed the old monetary system and ordered mintage of a 28-g silver ruble coin equivale-nt to 100 new copper kopek coins. As a result, the ruble became the world's first decimal currency. The ruble was the currency of the Russian Empire and of the Soviet Union (as the Soviet ruble). However, as of today, only Russia, Belarus and Transnistria use currencies with the same name. In 1992 the Soviet ruble (ISO code: SUR) was replaced with the Russian ruble (ISO code: RUR) at the rate 1 SUR = 1 RUR. In 1998 preceding the financial crisis, the Russian ruble was redenominated with the new code "RUB" and was exchanged at the rate of 1 RUB = 1000 RUR.

On December 11, 2013, the official symbol for the ruble was introduced, a Cyri-llic letter with a single added horizontal stroke - ₽, though the abbreviation "руб." is in wide use. (The Unicode Standard, Version 7.0. The Unicode Consortium. 16 June 2014, at https://www.unicode.org/versions/Unicode7.0.0/ retrieved on April 29th, 2019.)

All Russian ruble banknotes are currently printed at the state-owned factory Goznak in Moscow, which was founded in 1919 and operated ever since. Coins are minted in Moscow and at the Saint Petersburg Mint, which has been operating since 1724.

References

Kitroeff, N., & Weisenthal, J. (2014, December 16). Here's why the Russian Ruble is collapsing, Businessweek. *Bloomberg*.

Maternowskiy, D. (2009, December 16). Ruble gain versus Dollar 'inevitable,' Zadornov Says. *Bloomberg*.

Tanas, O., & Andrianova, A. (2014, December 16). Russia defends Ruble with biggest rate rise since 1998. *Bloomberg*.

Cryptocurrencies in Russia

Aleksandr N. Dubianskii

In conjunction with the emergence of new types of currency, central banks around the world face the challenge of developing an approach to cryptocurrencies in general and to bitcoin in particular. Many participants in the financial markets already actively use Cryptocurrencies, and their popularity is growing rapidly, especially among currency speculators. It is no longer possible to ignore the emergence of new monetary instruments, and regulators need to respond to the situation (Dubyansky, 2017a).

In most countries of the European Union and the United States, the reaction to cryptocurrencies is positive in general, and bitcoins are legal payment instruments, since there is no direct ban on their circulation in the legislation. In a number of other countries, such as Russia, China, India, Sweden, etc., bitcoins are still illegal means of circulation in official transactions. In Russia, the Ministry of Finance proposed the introduction of criminal liability for the use of cryptocurrencies, which include bitcoins. However, even in countries where the circulation of cryptocurrencies is not legally prohibited, they do not have a clear legal status. Critical currencies need a legal status for their mass use by major players in the currency and financial markets. Consequently, at present, the state would have to accept the cryptocurrency generated by the market and choose it as new kinds of currency.

The central bank as the representative of the interests of the state in the monetary system is to use the technology of the blockchain, or technology of distributed registries underlying bitcoin and other cryptocurrencies, to create a domestic counterpart bitcoin. The Russian analog of bitcoin could complement the ruble, operating in a special isolated "circuit," and be used for transactions in the financial markets. This circuit should not intersect with another circuit in which the "normal" Russian ruble would apply. A similar configuration of the monetary system existed in the

---

A. N. Dubianskii (✉)
Department of Economic History and Economic Thoughts, Saint Petersburg State University, Saint Petersburg, Russia
e-mail: a.dubianskii@spbu.ru

USSR, when the turnover of cash and non-cash money were divorced. In the context of the digital economy and the heterogeneity of the economic space, the prospects for the creation of multiple forms of money are becoming more real (Dubyansky, 2017b).

Cryptocurrencies are better suited for transactions in financial markets where a high level of trust and security of transactions are required. The regulator can create a centralized data bank for security purposes, but in this case, a high level of system reliability and continuity of its operation is required. In case of using blockchain technology, market participants can store all information on their own servers and check transactions, secured by cryptographic algorithms. Due to the absence of intermediaries, transactions can be cheap or even free.

Russia already took the first steps to introduce cryptocurrencies as legal currency. In particular, the Ministry of Finance has put forth legal definitions for mining, cryptocurrency, token, etc.[1] For example, a cryptocurrency is defined as a digital financial asset that is created and recorded in the distributed register of digital transactions by the participants of the register in accordance with the rules of the register.[2] This writer believes that in the future, the relevant legislation will be adopted, which will introduce cryptocurrencies into the legal field and the state will be able to effectively manage the cryptocurrency market.

References

Dubyansky, A. N. (2017a). Theory of the origin of money and cryptocurrency. *Money and Credit, 12,* 97–100. [Dubjanskij A.N. Teorija proishozhdenija deneg i kriptovaljuty// Den'gi i kredit 2017. #12. S.97-100].

Dubyansky, A. N. (2017b). Local currencies as a way of money circulation decentralization. Vestnik Saint Petersburg. UN TA. Episode 5. *Economy, 33*(1), 104–118. [Dubjanskij A. N. Mestnye valjuty kak sposob decentralizacii denezhnogo obrashhenija // Vestnik Sankt-Peterburg. unta. Serija 5. Jekonomika. 2017. T. 33. # 1. S. 104–118].

---

[1]Ministry of Finance of the Russian Federation https://www.minfin.ru/ru/document/?id_4=121810, retrieved on October 29th, 2020.

[2]Информационный портал «Майнинг Криптовалюты» at https://mining-cryptocurrency.ru/minfin-zakon-o-kriptovalyute-i-majninge/ retrieved on Apr. 29th, 2019.

Russian Energy: Hanging on the Needle?

Christian Altmann

Introduction: Oil and Gas as National and International Forces

Russia is a leading supplier in world energy and a major participant in international energy markets. Reserves and production figures of the country are impressive: Russia has the largest world reserves of gas and is by far the largest exporter of gas worldwide. It has the eighth largest oil reserves and is one of the largest producers of oil. Russia has the second-largest coal reserves (Fig. 12.1).

As these energy reserves in Russia are seemingly endless, efficient consumption of energy was never a political goal of high priority. This made Russia—the 11th biggest economy in the world—the third-largest energy user worldwide, only topped by the USA and China. Russia has one of the worst energy efficiency rates in Europe. The World Bank stated that Russia could save 45% of its total primary energy consumption by using modern concepts for energy infrastructure, insulation of buildings, or energy pricing.

Sales of oil and gas is the main revenue source. This makes the country heavily dependent on a sustainable export of oil and gas for sufficient prices in other countries. Due to the strategic importance of natural resources, energy exports heavily influence the budget of the Russian Federation, all sectors of domestic politics, and directly determines the stability of the Russian Ruble.

There is little doubt that the energy sector will continue to remain the core of Russia's economy for many more years to come. Only when manufacturing and production efficiency will come closer to levels of western economies new export opportunities will open up. Until then, Russia's strategic goal must be to get access to high-yield energy markets. This includes in particular the EU with its highly developed economies and that offer sustained energy demand (Fig. 12.2).

C. Altmann (✉)
Dortmund, Germany

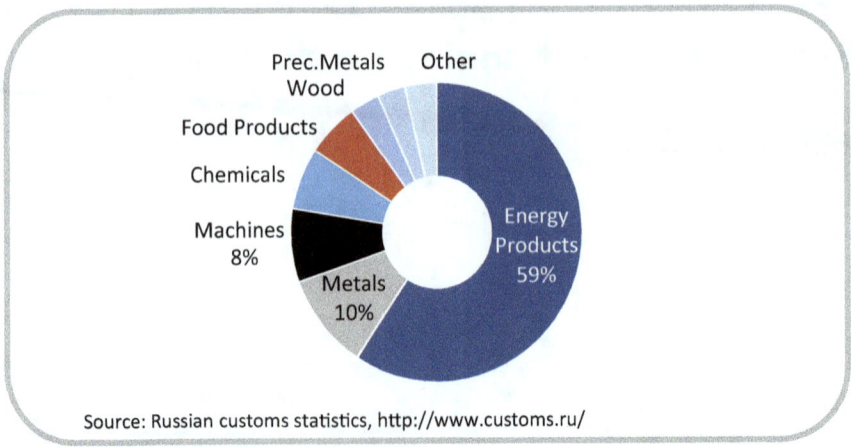

Fig. 12.1 Export share of Russian products

Domestically, the oil and gas industry in Russia is by far the biggest industry of the economy. Combined all energy-related industries account for roughly one-third of the Russian economy. Due to its central role, it affects all the other parts of the Russian economy and has even an impact on the stability of the governmental sector (section "Mineral Resources" of Chap. 16). Therefore, the development of the domestic Russian Energy sector has a significant impact especially on:

- Development of all industrial sectors
- Environment and nature
- Quality of life in Russia
- Political stability of the country
- Technological development and competitiveness

Accordingly, Russia aims to protect this key sector by controlling operational transit routes and keeping them as reliable as possible. Furthermore, it has a strategic interest in diversifying the oil and gas export infrastructure to keep different transport options while minimizing the role of transit countries. Here, the internationally disputed gas pipeline North Stream 2 comes into play, which runs from Russia via the Baltic Sea to Germany, and into other European countries. It is an alternative to existing routes, which transit countries like Ukraine and Poland before reaching the EU.

Russia's long-term strategy is to maximize the effective use of natural energy resources and the potential of the energy sector. It is obvious that the country cannot exclusively rely for this century only on natural resources. Russia needs to improve its production efficiency in order to develop competitive export products. However, until production efficiency reaches competitive levels natural resources have to secure economic growth and improve the quality of life in the country.

Fig. 12.2 Map of the major existing and proposed Russian natural gas transportation pipelines to Europe

Another challenge is that Russian energy consumption is high. Russia has understood that it needs to reduce its energy intensity and has set accordingly ambitious targets for 2030 (56% energy intensity reduction compared with 2005) (Fig. 12.3).

However, the low energy prices in recent years make it difficult for renewable energy to gain a significant market share without subsidies from the government. Even though Putin declared the year 2017 as the *Year of Environment*, renewable energy remains a niche product in the Russian energy market.

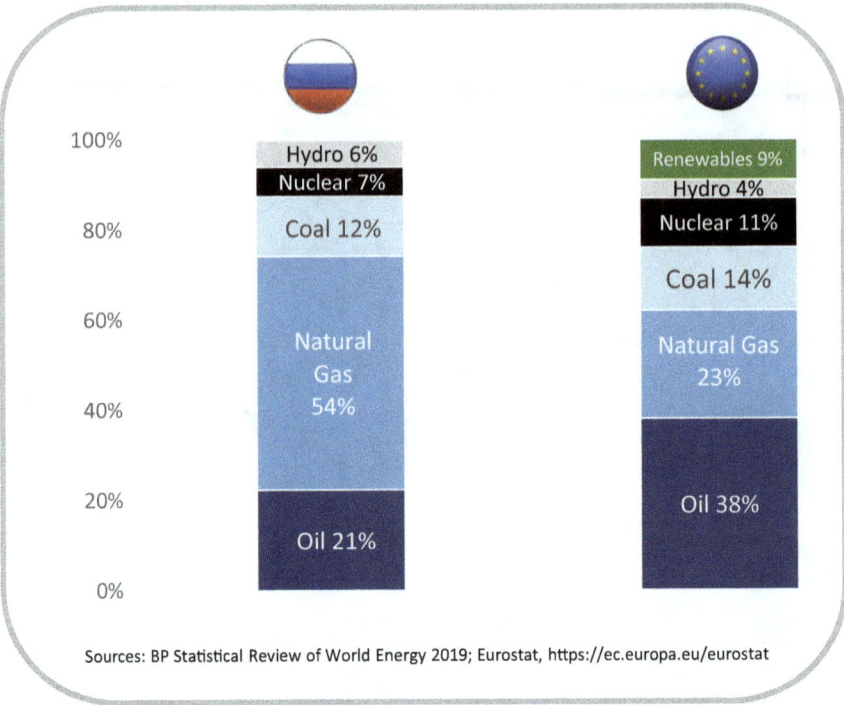

Fig. 12.3 Split of EU and Russian energy consumption

The EU and Russian Energy

The strategy of the EU and its member states is to provide its member countries with secure, competitive, sustainable, and affordable energy. In order to deal with these potentially conflicting targets, a project called *Energy Union Strategy* was founded in 2015 by the European Commission to coordinate the transformation of European energy supply.

In its detailed long-term energy strategy, the EU outlines various targets for the next decades with the ultimate objective to become climate neutral by mid of the century. The EU strategy includes emissions reduction targets, improved energy efficiency, an increased share of renewables in the EU's energy mix. It also describes the vision of an economic, political, and societal transition of its member states to become climate-neutral economies by 2050. Executing the strategy will require action in seven strategic areas:

- Energy efficiency
- Deployment of renewable alternatives
- Clean, safe, and connected mobility

- Competitive industry and circular economy
- Infrastructure and interconnections
- Bio-economy and natural carbon sinks
- Carbon capture and storage to address remaining emissions

EU policies are in line with the *Paris Agreement* to keep the global temperature increase at 2 °C above pre-industrial levels or even lower.[1] It is clear that based on these EU targets, imports of Russian coal and oil should not gain more weight. The EU considers gas a temporary solution to improve its CO2-balance by replacing coal but not as a mean to become neutral. Some EU countries fear that the EU member states, which buy gas from Russia, will become more politically dependent on it. Accordingly, they heavily oppose the operation of North Stream 2. Some other European governments view it as a sustainable, affordable, and very secure energy option. From their perspective, Russian gas has been reliable energy source for decades.

Russian Gas for the EU

Historically, gas-trade dates back to the 1970s, when the USSR started to deliver gas to Western Europe. Initially, the US government objected heavily against these gas deliveries because it feared that American allies might become dependent on the "enemy" and could become less reliable partners. Despite all political differences, Russia has consistently secured a reliable supply of energy to its EU customers without major interruptions. In recent years though, the disputes between Russia and Ukraine raised again questions in Washington and within the EU over the future of the pipeline network. In 2006 and 2009 these disputes caused temporary cut offs of gas supplies to downstream customers in Europe. It became obvious that Ukraine's *Orange Revolution* and its subsequent orientation toward the West had could have an impact on gas delivery to Europe.

Legally it was never and still is not easy for an energy supplier from outside the EU to provide member countries with energy. The legal context is generally defined by EU energy regulation, and particular in the shape of the 2009 Third Energy Package (TEP). Since then, all eyes are on the construction and operation of the gas pipeline North Stream II that had to meet conditions of the TEP.[2] One of the main conditions for the operation of gas infrastructure is the unbundling requirement, which warrants the separation of pipeline operation from ownership in order to allow Third-Party Access (TPA). In theory, it would make sense for any pipeline operator to grant access to several market suppliers in order to stimulate competition. However, there is no rule without exception: Article 36 of the Gas Directive provides

---

[1] Climate actions in the EU, at https://ec.europa.eu/clima/policies/eu-climate-action_en, retrieved on October 22nd, 2020.

[2] Members of the North Stream 2 consortium are ENGIE, OMV, Shell, Uniper und Wintershall.

the option to grant an exemption from TPA and unbundling requirements for major new infrastructure projects or projects significantly increasing the capacity of existing infrastructure. Germany counted on Paris along with the Netherlands, Belgium, Austria, Greece, and Cyprus to get the current set up—with Gazprom as operator of the pipeline and supplier of energy at the same time—approved. France demanded in 2019 a separation of gas sales and pipeline operating activities as well as third-party access to a pipeline.

It is very likely that the EU and Russia will find a common agreement for North Stream 2, but the incident shows that EU institutions, governments of member states, and political parties in Europe have different views on the project. The EU states continue to debate whether Nord Stream should be extended with new pipelines in the Baltic Sea. One side argues that it would undermine European energy security and makes its member states dependent from Russian energy. They claim the project ignores the EU's Energy Union, as the project is not in the common interest of all EU states. They opponents also argue that Gazprom acts as an instrument of Moscow's foreign and economic policy, which contradicts the political targets of EU and the USA. Other EU members focus less on the political but on the economic side of the project. They view it as a feasible and sustainable business partnership. Countries like Germany and Austria believe that North Stream 2 helps to secure energy for many years and could potentially improve relations with the Russian government.

Geopolitical Considerations and Outlook

A majority of the EU parliament would like to allow closer relations in the energy sector only if Russia fully implements the so-called Minsk agreements and starts respecting international law. Members of the EU Parliament demand that

- Russia must restore Ukraine's territorial integrity.
- Global challenges must be addressed through selective EU-Russia cooperation.
- EU should be ready to adopt further sanctions against Russia if conditions of the Minsk agreement are not met.

Since 2014, the EU and the US targeted certain individual representative from Russian companies, its bank accounts, the respective companies, and its products with economic sanctions. In return, Russia imposed economic sanctions such as the import stop of EU products and foods. As these political conditions seem to be difficult to be met, it is unlikely that the sanctions will be waived soon.

How Do Western Sanctions Affect Russia's Oil and Gas Sector?

Energy experts are divided. Some point out those sanctions have no positive political effect and hardly any negative economic impact. They think long-term sanctions stimulate technological development in the country because the domestic industry

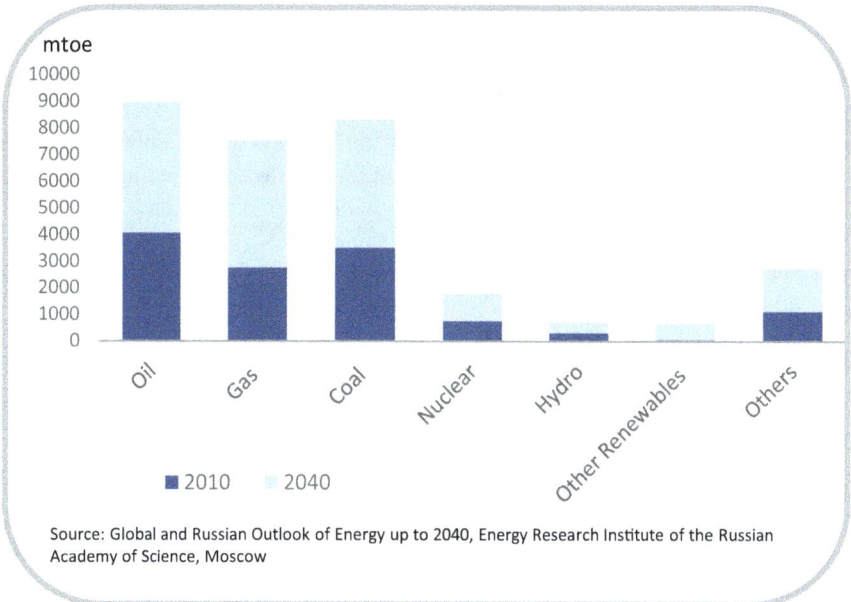

Fig. 12.4 Growth of primary energy consumption worldwide from 2010 to 2040

sectors are relieved from international competition. Others believe sanctions will have severe consequences due to the dependence on foreign financing and technology. If sanctions remain for a longer period, they will hinder the development of modern infrastructure. Furthermore, sanctions could give customers time to systematically replace Russian oil and gas in international trade or competitors to win market shares.

With these uncertainties in mind, the EU secured gas supply by expanding its liquefied natural gas (LNG) infrastructure, building additional storage capacities, implementing pipeline reverse flow capabilities, eliminating restrictive destination clauses, and constructing a multitude of energy infrastructure projects. It is now well on its way to achieving a highly competitive, liquid, and transparent internal gas market. Today, the EU has roughly 30 LNG import terminals with a balanced distribution across countries, e.g., nearly half of all EU countries have import terminals.

The EU strategy is based on the understanding that the structure of the world energy mix becomes more diversified, however—against all political attempts—the share of fossil sources remains high and gas will gain more importance (Fig. 12.4).

The USA: A New Energy Giant

For decades the US was dependent on importing energy from all over the world. The picture changed when the government lifted its national crude oil export restrictions in 2015 and was able to export LNG. Immediately the EU gained importance as an important energy customer for Washington. Europe was identified as a potential LNG market with high energy demand, stable economies, and geostrategic importance.

The first shipment of US LNG was in February 2016 and since then the USA has shipped LNG to Europe, Asia, and South America. The US claim that the export of LNG gas is creating greater certainty of supply, puts downward pressure on prices around the world especially in Europe. From a geopolitical perspective, increased LNG exports from the USA and its allies would shift revenues away from traditional suppliers like Russia, which has always been seen as a power working against US national security interests. US LNG competes with Russian gas for market shares in the EU and the rest of the world.

US President Trump tried to support US LNG gas by attacking Germany during his speech in the UN General Assembly on 25. September 2018: "Germany will become totally dependent on Russian energy if it does not immediately change course. Here in the Western Hemisphere, we are committed to maintaining our independence from the encroachment of expansionist foreign powers."

The 2014 imposed sanctions from the US have been gradually increased and started to target Russian energy sectors more and more in order to give US energy exports a competitive advantage. Negative effects for the Russian gas sector may especially come from the expanded application of the sanctions to export pipelines under the Countering America's Adversaries Through the Sanctions Act, which was signed by President Donald Trump in August 2017. The act allows the US president to impose sanctions blocking any operation worth more than US$5 million annually that provides equipment and services for the construction of new gas pipelines or maintenance of existing ones. The US imposed the sanctions after consultations with European partners. However, most EU governments reject these sanctions because European companies can become target by US sanctions, if they significantly support the Russian energy sector as described above. In addition, the US president signed the end of 2019 a National Defense Authorization Act, which allows sanctions against companies that provide pipe-laying vessels for North Stream 2. Consequently, western vessels left the project and Russia has been forced to rebuild own vessels in order to continue with the completion of North Stream 2. It certainly could be possible that the US government will consider a total embargo of all goods and services in the future. At the current state, with both Russia and the USA heavily hit by the corona virus, initiatives that are more radical have not been seriously considered.

Russia's Position and Outlook

It became obvious that the EU with its hunger for energy and 500 million citizens would be a lucrative but highly competitive energy market, especially the gas market for future decades. Russia as a neighbor of the EU is generally in a strategically strong position, although geopolitical, economic, and environmental challenges are enormous.

The Energy Research Institute of the Russian Academy of Science claims that "natural gas will account for the most substantial increase in absolute volumes of consumption and the share taken by gas in primary energy consumption will increase more than that of any other fuel. The next 30 years could be quite reasonably considered as the era of gas. But Russia runs risks of missing the resulting opportunities."

Russian production of natural gas reached a record high of 679 billion m^3 in 2019, making it the second-largest producer after the USA. However, it is the world's largest exporter of natural gas, as the USA consumes most of its domestic production. Russia exports almost all of its natural gas to Europe via pipelines. At the same time, Russia's exports of LNG are increasing, destined primarily for Japan and other Asian countries. The BP 2018 Energy Outlook expects Russian production of natural gas to continue to rise steadily for the near future, with further increases in LNG exports.[3]

The EU will remain an import market in gas going forward, and if its consumption rises then its import gap will widen. In order to expand its market share in Europe and meet it is legal and market conditions Russia has primarily focused on:

- Developing new gas suppliers
- Unbundling infrastructure
- Restructuring Gazprom
- Build additional LNG facilities
- Support of renewable energy
- Common understanding with transit countries

It will be crucial for Russia that *Gazprom* and its counterpart *Naftogaz Ukraine* will find an agreement that will probably guarantee Ukraine a certain minimum of transit revenues because if Nord Stream 2 is completed the volume of transit through Ukraine will decrease. It can also be concluded that whatever role Ukrainian transit plays after 2020, the considerable investment will be required in the transportation network in the future.

It also seems obvious that western sanctions have an impact on Russia. The silent power of sanctions lies in its long-term effect: The more time passes, the greater the potential technological backlog, financing gap, and negative consequences for the pipeline infrastructure could be. Over a longer period, they even might have the

---

[3]BP Statistical Review of World Energy, at www.bp.com, retrieved on June 2nd, 2020.

power to jeopardize Russia's oil and gas production volumes and thereby bringing the stability of the Russian economy in danger.

Energy markets tend to be heavily influenced by geopolitical considerations. All too often, the political influence limits competition and eco-friendly developments. For the future, it would be beneficial for both sides, if Western nations and Russia decouple market accessibility from their geopolitical objectives. E.g., EU climate goals would be more efficient, if they would be accompanied by similar measures in Russia. One solution could be that EU institutions grant energy providers from Russia conditional access to its markets, if Russia would commit to investments in eco-friendly and renewable energies.

Suggestions for Further Reading

BP Energy Outlook 2018	www.bp.com
Energy Research Institute of the Russian Academy of Science, Moscow: *Global and Russian Outlook of Energy up to 2040*	www.eriras.ru
Infothek der AHK, Deutsch-Russische Auslandshandelskammer	www.russland.ahk.de/
International Energy Agency: *World Energy Outlook 2018*	www.iea.org/weo
Kings College London: *Assessing North Stream 2*	www.kcl.ac.uk
World Bank Report: *Preserving stability, Doubling Growth, Halving Poverty*, November 2018	www.documents.worldbank.org

Import Substitution in Russia

Christian Altmann

Incentives, Restrictions, Regulations

Since 2000, the Russian government has tried hard to develop the local manufacturing sector and domestic service industry in order to replace foreign products with Russian goods (import substitution). The main goal of this strategy was to increase domestic production and to diversify the Russian economy, which was heavily dependent on oil and gas exports.[1]

The government started to use a wide range of economic measures such as incentives for locally producing companies, restrictions against unwanted foreign exports and political restrictions to protect and support selected local industry sectors. For instance, Russia's automotive sector has received plenty of incentives and customs advantages which helped to shift production or at least to push local assembling of cars and trucks in the last decade to Russia.

In the last years, industrial policies became more and more restrictive. Political measures such as high customs tariffs or in-transparent tender regulations made it difficult or even impossible for foreign export companies to sell their products freely on the Russian market.

The situation for foreign companies exporting to Russia became even more difficult when EU and US sanctions, together with Russia's countersanctions, led to even more restrictive and protective market. The sanctions against the import of EU foods into Russia had an especially noticeable impact on the market. With practically no competition from EU, the domestic agricultural sector grew year by

---

[1]KFW Report on Import Substitution in Russia, https://www.kfw.de/PDF/Download-Center/Konzernthemen/Research/PDF-Dokumente-Fokus-Volkswirtschaft/Fokus-englische-Dateien/Fokus-2017-EN/Fokus-No.-173-June-2017-Russia-emerging-from-recession.pdf retrieved on August 8th, 2019.

C. Altmann (✉)
Dortmund, Germany

year with 2–3% p.a. and allowed Russia to become the biggest wheat exporter in the world.[2] However, the quality and variety of domestic foods often do not reach the level of formerly imported products.

Import Substitution Since 2014

In 2015, the Russian Government introduced an action plan for import substitution in 22 sectors of the Russian industry.[3] Proposed measures are intended to achieve a gradual reduction of foreign-made industrial products used in Russia and their replacement by domestic ones by up to 100% in the next decade.

In the same year, President Putin introduced Industrial Policy Laws, which gave priority to Russian products in public procurement. It is intended to limit access of foreign-made products to both public procurement and state-owned companies' procurement—even if the quality or price of foreign imported goods was advantageous. In order to join public tender, a product had to be mainly produced in Russia.

The new Russian legislation shows an ambivalent character. On the one side, it provides for various incentives and support measures for local producers. On the other side, it makes it difficult for foreign products to enter and remain in the Russian market without investing into local production.

Made in Russia

The only way to participate in a public procurement tender as well as to prevent discrimination in a general tender is to classify one's product as a "Made in Russia." As the public sector and its related companies play a dominant role in the Russian economy, the pressure to produce local products represents a significant challenge for companies focusing on the Russian market.

On one hand, special investment contracts for investors, special economic zones, and modern technological parks offer different kinds of incentive and create attractive conditions to localize production in Russia. However, not every SMEs is in the situation to move its production to Russia as the respective market is not relevant enough to build up a new production or to justify new investments. In fact, some companies, which tried to localize their production, face the challenge that important supplier or certain materials are not available in Russia.

Customs laws and regulations of the EAEU will determine whether a product may be regarded as a Russian. A product receives a certificate of Russian origin when fully manufactured or sufficiently processed in Russia. The sufficiency of

---

[2]https://www.world-grain.com/articles/13316-russia-forecast-to-remain-top-wheat-exporter, retrieved on October 27th, 2020.
[3]Ministry of Industry and Trade of the Russian Federation, at https://gisp.gov.ru/plan-import-change retrieved on August 8th, 2019.

processing is achieved when one of the first four digits of the customs classification code of an imported product is changed after such a product is processed into a final product (formal criterion).[4] The status can be achieved as well if the product has undergone an industrial, intellectual, or technical process leading to a high percentage of added value in the final product.[5]

Results and Future of Import Substitution

Although some positive results have been achieved (in the agricultural industry or the pharmaceutical industry), it is common sense that import substitution and protection of domestic companies against international competition can only be a temporary political measure as it has negative side effects. Accordingly, Putin stated in 2018: "The idea of import substitution itself is not universal and is not what we should strive for in the long run, because import substitution should not undermine competition. This is an extremely important thing."[6]

Russia introduced roughly 380 protective measures, mainly protecting the car industry, construction business, chemical production and agricultural sector.[7] Hardly any of these protective measures have been taken back and therefore think tanks as the *Global Trade Alert (GTA)* show that Investment freedom in Russia has been gradually reduced. Investment freedom was in the mid of 1990 on the same level as Germany and well above the world average. In 2019, Russia is ranked 41st among 44 countries in the Europe region, and its overall score is below the regional and world averages.[8]

Only one decade ago, Russia and other G 20 governments made a "No Protectionism" pledge in Washington. Today, it is obvious that Russia—as almost all other G 20 countries—have in multiple ways ignored the idea of free trade. Ironically, Russia's comparably low level of global economic integration turned out to be an advantage during the corona crisis when the breakdown of global supply chains hit its manufacturing base not as hard as well-integrated Western economies. However, the country's export trade balance was deeply affected by record low oil prices and the sharp decline in demand. The main challenge for the Russian government will be to carefully lift the protective barriers and to open its market for competition without putting its key domestic industries at risk.

---

[4]CMS, Tax.Law., Practical Guide on Import Substitution in Russia, at https://cms.law/en/RUS/Publication/Practical-Guide-on-Import-Substitution-in-Russia, retrieved on October 26th, 2020.

[5]Switzerland Global Enterprise, Import Substitution in Russia, at https://www.s-ge.com/sites/default/files/cserver/mig/sites/default/files/censhare_files/swiss-business-hub-russia-practical-guide-import-substitution-russia_14.pdf, retrieved on August 8th, 2019.

[6]Vladimir Putin in TASS Interview 7 MAR 2018, at https://tass.com/economy/993242, retrieved on August 8th, 2020.

[7]GTA, at https://www.globaltradealert.org/reports, retrieved on August 8th, 2019.

[8]GTA, at https://www.globaltradealert.org/reports, retrieved on August 8th, 2019.

Suggestion for Further Reading

Germany Trade & Invest, GTAI	https://www.gtai.de/GTAI/Navigation/EN/invest.html
German Russian Chamber of Commerce	https://russland.ahk.de/
Association of European Business	https://aebrus.ru/
Kreditanstalt für Wiederaufbau, KfW Research	https://www.kfw.de/KfW-Konzern/KfW-Research/index.jsp
Cherkesova, E. YU. a.o.	*Sustainable Import Substitution in Russia: Institutional Conditions and Efficiency Imperatives*, in European Research Studies Journal Volume XXI, Special Issue 1, 2018

The Russian Start-Up Ecosystem

Dmitrij Kononenko

The USA, the UK, Israel, Germany, and Singapore—these are some of the countries that might come to one's mind when thinking about competitive and innovative start-up ecosystems. Russia, on the other hand, is usually associated with a commodity-based economy, mighty oligarchs, and cumbersome state-owned holdings, but not with a thriving start-up community.

Most start-up companies are SMEs by definition—small and medium enterprises (SMEs). However, they only represent a fraction of the Russian economy with a share of GDP of only around 20%.[1] There are several reasons for this shortfall: one certainly being Russia's communist decades. While technological corporations as *Apple* and *Microsoft* emerged in the US in the 1970s driven by the exceptional entrepreneurial skills of their founders Steve Jobs and Steve Wozniak, Bill Gates and Paul Allen, a skilled programmer in Russia might have ended up in prison for trying to launch a private business. It was not until the 1990s, when Russia's private entrepreneurs started to catch up, and it was not until the early 2010s, when a full-fledged start-up ecosystem emerged. This article will explore this ecosystem and its key players, and it will explain why Russia's start-up ecosystem, while not being one of the first-tier ecosystems of the world, is definitely worth a look.

---

[1] https://www.themoscowtimes.com/2020/01/28/russias-small-businesses-contribute-20-percent-russia-economy-a69063, retrieved June 30th, 2020.

D. Kononenko (✉)
Initiative for Digitalization Project Leader Government Relations Department, German-Russian Chamber of Commerce (AHK), Moscow, Russia
e-mail: kononenko@russland-ahk.ru; http://www.russland-ahk.ru; http://www.facebook.com/ahkrussland

Where Do Russian Start-Ups Come from?

Like in many other countries nowadays, IT is the source of some of the most dynamic start-ups in Russia with IT-based solutions and products both for B2C and B2B—be it service aggregators, e-commerce, e-health, blockchain, big data, robotics, virtual and augmented reality (VR/AR), artificial intelligence (AI) or the internet of things (IoT). This is largely because many Russian start-up founders have a professional background in IT and software engineering.

The Russian higher education system in these areas has been excellent for many decades with universities like the Moscow State University, the Bauman Moscow State Technical University, the Moscow Institute of Physics and Technology, the St. Petersburg State University, the St. Petersburg Polytechnic University, and the St. Petersburg ITMO University being ranked among the best universities worldwide. Teams from these universities regularly win the International Collegiate Programming Contest (ICPC), thus becoming world champions in coding.

Their deep fundamental training in mathematics and data science paves the way for the success of Russian entrepreneurs developing rather complex technologies, with start-ups like *VisionLabs*, *NtechLab*, and *Vocord* (three machine vision companies), *Robot Vera* (an AI-based HR recruiting robot), *Promobot* (a versatile service robot), and *DATADVANCE* (data analysis in engineering) being among the global technological leaders in their respective market niches.

It is not only due to the locations of the best Russian universities, but first because of the geographic distribution of wealth and economic strength in Russia, that most Russian start-ups arise either in Moscow or in St. Petersburg. These two cities are by far the most important centers of the Russian start-up ecosystem.

Founding a company is relatively cheap and easy in Russia. The minimum paid-in capital requirement for a limited liability company is 10,000 rubles and the state company registration fee amounts to only 4000 rubles, with additional 2000 rubles for notary fees and minor expenses. The whole registration process takes approximately 11 days. That is the reason why Russia was ranked 32nd in the category "Starting a Business" by the World Bank in its Doing Business 2019 report, outperforming countries like Finland, Israel, the USA, and Germany.

Consequently, it is not the bureaucracy that hinders Russians with good ideas from founding a company, but a lack of entrepreneurial skills and a low awareness of market demand. All too often, Russian programmers or engineers develop innovative and sophisticated technologies but have very limited understanding of their commercialization and of customer development techniques. And this is where a great variety of ecosystem institutions come into play that teach Russian company founders how to convert their ideas into a business concept, how to advance in customer development, how to grow their businesses, and how to raise investments.

Incubators and Accelerators

The first type of ecosystem players facilitating the development of Russian start-ups is business incubators run by universities. The Russian university incubators work quite similar to their peers in other countries. Their goal is to mentor students and graduates in order to turn them into successful entrepreneurs by supporting them at the earliest stages of their entrepreneurial career. Over the last 10 years, university business incubators in Russia introduced and adapted most of the globally proven instruments for fostering innovative entrepreneurship. Some of their successes were acknowledged internationally. For instance, in 2018 the business incubator of the Moscow-based Higher School of Economics was ranked seventh best in the world by UBI Global, a Swedish analytics company examining global innovation hubs.

Any company can participate in a variety of acceleration programs after its launch, which are offered by both state-owned and private institutions. Many Russian accelerators take small equity shares from start-ups in return for their participation in such programs.

A very distinctive feature of the Russian start-up ecosystem is that the state plays a leading role in it. This partially results from the state's dominant position with state-owned companies. Therefore, some of the biggest acceleration programs in Russia are run by state-owned venture capital (VC) funds. For example, the *Russian Venture Company (RVC)* operates the "GenerationS" accelerator—the biggest acceleration program for technology start-ups in Eastern Europe. Another state VC company, the *Internet Initiatives Development Fund (IIDF)*, runs several acceleration programs specifically tailored for IT entrepreneurs. Although being controlled by the state, both institutions closely cooperate with industrial partner companies.

A counterweight to the big state-owned accelerators is the acceleration programs offered by private Russian VC companies like *iDealMachine* and *Starta Ventures* or by the Russian branches of global accelerators like *Techstars* and *500 Start-ups*. The latter closely collaborates with the state-owned *Sberbank*. Furthermore, there are corporate accelerators independently run by private Russian companies like the telecommunication provider *MTS* ("MTS Start-up Hub") or the IT system integrator *CROC*. Both state-funded and private accelerators offer co-working spaces to their participants or grant access to production premises for testing product prototypes.

Venture Capital and Grants

Finding investors is crucial for most Russian start-ups, as VC is the fuel of any start-up ecosystem and Russia is no exception here. However, unlike in the first-tier start-up ecosystems of the world, the Russian economy definitely lacks VC. The total Russian VC market is only a tenth of the size of the VC market (according to EY and PwC, respectively).

One reason for this tiny market volume is Russia's undeveloped business angel community with only a relatively small number of individual investors willing to deal with start-ups. A further reason is the geopolitical tensions between Russia and the West, which induced Western investors to reduce their presence in Russia and Russian private investors to invest their money in foreign rather than in domestic assets. In addition, the economic downturn in Russia in 2014–2016 led to a serious devaluation of the ruble, reducing the volume of the VC market when counted in USD. There has been a trend among start-ups worldwide to compensate a lack of VC by initial coin offerings (ICOs), but this trend seems to abate in Russia now.

The Russian state is aware of the insufficient amount of VC being a severe hindrance for the further development of the start-up ecosystem. That is why it has established the aforementioned Russian Venture Company in 2006 and the Internet Initiatives Development Fund in 2013 with the goal to create a mature venture capital market, compensating for the insufficient number of private VCs. While the *RVC* is a "fund of funds," pumping state money into the market by establishing sector-specific VC funds with co-investors (currently 27 funds), the *IIDF* does direct investments and has currently an investment volume of over six billion rubles with more than 300 investments in start-ups. Thanks to its clever investment strategy the *IIDF* was ranked eighth worldwide by Forbes in the "10 Startup Accelerators Based on Successful Exits" list in 2018.

Similar to the accelerator market, where private providers complement the big state-owned players, there are also some private VC firms replenishing the Russian VC market. The biggest and most active of them are *AltaIR Capital, Runa Capital, Almaz Capital, Flint Capital,* and *The Untitled* as well as the aforementioned *iDealMachine* and *Starta Ventures*. While having Russian roots and staff, some of these companies are registered outside of Russia and do investments worldwide. In addition, there are several corporate VC funds run by big Russian corporations, like *AFK Sistema's* venture fund called *"Sistema VC"* and the corporate VC funds of the industry giants *Severstal* and *Rosatom*, which both were launched in 2018.

Another way for Russian start-ups to raise capital is to get grants, which again are mostly provided by the state via organizations like the *Fund for the Assistance to Small Innovative Enterprises* (FASIE, often called "The Bortnik Foundation") or the *Skolkovo Foundation*.

The *FASIE* was founded in 1994, thus being a veteran facilitator of private entrepreneurship in Russia. It provides grants to innovative start-ups of different sizes and stages of maturity.

The *Skolkovo Foundation* was founded in 2010 and runs not only a grant program for start-ups, but also a giant innovation center on the western outskirts of Moscow, which is virtually a whole new city built entirely greenfield. This innovation center hosts a huge technology park with five industrial clusters that offers laboratories, co-working spaces, and significant tax benefits for innovative companies. About 2000 start-ups take advantage of these benefits at the moment, being physical or virtual residents of Skolkovo's technology park and making it the biggest of its kind in the whole of Eastern Europe. In addition, the Skolkovo innovation center hosts a technical university called Skoltech with an emphasis on innovations in its teachings as well as several R&D centers of companies like Boeing, FANUC, and Cisco Systems, thus enabling synergetic effects between the start-up residents of its Technology Park and global corporations.

International Ambitions

Notwithstanding this extensive network of institutions supporting Russian entrepreneurs, the long-term success rate of Russian start-ups is quite similar to start-up companies in other countries—it is approximately 10%. At the same time there is hardly any "culture of failure" in Russia, which means that once an entrepreneur has failed to succeed with his first company, serious problems with getting acceptance and investments for starting a new business will follow. Although this mentality is changing gradually, it is still widely spread.

A promising way to increase a start-up's chances of success is the international scaling up of its business right from the very first day of its existence. Many Russian entrepreneurs realize this and actively seek for foreign clients and partners. They do this particularly in view of the relatively small market for innovations in the Russian B2B segment where the notoriously sluggish state-owned holdings only very hesitantly deal with disruptive innovations.

Russian start-ups typically face several challenges that keep them from successful international expansion. One of them is a lack of international marketing and sales skills due to the limited international experience and exposure of many company founders. At first glance, trivial reasons like bad English skills or the absence of a visa detain them from a close interaction with fellow founders in other countries, thus impeding an exchange of experience and the adoption of international best practices. This kind of remoteness corresponds with another problem, which disturbs start-up companies worldwide, but is particularly serious in Russia: the brain drain of internationally sought-after human capital. Many talented start-up founders and employees with foreign language proficiency and with an international mindset leave Russia for better opportunities to make money, to find investors, or to self-realize. This brain drain issue has been regularly addressed by Russian authorities at public debates but has not been solved yet (section "International Migration: Brain Drain and Muscles Inflow" of Chap. 19).

Nevertheless, the state has established institutions that help start-ups to enter foreign markets by using a variety of financial and non-financial instruments. The most powerful of such export promotion agencies is the *Russian Export Center (REC)*. Inter alia, it promotes the participation of Russian companies in international trade shows by partially reimbursing the costs for a booth. The *REC* also helps start-ups to sell their goods on foreign online marketplaces, supports them in certification and customs matters, and has an "exporter's school" for entrepreneurs.

There are quite a few success stories of Russian start-ups entering foreign markets. For instance, *Vocord* is implementing its face recognition technology in the municipal video surveillance system of Jakarta (Indonesia), while *Promobot* has signed a big deal in 2018 on delivering 2800 of its service robots to the U.S. within the next few years. Another above-mentioned company, *DATADVANCE*, is one of Russia's internationally most successful start-ups as it has been selling its software platform to corporations like *Airbus, Michelin, Porsche*, and *Toyota* for many years and has an own representative office in Toulouse.

An increasing number of western corporations are recognizing the potential of the Russian start-up ecosystem and have opened up their global partnership and co-innovation programs for Russian entrepreneurs. For example, Bayer has a Russian branch of its Berlin-based "Grants4Apps" program, which prepares start-ups for different cooperation models by offering them workspace, mentorship, access to corporate expert knowledge, and financial awards. *SAP*, on the other hand, actively scouts Russian start-ups for its global partnership formats like "PartnerEdge—Build" that give third-party companies an opportunity to develop applications based on SAP technologies and to engage with the *SAP* ecosystem. Both corporations do this, because they expect a benefit for themselves and for their clients from interacting with Russian start-ups, which means that Russian founders definitely generate ideas and products relevant to the global market.

The Russian-German Chamber of Commerce *(AHK)* shares these companies' optimistic view on Russian start-ups and has launched projects on its own to bring together Russian entrepreneurs and German corporations. The most important of them is a yearly roadshow called *"Start.up! Germany,"* where six up-and-coming Russian start-ups from different industries travel across Germany's economic heartlands and meet senior representatives of large German corporations, which in turn are interested in dealing with foreign start-ups. The results of two such business missions in 2017 and 2018 show a clear trend: while an increasing number of German corporations are interested in the innovations and technologies offered by Russian start-ups, more and more Russian entrepreneurs recognize Germany as an attractive export market. This "going global" trend might help the Russian start-up ecosystem to overcome its internal difficulties.

Suggestions for Further Reading

Universities

Moscow State University	msu.ru/en
Bauman Moscow State Technical University	bmstu.ru/en
Moscow Institute of Physics and Technology	mipt.ru/english
Higher School of Economics	hse.ru/en
St. Petersburg State University	english.spbu.ru
St. Petersburg Polytechnic University	english.spbstu.ru
ITMO University	en.itmo.ru/en
Skoltech	skoltech.ru/en

Start-Up Companies

VisionLabs	visionlabs.ai
NtechLab	ntechlab.com
Vocord	vocord.ru/en
Robot Vera	ai.robotvera.com
Promobot	promo-bot.ai
DATADVANCE	datadvance.net

Accelerators

GenerationS	en.generation-startup.ru
Internet Initiatives Development Fund	accelerator.iidf.ru
iDeal Machine Accelerator	idealmachine.ru/programs.html
Starta Ventures Accelerator	startaventures.com/accelerator
Techstars Moscow	communities.techstars.com/russia/moscow
500 Startups & Sberbank	sberbank-500.ru
MTS Startup Hub	startup.mts.ru
CROC corporate accelerator	startup.croc.ru

Venture Capital Funds

Russian Venture Company	rvc.ru/en
Internet Initiatives Development Fund	iidf.vc
AltaIR Capital	altair.vc
Runa Capital	runacap.com
Almaz Capital	almazcapital.com
Flint Capital	flintcap.com
The Untitled	theuntitled.net/en
iDealMachine	idealmachine.ru
Starta Ventures	startaventures.com/invest
Sistema VC	sistema.vc

Grant-Givers

FASIE ("The Bortnik Foundation")	fasie.ru
Skolkovo Foundation	sk.ru

Export Promotion Agency

Russian Export Center	exportcenter.ru/en

Global Corporate Partnership Programs and the AHK's Activities

Bayer Grants4Apps	g4a.health
SAP Partnership Programs	sap.com/partner/become.html
Start.up! Germany	startupgermany2018.de

Part II
Society

Brief Overview over Russian History

Henk R. Randau

The Origin of the Land of Rus'

The Russia we know today has its humble beginnings over 1000 years ago. Since then, some previously foreign lands have become incorporated into Russia and some lands that once belonged to Russia now lay outside its reach. Russia's history is a history of changing borders. At the peak of their power, the empire of the tsars spanned one sixth of the globe. Within these borders were multiple races, cultures, and ethnic groups (Slavs, Turks, Mongols, Fins, and others) all of whom had different practices, spoke different languages and had no sense of being part of a coherent land at all. Russia was a nation of many groups.

In the ninth century, Viking explorers sailed down major rivers at the edge of Europe such as the Dnieper, the Don, and the Volga, and pioneered new trade routes. They spawned short-cuts to the riches of the Silk Road, the Fertile Crescent, and Constantinople. The Vikings called the native Slavs along the rivers "the Rus." Upon the Dnieper, the Vikings settled in the city of Kiev and assimilated into the native Slavic ruling class. Their kingdom became known as the "Kievan Rus". This frontier between Europe and Asia would later become known as Russia.

By the late tenth century, this land was a patchwork of warring city-states that battled for supremacy. Kiev, being the greatest city, was also the home to the grand prince of Kiev, Vladimir, who was the most powerful man in the land of the Russ. Prince Vladimir had united the land of the Russ through the orthodox Christianity but at his death, he left the land divided by his sons, which led to civil war and threatened to tear the country apart.

H. R. Randau (✉)
Weinheim, Germany
e-mail: hrandau@whu.edu

> **TIPS, OPPORTUNITIES and WARNINGS**
> Warning: History is controversial
>
> With each new ruler, Russian history is interpreted in a new way. In recent decades, perceptions of Russian history have changed again. With new research, "forgotten" or "lost" information has made its way into the mainstream historical narrative while some things, which were previously considered important, have been phased out. Views of historical figures like Stalin or Nicolaus II have altered 'and even the view of the old Rus kingdom's history has changed. There are many different perspectives and viewpoints on history in Russian society so it is a touchy subject and should be avoided in small talk.

In 1237–1240, the Mongol horde invaded from the East and occupied most of the land of the Russ in only 3 years. Led by Batu Khan, they were one of the greatest war machines in history. They would go on to create the largest contiguous land empire of the world, yet were only interested in collecting payments from Russ' princes and not on enforcing any Mongol culture, lifestyle, or religion on the natives. This marked the beginning of the reign of the golden horde that would last 250 years. As time went on, the city of Moscow grew in power and was able to build an army to fight against these invaders. The end of Mongol rule came slowly over time, not decisively. When Moscow gained independence in 1480, the city's new grand prince Ivan III (the Great) united the nation. Soon Ivan the Great would take a new title for himself: "tsar" (Russification of Caesar) which means absolute imperial ruler of all Russians.

By the mid-sixteenth century, Ivan the Great's grandson, Ivan IV (the Terrible), took steps to concentrate all power in the hands of the tsar and began an era of autocracy. Ivan IV was the first prince who was formally crowned tsar in 1547. He waged internal wars for nearly 8 years. Tsar Ivan the Terrible had elevated Moscow from a kingdom to an empire but his own brutality had killed his son and ended his dynasty.

In 1613, Michael Romanov was crowned as grand prince of Russia ending a long period of instability and foreign intervention. It was the birth of the Romanov family rule (Romanov Dynasty) that lasted for more than three centuries.

By 1689, Michael Romanov's grandson, Peter I (the Great), took the throne. Russia was behind other nations in technological and societal advancements, having not yet reaped all the benefits of the Renaissance, or the Scientific Revolution of the seventeenth century. In 1697 Peter left the kingdom to seek technical know-how and bring innovations and reforms from Europe to Russia. He wanted to take Russia out of its Muscovite isolation and backwardness and to exchange goods and technologies with the West. Peter sought warm-water ports at the Baltic Sea and the Black sea to aid in his ambitions of creating a formidable Russian navy. Peter would later found the city of St. Petersburg. His "Window to Europe" grew and flourished until it replaced Moscow as the capital of the Russian Empire. As a reforming tsar, Peter transformed Russia into a "Westernized" nation, with a government that followed along European lines, and helped form Russia into a modern global power.

Between 1721 and 1815, Russia established naval presence in the Baltic Sea and gained new territories such as modern Estonia, Latvia, Ukraine, and the long-sought-after symbol of the Black Sea; Crimea. Moldova, Belarus, Georgia, and parts of Poland were also added to the Empire, especially during the rule of Catherine II (the Great). In the early nineteenth century, the Napoleonic Wars were raging across Europe, and in 1812, Napoleon invaded Russia. Tsar Alexander I led the Empire against Napoleon and the invading French. The Russian Winter famously defeated Napoleon and the loss of his army led to his eventual downfall.

In the latter half of the century, Russia continued with its ambitions for expansion due to the weakening of the Ottoman Empire (nicknamed "the Sick Man of Europe") but Russia's defeat in the Crimean War (1853–1856) showed that the Empire had fallen behind militarily compared to the rest of Europe. Russia's society was also somewhat backward as the institution of Serfdom was still heavily practiced. In 1861, the Emancipation Edict ended serfdom, allowing for the emergence of a small but functioning working class. Yet, the Emancipation Edict failed to create functioning economic mobility for many of the former Serfs as it kept them tied to the land through continuing labor obligations in a neo-feudalistic fashion. This mistreatment, coupled with rapid industrialization lead to discontentment and the spread of revolutionary ideas.

The Twentieth Century: Soviet Era

In 1905, the Russian Revolution forced Tsar Nicholas II to make constitutional reforms, which led to the formation of a parliament, the Duma, and basic civil rights for Russians. The Duma wanted radical reforms in Russia's political system but Tsar Nicholas II still believed that the Romanov family were the nation's rightful rulers. In 1914 (World War I), Russia fought alongside France and Britain as a member of the Entente. In 1917, Russia's economy was in ruins and casualties were high. The Russian people had to suffer high inflation, fuel, and food shortages. Bread lines were formed and riots sparked. After Nicholas II received an ultimatum by the Duma to relinquish his entire executive power to the assembly, he abdicated his throne on February 27, 1917, ending three centuries of Romanov rule. The Russian Provincial Government (Lvov Government) was established with Georgy Lvov and later Alexander Kerensky acting as the de-facto leaders. However, this did not last as the government was overthrown in another revolution in October of that same year (the October Revolution). The Radical Bolsheviks, led by Vladimir Lenin, dissatisfied with Russia's continued involvement in the war, overthrew the Lvov Government and established the new Soviet Union. In 1918, the Soviets signed the Treaty of Brest-Litovsk which effectively ended Russia's involvement in the war and ceded massive amounts of territory in the nation's western portion to the Central Powers, or to newly-formed independent nations (Finland, Latvia, Estonia, Lithuania, etc.).

The Soviet Union represented a massive shift in Russian domestic affairs as well as global affairs, since it was the first constitutionally socialist state. It changed the way Russia was seen by the rest of the world dramatically. It was a threat to many in the Western World who feared Communism's growing influence on their societies. Lenin, the architect of the October Revolution, passed away in 1924 causing a power struggle for leadership of the nation. In 1929, Joseph Stalin became General Secretary of the Communist Party in the Soviet Union. In this period, the Bolshevik government carried out a systematic annihilation of the "old regime." The Lenin-Stalin era (1918–1953) was characterized by civil wars, the Red Terror (a campaign of mass killing, torture, and oppression by the Bolsheviks), political oppressions, forced labor camps, and prisons, comparable to those commonly known to have occurred during the Second World War.

Following Russia's victory in World War II and the nation's outstanding industrialization, Russia began competing with the West about being the global nuclear superpower and the first humans landing on the moon. In 1947, the "Cold War" had begun. At that time, the Union of Soviet Socialist Republics (USSR) ruled over the largest area in its history and rose to become the world superpower. After the Cuban Missile Crisis in 1962 and the removal of the Communist Party's leader Khrushchev, Russia suffered under economic and political stagnation under Leonid Brezhnev.

Perestroika and Glasnost

Between 1985 and 1991 General Secretary of Russia, Mikhail Gorbachev published reforms with the purpose of the reorganization and democratization of the Communist Party and the recovery of the nation's economy, generally known as 'perestroika'. Perestroika literally means "rebuilding" or "restructuring." It was Gorbachev's campaign to revitalize the communist party, the Soviet economy, and Soviet society. It planned to reform economic, political, and social mechanisms in the USSR. Perestroika was mostly directed at the economy, but it was meant for society in general. Gorbachev always said that his goal was to modernize Socialism and to keep the Communist Party in power. In the beginning, Gorbachev spoke of perestroika often, but in 1987, the slogan came into practice. In economic terms, perestroika meant greater freedom in decision-making for managers, allowed for individual initiative to a certain degree, and created the opportunity to make profit.

In January 1988, the new Law on State Enterprises went into effect, allowing businesses to set many of their own prices and wages. However, the results were disappointing as workers demanded huge wage increases. The government printed more money and Russian products began to drop in value on the open market. Speculators took advantage of this and snatched up whatever they could find in bulk and many Russian stores were left with empty shelves. Towards the end of 1988, it was difficult to find staple products even in Moscow.

The second set of reforms were known as "Glasnost." A word that is meant to describe public discussion and the availability of information to the public. Gorbachev designed it to foster discussion to rally support for Perestroika among the public. Glasnost reduced censorship and allowed the press to criticize the actions of the Communist Party in the past. During this time, Russians began to see the first news reports critical of the Stalin Era, the War in Afghanistan, and other things.

End of the Soviet Era

Following immense pressure from the other Soviet Republics, Gorbachev urged in 1991 that the republics should adopt a new system as a federation of independent states. An unsuccessful coup in 1991 resulted in the shift of Russia's power from Mikhail Gorbachev, the Communist Party leader, to Boris Yeltsin, the first elected president of the Russian Republic. Gorbachev resigned from office and dissolved all units of the Communist Party. Fearing another coup, the republics declared independence. The leaders of the Russian SFSR, the Ukrainian SSR, and the Byelorussian SSR met in December of 1991 to sign the Belovezha Accords, which formally ended the Soviet Union and replaced it with the Commonwealth of Independent States (CIS), a loose confederation of independent states with no central authority made up of all former republics except Latvia, Lithuania, and Estonia.

The new president of the Russian Federation, Boris Yeltsin faced chaotic political and economic challenges until he resigned. Yeltsin was re-elected in 1996 and followed by Vladimir Putin who was elected president in March 2000. President Putin strove to consolidate his power and to restore the authority of the new Russia to Soviet era levels. Since then, Russia has flexed its military muscles around the world in various conflicts such as Abkhazia in 2008, the Donbass in 2014, and now Syria. Putin would go on to win the presidential elections of 2000, 2004, and 2012. He has been recognized for restoring the nation's stability but has also being accused of authoritarianism and of suppressing democracy. The Russian annexation of Crimea in 2015 resulted in sanctions of the EU and the USA against the Federation. During the same year, a crackdown on the Russian independent media gave the president practically absolute power of the Russian public opinion. Putin's loyal ally Dmitry Medvedev won the presidential election in 2008 and took over in May of that year. Mr. Putin returned to the presidency for a third term in May 2012. Following a constitutional change, his term will last 6 years, to 2018.

Following the dissolution of the USSR, Russia was now officially known as the Russian Federation. For the first time since the sixteenth century, Russia became a relatively ethnically homogenous country. With the new borders that had been drawn after the independence of the SSRs, the margin by which ethnic Russians made up the majority had increased dramatically. However, the federation still included several autonomous republics, regions, and one autonomous oblast, each designated for a particular ethnic group. In 1991 Leningrad took back its former name; St. Petersburg. Along with it, several other cities changed their name: Gorky, named after a Marxist writer, returned to Nizhniy Novgorod. Andropov became Rybinsk and Sverdlock, named after an executioner of the royal family, was rechristened "Ekaterinburg," for Catherine the Great.

The transition to a market economy in the early 1990ies was accompanied by a collapse in industrial production and a sharp drop in living standards. A contested privatization process led to a highly concentrated ownership structure. Executive weakness and bureaucratic dysfunction contributed to a sharp decentralization of power. After becoming president in 2000, Vladimir Putin sought to restore central control over the regions and tame independent corporate interests. Mr. Putin presided over a period of strong economic growth in his first two terms. His re-election as president in 2012 has heralded the development of a more authoritarian domestic environment. Putin's second term in office was characterized by increasing centralization of the state.

Suggestion for Further Reading

Russia—Land of the Tsars, The History Channel, 2003

Anastasia Edel: *Russia—Putin's Playground—Empire, Revolution and the new Tsar*, (Lightning Guides, Berkely California, 2015)

BBC: Russia profile—Timeline   http://www.bbc.com/news/world-europe-17840446

Geography 16

Olga Medinskaya

The Russian Federation (RF) is still the largest nation in the world with a territory amassing 17 million km^2. Covering 1/9 of the world's land surface, (about 10,000 km from West to East and 4000 from north to south) it is twice the size of China or the USA, five times of India, and 70 times the size of the UK. The country borders with 16 other countries and covers 11 time zones. About 1/4 of the territory lies in Europe. The other part of the country is considered Asia. The two parts are separated by the 2000 km long Ural Mountain range, which acts as a natural border (Fig. 16.1).

Russia is disadvantageously located far from major sea routes and closer to the Arctic than to the Equator. More than 70% of the territory is plains and lowlands. The mountains are located in the southern and eastern parts of the country. It has land borders with Norway, Finland, Estonia, Latvia, Lithuania, Poland, Belarus, Ukraine, Georgia, Azerbaijan, Kazakhstan, China, Mongolia, North Korea, and maritime borders with Japan and the USA.

Climate

The RF has a predominantly continental climate, characterized by a distinct division of the year into cold and warm seasons and large temperature differences. Due to its big territory, Russia's climate contrasts immensely depending on the region. Summers are hot in the Prairielands but cool along the Arctic coast—where it is only warm enough to melt snow. Winters range from cool along to the Black Sea to frigid in sub-arctic Siberia. Normally the whole territory is covered by snow with exception of some areas along the Black Sea. In 93% of Russia, the average temperature in January is below −10 °C and 65% of the territory has Permafrost (north of the

---

O. Medinskaya (✉)
Cultural Connectors, Mannheim, Germany
e-mail: info@cultural-connectors.com

© The Author(s), under exclusive license to Springer Nature Switzerland AG 2021
O. Medinskaya et al. (eds.), *Russia Business*,
https://doi.org/10.1007/978-3-030-64613-4_16

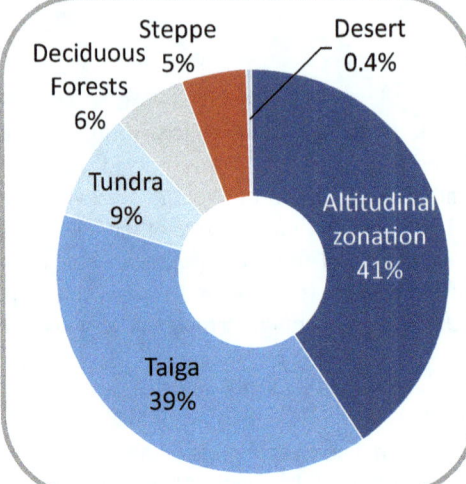

Fig. 16.1 Geography in a nutshell

European part, Siberia, and the Far East). Climate causes almost ¾ of the territory of RF to have unfavorable living conditions for human life (Лопатина & Назаревский, 1972) (Fig. 16.1).

The Federal Service for Hydrometeorology and Environmental Monitoring of Russia in its yearly report noticed that the country is undergoing a climate change. The effects of global warming are felt through increased precipitation, record-breaking warm summers, continuous decrease in the duration of snow cover, and

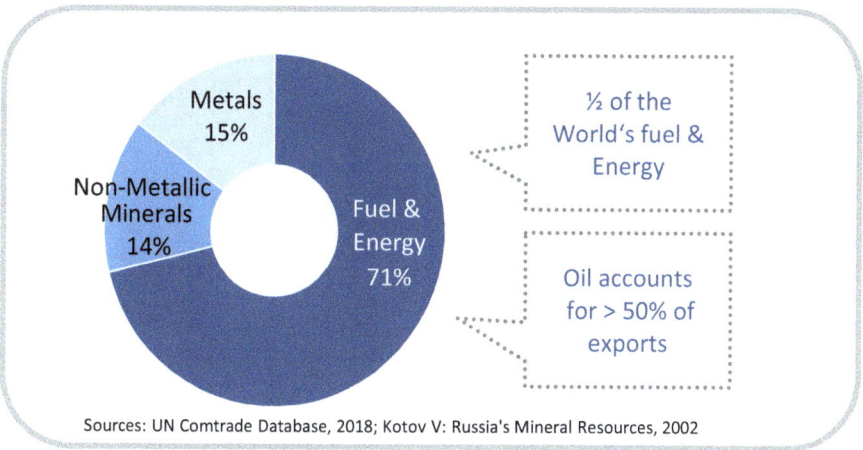

Fig. 16.2 Structure of the Russian mineral resource base

the absence of exceptionally cold days in vast areas of the northern and eastern part of European Russia. For the first time ever in 2016, a mini-ozone depletion over the north of the Urals and Siberia was observed. It lasted for 5 days.[1]

Mineral Resources

Russia is likely to be richer in natural resources than any other country in the world. It has abundant supplies of oil, natural gas, timber and valuable minerals such as copper, diamonds, lead, zinc, bauxite, nickel, tin, mercury, gold, and silver. Most of these resources are located in sparsely populated areas in the North and the East of the country. Despite 90% of reserves being concentrated here, 3/4 are consumed in Western Russia. The exploitation of these resources is hindered by the challenges brought forth by climate, terrain, and distance making the cost for the acquisition of those resources so high that extracting them is not economically feasible (Симагин, 2014). About 20,000 mineral resource deposits have been discovered in the country, however, only about 1/3 of this amount is being developed.

In the value structure of the country's mineral resource base, around 70% of the value belongs to the fuel and energy complex (oil, gas, coal, etc.), 15% are non-metallic minerals, and about 15% are metals. This gives the Russian fuel industry disproportionate importance (Kotov, 2002) (Fig. 16.2). More than half of the world's fuel and energy reserves are concentrated in the Russian Federation and they account for about a half of the country's total export[2] (Chap. 12).

---

[1]Federal Service for Hydrometeorology and environmental monitoring, (www.meteorf.ru).
[2]UN Comtrade Database, 2018.

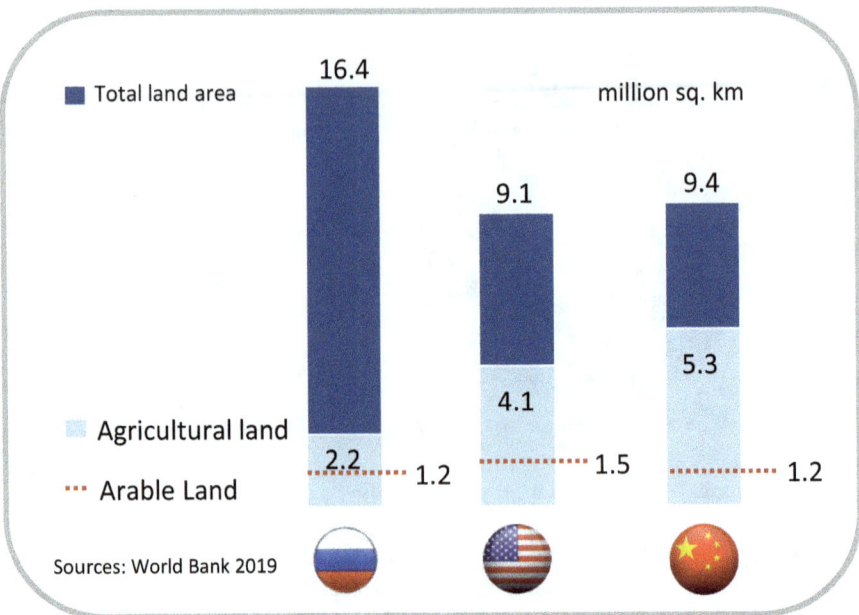

Fig. 16.3 Land used for agriculture

Agriculture and Animal Husbandry

In general, the agricultural growing season is short due to unfavorable climate conditions. It lasts in the biggest part of Russia only 2–4 months (in contrast, it averages 8–9 months in Europe and the USA). Only 13% of the land (or 2.2 million km^2) can be used for agriculture—it is either arable, under permanent crops, or under permanent pastures (China 56%, the USA 44%) (Fig. 16.3). 7.5% of the land (or 1.2 million km^2) is arable and used for temporary crops such as cereals, temporary meadows for pasture or gardens (Fig. 16.4). This makes up 9% of all arable land in the world. In the international context, the amount of arable land is comparable with China (1.2 million km^2) or it is 19% lesser than in the USA (1.5 million km^2).

The natural quality of the soil is high—more than 50% of the world's *chernozem* (around 1.2 million km^2) is located there. This kind of soil can produce the highest agricultural yield[3] (Fig. 16.5). However, during the last 100 years, the quality of Russian *chernozem* fell dramatically. Humus content is a key determinant of soil fertility. In 1883, the soil of the Tambov region contained up to 12.6% of humus—today it is not more than 7%. Loss of humus is associated with increase in the intensity of soil processing together with insufficient intake of organic fertilizers, burning of stubble and straw, and exposure to water and wind erosion. The poor

---

[3]The World Bank Data. Agricultural land (% of land area), last available date 2015.

16 Geography

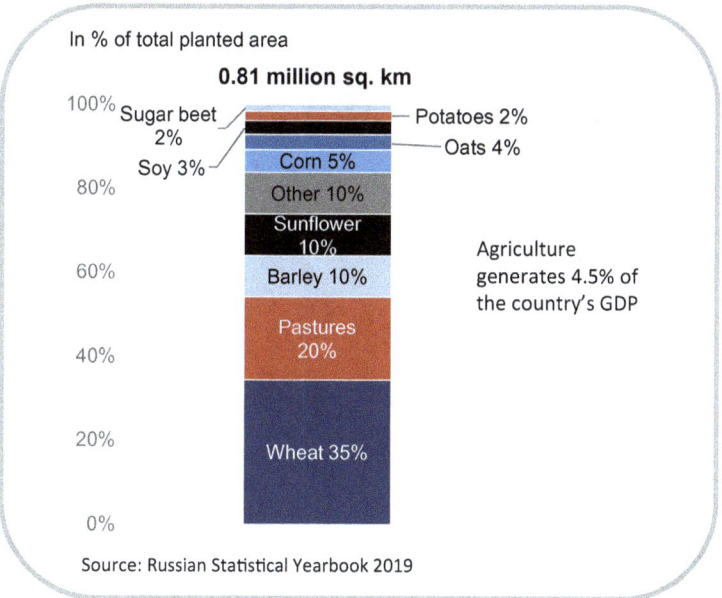

Fig. 16.4 Structure of planted crop area

Fig. 16.5 Traditional grain belt: production in percent of total wheat output

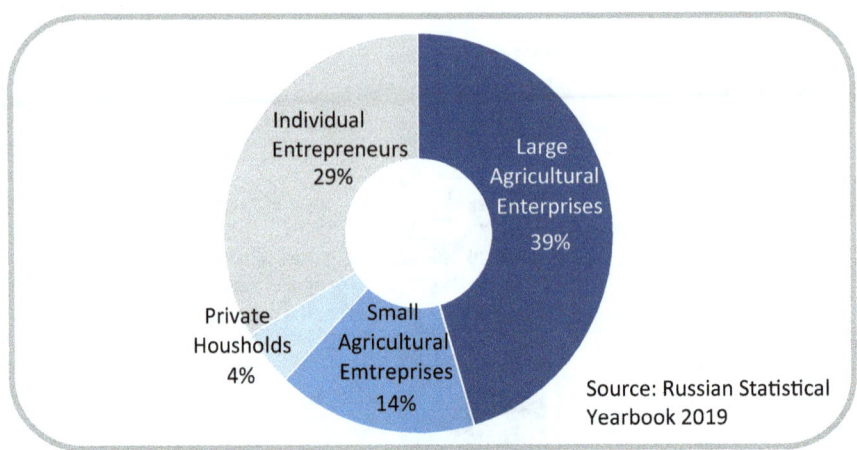

Fig. 16.6 Planted corps by farm type

economic condition of farms as well as reducing of the number of animals caused reduced usage of organic fertilizers (Федоров & Воронцов, 2009) (from 4 ton per hectare in the 1980s to 1.5 in 2017[4]), which is one of the main reinforcements of organic soil matter.

Agriculture represents an important industrial pillar, generating 4.5% of the country's GDP and employing 7% of the working population.[5] The 1990s saw a dramatic drop in agricultural and animal husbandry output. With the transition from the command economy to a market-oriented economy, large collectives, and state farms lost their state-guaranteed marketing and supply channels. These farms had served as the backbone of Soviet agriculture until then (Fig. 16.6). As a result, the livestock inventories in the following 10 years were halved and crop inventory dropped by 25% (Fig. 16.7). However, since 2000 the total production volume has started to climb back to former levels. In 2016, it reached the 1989 level and made Russia the world's leading wheat exporter by 2017 for the first time since the Soviet Union collapsed.[6] Russia exports around 50% of the yearly wheat production making around 20% of the world wheat trade (the USA 16%; Canada 13%; EU 13%)[7] (Fig. 16.8).

---

[4]Russian Statistical Yearbook (www.gks.ru) retrieved on October 7th, 2020.

[5]Russian Statistical Yearbook (www.gks.ru) retrieved on October 7th, 2020.

[6]https://www.bloomberg.com/news/articles/2018-03-16/russia-wheat-stocks-to-rise-to-record-in-blow-to-european-rivals, retrieved on February 7th, 2020.

[7]U.S. Department of Agriculture: World Markets and Trade: Commodities and Data, 2018.

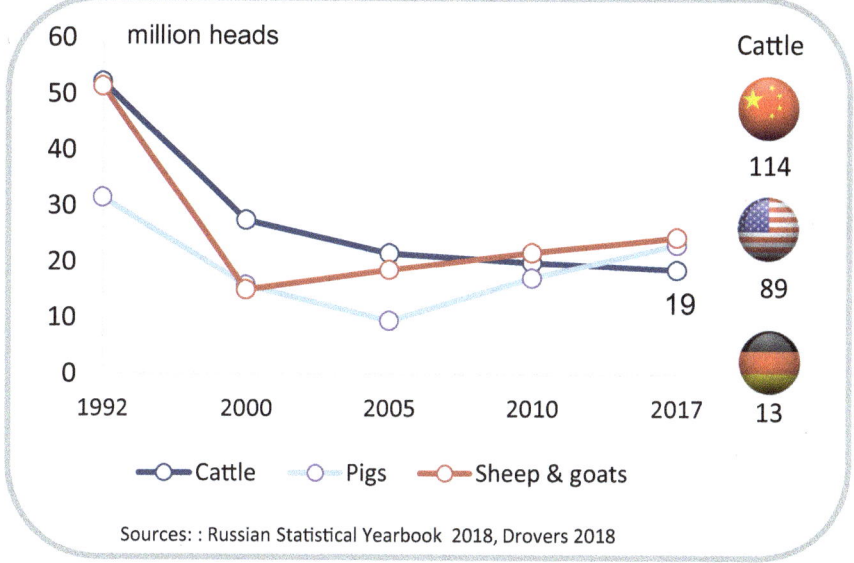

Fig. 16.7 Livestock population

Forecast 2020 / 2021

Total Production in thousand tons	77,000	50,784
Export	35,000	26,000
Share of world export	19%	14%
Planted acreage (million acres)	75	55

Source: US Department of Agriculture 2020; Ministry of Agriculture in Russia, June 2020

Fig. 16.8 Wheat production and trade

Drinking Water

Although the country uses no more than 3% of its river flow annually, some regions suffer from an acute shortage of clean water. This is difficult to understand given the fact that Russia has 2.8 million rivers and 2.7 million lakes, making it one of the water-richest countries in the world. Lake Baikal, the world's deepest lake and most prominent of Russia's freshwater bodies, contains over 1/5 of the world's fresh surface water alone.

Shortages in freshwater for some regions are caused by the inequality of the water distribution. The most developed and populated areas of the European part of Russia (central and southern) account for only about 8% of the total water resources. The other reason is low water quality in these regions, especially surface water bodies. The most pressing problem is the supply of drinking water to large cities (Moscow, St. Petersburg, Yaroslavl, Kostroma, Ivanovo, Nizhny Novgorod, Novosibirsk, Omsk, Khabarovsk, and others) which use surface water for their water supply.

The reasons for the low drinking quality are manifold. For one, the overall water treatment capacity and low technical standards are inadequate. Beginning in 1978, biological wastewater treatment facilities were erected in almost all cities in Russia, but their combined total capacity is only about 75% of the required volume. Unfortunately, the treatment efficiency does not comply with the existing standards for safe water conditions.[8]

Another reason is the weak or inadequate enforcement of legal acts and regulations relating to water.[9] Often highly polluted runoff water is dumped in local rivers by manufacturing centers that have never passed contemporary water quality control inspections.[10] There is also usually a lack of compliance with the required controls on human activities in water protection zones. As a result, the surface water contains large quantities of anthropogenic pollutants from wastewater of industrial enterprises. This water drains from residential and industrial areas, transport routes, agricultural lands, etc.[11]

References

Лопатина, Е. Б., & Назаревский, О. Р. (1972). *Оценка природных условий жизни населения*. Москва: Наука.

Симагин, Ю. А. (2014). *Экономическая география и прикладное регионоведение России*. Издательство Юрайт.

Kotov, V. (2002). *Russia's mineral resources: Reconfiguration of institutional framework*. Conference paper, Political Economy Research Institute University of Massachusetts Amherst.

Федоров, В. А., & Воронцов, В. А. (2009). Чернозем наше богатство. *Вестник ТГУ*.

---

[8] http://wto.int/water_sanitation_health/resourcequality/wpccasestudy10.pdf, retrieved on April 2nd, 2018.

[9] http://wto.int/water_sanitation_health/resourcequality/wpccasestudy10.pdf, retrieved on April 2nd, 2018.

[10] Federation Council, at http://council.gov.ru/activity/activities/roundtables/31980/ retrieved on October 2nd, 2020.

[11] Federation Council, at http://council.gov.ru/activity/activities/roundtables/31980/ retrieved on April 2nd, 2020.

Population and Demography

17

Olga Medinskaya and Henk R. Randau

Although Russia's territory is nearly twice the size of the USA, it has only roughly half of the USA population. This leads to an average population density of only 8.6 per km^2 (e.g., Germany is around 231 people per km^2) (Fig. 17.1). Although, this average does not tell the story well, as the population density differs dramatically by region (Fig. 17.2). Historically, favorable agricultural conditions in the European part and some southern regions of Siberia and the Far East were the reasons for the unequal distribution of the population. The high centralization of political power around Moscow and a few other economic centers has fueled the imbalance. Today, more than 5000 people per square km live in the mega metropolitan of Moscow.[1] The population density in the countryside around Moscow (Moscow Region) drops already to roughly 170 people per km^2. In comparison, other regions of the European part like the south federal district have around 37 people per km^2, while regions with harsh climate conditions like the north and eastern parts of the country only have a density of one person per km^2.

---

[1]Project "New Moscow" started in 2012. It was an expansion of Moscow's administrative borders at the expense of the territory of the Greater Moscow Region where less than 250,000 people lived. It changed the statistic of population density in Russian Capital dramatically. Since then, the territory of Moscow has grown by 240%, at https://stroi.mos.ru, retrieved on February 7th, 2020.

O. Medinskaya (✉)
Cultural Connectors, Mannheim, Germany
e-mail: info@cultural-connectors.com

H. R. Randau
Weinheim, Germany
e-mail: hrandau@whu.edu

© The Author(s), under exclusive license to Springer Nature Switzerland AG 2021
O. Medinskaya et al. (eds.), *Russia Business*,
https://doi.org/10.1007/978-3-030-64613-4_17

Fig. 17.1 Population and density

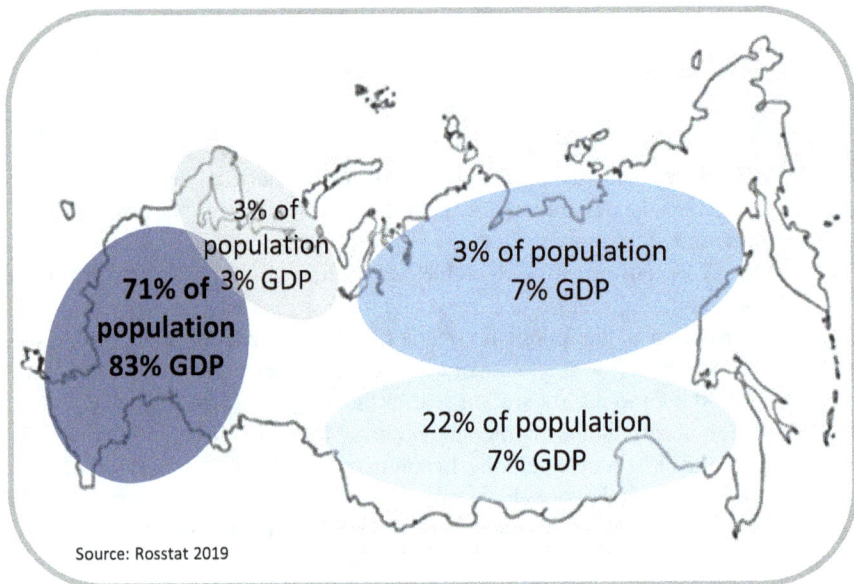

Fig. 17.2 Population and GDP

Demographic Crisis

The decline of the population has become an acute problem for Russia. An overall low birth rate and high mortality rates have led to a decline in population. The Russian political philosopher *Sergey Kara-Murza* is credited with being the first to label the excess of death rates over birth rate in the 1990s and 2000s as the "*Russian Cross*" in his book *Soviet Civilization* (Fig. 17.3). The name comes from the cross-formed when both lines are plotted on the same chart. This label certainly sounded dramatic and resonated within Russian ears, as the term cross is associated with gravestones and surrender.

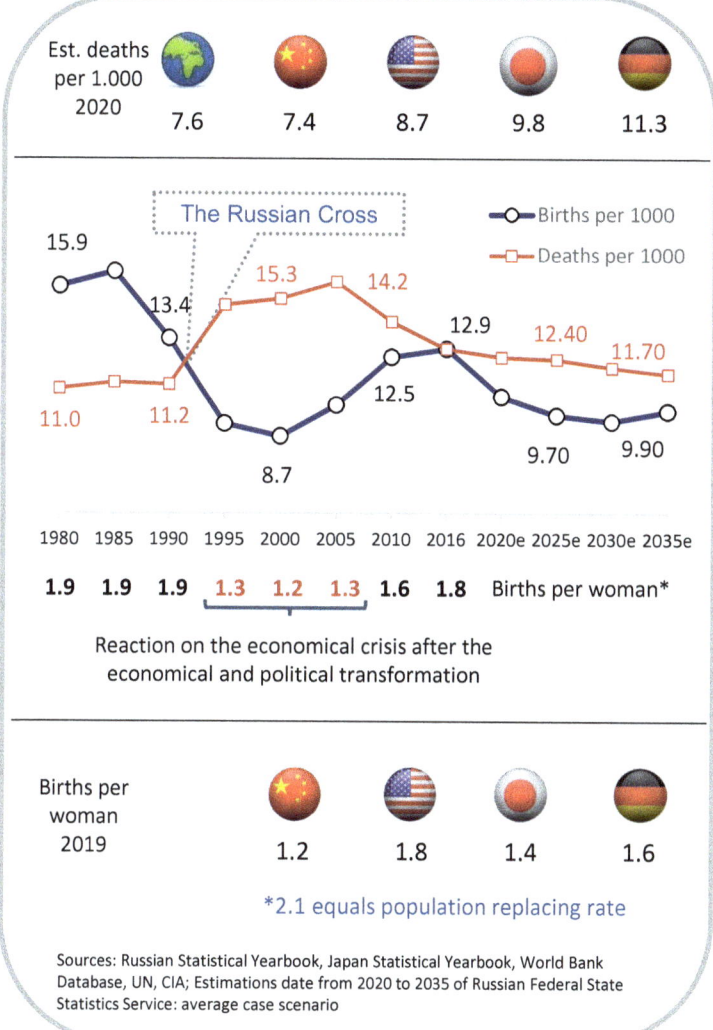

Fig. 17.3 Demographic crisis: Russian Cross

Birth Rates

Since 2006, the birth rate has started to climb back and is coming today closer to the rate of the early 1990s. Since birth rates were so low for many years, the *Federal State Statistic Service* expects that even with a further recovery in birth rates, the decline of the natural population will continue for several decades.

When discussing the birth rate in Russia, there are also major regional differences that need to be taken into account. Regions with a majority Slavic population (e.g.,

Central Federal District, North-West, Volga) display a declining natural population, whereas in other regions where traditionally large families are highly valued (e.g., North Caucasian republics) the natural population continues to grow.

The Russian government has taken comprehensive measures to reverse the overall trend. Since 2007, it has implemented multiple measures to support families by bringing up children.[2] Although it is difficult to estimate the influence of the government efforts exactly, surveys indicate that up to 90% of all citizens know about these supporting programs and 38% believe that they may significantly increase the birth rate. However, in practice, 79% of Russian citizens who already have children are not ready to have another child.[3]

The Aging Population and High Death Rates

Besides the low birth rate, the extraordinarily high mortality rates have contributed to the Russian demographical crisis (Chap. 24). One of the key differences between Russia and the West is the "jumps" of the aging pyramid due to wars and due to the economic and social crisis that followed the collapse of the Soviet Union. The Life expectancy at birth (LEB) dramatically dropped in the 1990s and remained as low as around 58 years for males and 72 years for females over a course of 15 years.[4] The LEB started to slowly climb again from 2005 onwards and in 2017 it reached an average of 70.5 years (67 years for males and 77 years for females) (Fig. 17.4). Although the Russian media enthusiastically sees the gain as the longest in the history of Russia, it remains low in comparison to western countries.[5] The mortality rate, mostly amongst men of working age, stems from cardiovascular diseases, cancer, and external causes (trauma, alcohol poisoning, homicide, and suicide). It remains much higher (Chap. 24) than in other developed countries (Fig. 17.5).

All this leads to an aging population, as in so many other industrial and post-industrial countries. According to Bloomberg,[6] Russia only has 2.4 working people supporting one senior (France 2.2; China 3.5; USA 4.4). It is one of the top ten most at risk countries in the world with regards to the aging population problem. While Western European countries have started to gradually raise their retirement age up to 67 years, Russia has only raised the retirement age for civil servants. The government still has no official plans to raise it for other workers, though Putin stated that

---

[2]For example, as part of the "Maternity capital program", a family received a one-time payment of around USD8000 for their second and following children. This was intended to be spent on either the education of the children, the buying a property or investment in the parents' pension.

[3]Russian Public Opinion Research Center: Рождаемость в России: меры и мнения, at https://wciom.ru/index.php?id=236&uid=116649, retrieved on February 2nd, 2020.

[4]Rosstat (www.gks.ru) September 2nd, 2020.

[5]http://www.aif.ru/society/muzhchiny_v_rossii_v_srednem_stali_zhit_dolshe retrieved on October 25th, 2020.

[6]Bloomberg Sunset index.

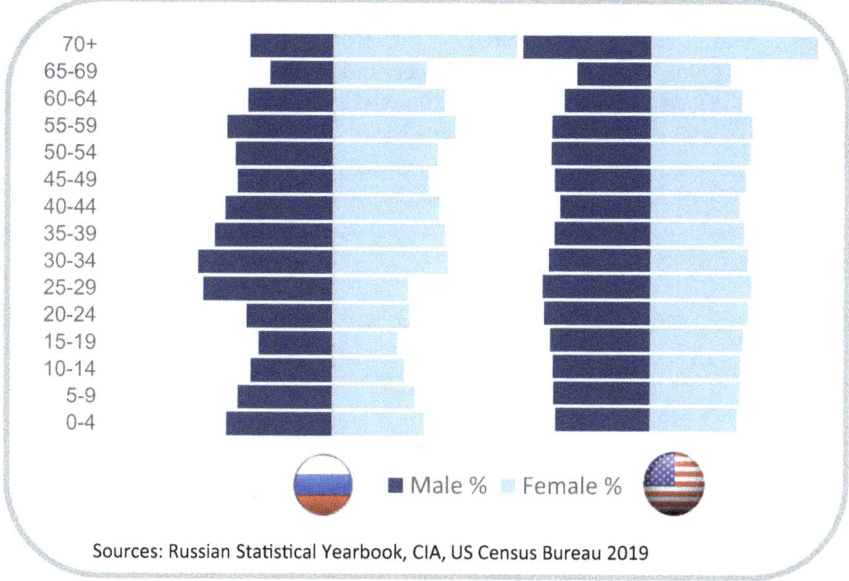

Fig. 17.4 Population by sex and age

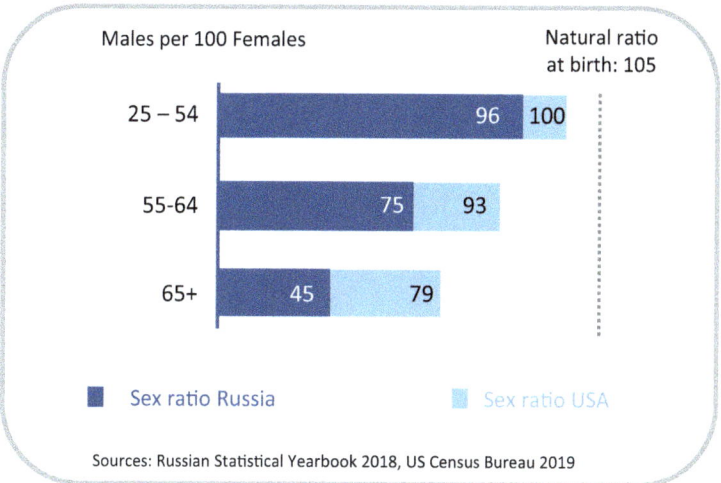

Fig. 17.5 Russia missing men: Sex ratio

the increase would be gradual and smooth.[7] One of the popular arguments for keeping the retirement age from 1932 (60 for males and 55 years for females) is that most of the population will die even before entering the age range. Another

---
[7]Interfax, at http://www.interfax.ru/russia/591813, retrieved on August 2nd, 2020.

argument against the raising of the retirement age is the higher rate[8] of unemployed young people in comparison to older people. However, due to the demographical crisis of the 1990s, the number of 10–19 year olds is around 25% fewer in number than the 45–54 year olds. Additionally, the work skills and qualifications of both generations are so vastly different in nature that the professional roles they seek to fill are oftentimes incomparable and/or incompatible (Бобков et al., 2015).

Reference

Бобков, В. Н., Забелина, О. В., & Локтюхина, Н. В. (2015). Повышение пенсионного возраста в Российской Федерации: социально-трудовые последствия. *НАРОДОНАСЕЛЕНИЕ, 4*(70). Retrieved February 2, 2020, from http://www.isesp-ras.ru/narodonaselenie/

---

[8]Rosstat, http://www.gks.ru/bgd/regl/b17_44/Main.htm, retrieved on August 2nd, 2020.

Ethnicity and Languages

Olga Medinskaya and Henk R. Randau

The Russian Federation is home to about 100 indigenous ethnic groups (with main ethnic territory in Russia) and more than 60 ethnicities whose majority live outside of Russia (like Korean or Germans) (Богоявленский, 2013, p. 93). The ethnic majority with 81% of the population are Russians.[1] Only in five of 85 Federal Subjects, the Russians are the ethnic minority (Российская академия наук, 2008) (Fig. 18.1). The mostly minorities live in Caucasian, Ural, and Volga regions, as well as in the Far North, Siberia, and the Far East (Table 18.1).

One may also categorize groups in Russia based on different linguistic and cultural formations—see Fig. 18.2, which shows the language groups that have at least 100 thousand speakers.

Three of the "World" religions; Christianity, Islam, and Buddhism are the dominant faiths within the Federation. They are predominantly bound on a regional or ethnic basis. Though they are typically found within one of these three major faiths, minority ethnic groups usually, exist within denominations unique to their region or group complete with their own customs and traditions which sets them apart to a degree. Additionally, many Russians across the religious spectrum share beliefs and superstitions rooted in ancient Slavic folklore (Fig. 18.2).

---

[1] From whose who indicated the ethnicity by the census 2010.

O. Medinskaya (✉)
Cultural Connectors, Mannheim, Germany
e-mail: info@cultural-connectors.com

H. R. Randau
Weinheim, Germany
e-mail: hrandau@whu.edu

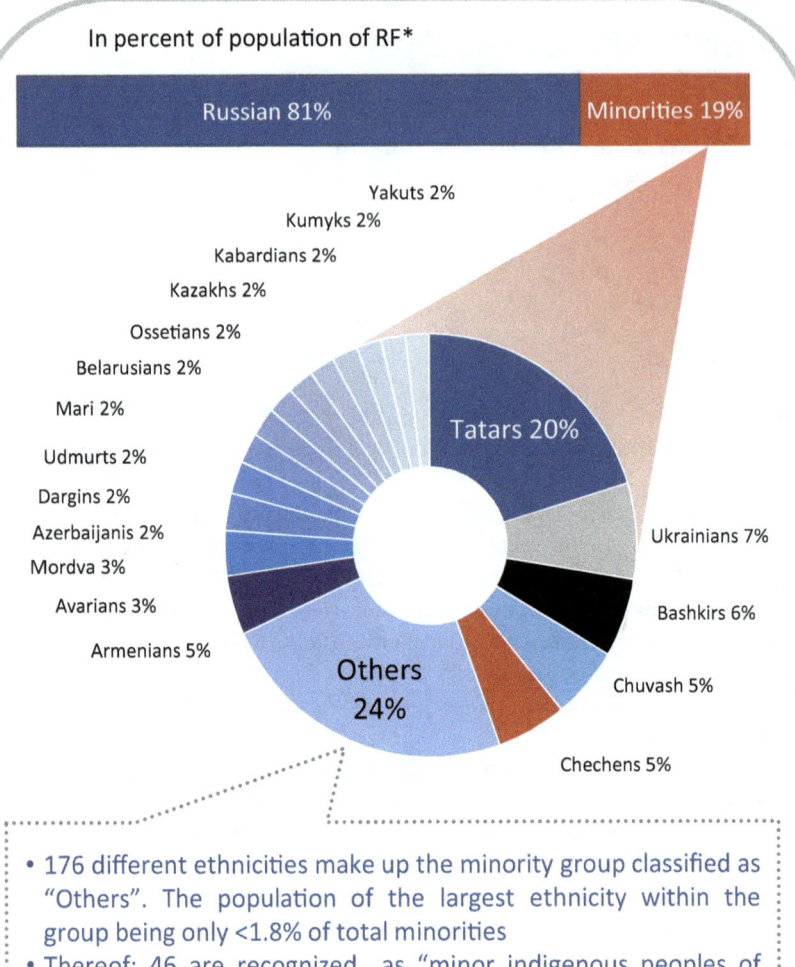

Fig. 18.1 Ethnic structure

Table 18.1 Geographic distribution of ethnic minorities

Percent of Russians	Federal subject	Federal district
<5	Ingushetia, Chechnya, Dagestan	North Caucasian
<30	Tyva	Siberia
	North Ossetia-Alania, Kabardino-Balkaria	North Caucasian
	Chuvashia	Volga
<40	Kalmykia, Tatarstan	Volga
	Bashkortostan	Ural
<50	Mari El	Volga

Subethnic Groups: Cossacks

Different subethnic groups, which belong to the big ethnos (e.g., Russian) but developed own dialect and culture contribute to ethnic diversity in Russia. One of the most famous subethnic groups is Cossacks which is actually an ethno-social formation, including Russians (majority), Ukrainians, Kalmyks, Ossetians, Bashkirs, etc. Runaway serfs formed the democratic, self-governing "troops" of Cossacks over the sixteenth–eighteenth centuries mostly in the southern steppes of the country. The Name Cossacks come from Turkic languages and mean "free warrior." They were used by the Tsarist government for border protection. Cossacks were actively involved in the Civil War of 1917 and because of repression during Soviet time the Cossacks lost a large part of their lands. Religion: mostly Russian Orthodox.

> **TIPS, OPPORTUNITIES and WARNINGS**
> "Nationality" mean "ethnicity" in Russia.
>
> In the mind of Russians, the ethnicity (called in Russian "Nationality") is an unchangeable feature, received at birth and determinate thought nationality of the parents, mostly of the father. The official record of it in many Soviet documents inclusive passports reflected and strengthened this opinion. Interestingly in Russian Empire the religious believes determinates "Nationality" in the official documents. Since 1990, the column "Nationality" disappeared from the personal ID in order to avoid conflicts and discriminations at school and on the jobs, but the discussions to return the paragraph back at least as voluntary statement never stop in the government. Some minority members fear the return of the column, some are proud to belong to their minority, some changed their name to not be recognized as a minority at all, especially by looking for the job in the capital.[188] The typical for the particular minority name, birthplace, sometimes the appearance and possible accent let others to recognize someone as a minority.

	Branch	Language	Religion of Majority (ordered largest to smallest)
Indo-European languages	Slavic	- East (Russian, Ukrainian, Belarusian, Rusyns) - West (Poles) - South (Bulgarian	✝
	Armenian	Armenian Hemshin	✝ ☪
	Germanic	German Iddisch*	✝ ✡
	Iranian	Ossetians Yezidi Kurds Caucasus Jews Tats	☸ ✝ ☪ 🌑 ☪ ✡ ☪
	Neo-Latin	Romanian Moldavan	✝
	Indo-Aryan	Romanian	✝
	Greek	Greek	✝
	Baltic	Latvian Lithuanian	✝
Altaic languages	Turkic	Tatar Bashkir Chuvash Kazakh Azeri Yakut Kumyks Tuvans Karashay Balkar Uzbekh	☪ ☪ ☸ ✝ ☸ ☪ 🌑 ☪ ✝ ☸ ☪ ☸ 🛕 ☪ ☪ ☸ ☪
	Korean	Koreans	✝ 🌑
	Mongolic	Buryat Kalmyks	🛕 ☸ 🛕
	Manchu-Tungus	Indigenous small-numbered peoples (Evenks, Evens, a.o.)	☸ ✝

*Ashkenazi (European Jews) ethnolect, formed in Germany in the X-XII centuries

Fig. 18.2 Language and religion diversity

18 Ethnicity and Languages

	Branch	Language	Religion of Majority (ordered largest to smallest)
North Caucasian	Nakh-Daghestanian	Chechens	☪
		Avars	☪
		Dargins	☪
		Ingush	☪
		Lezgins	☪
		Laks	☪ ✿
		Tabasaran	☪ ✿
	Abkhaso-Adyghean	Kabardians	☪ †
		Adyghe	☪
		Circassians	☪ †
		Abkhazians	† ☪
Paleosiberian	Chukotko-Kamchatkan	Indigenous small-numbered peoples (Chukchi, Koryaks, Itelmens a.o.)	✿ †
	Eskimo-Aleut	Indigenous small-numbered peoples (Eskimo, Aleut, a.o.)	✿ †
Uralic–Yukaghir	Finno-Ugric	Mordvins Udmurt Mari Komi	† ✿
	Samoyed	Indigenous small-numbered peoples (Nenets, Selkup, Enets a.o.)	✿
Others	Kartvelian	Georgian	† ☪
	Sino-Tibetan	Chinese	🧘 🌐

Religion of Majority:

† Christianity   ✡ Judaism   🧘 Buddhism
☪ Islam   ✿ Traditional Beliefs   🌐 Others

Source: Российская академия наук: Народы России. Атлас культур и религий, Москва, 2008

Fig. 18.2 (continued)

Languages

Russian is the official language at the national level. The republics can additionally establish their own official languages. Besides that, more than 130 languages are spoken in the Russian Federation because many of the ethnic groups in Russia speak their own language, with Russian being either their first or second language. However, around 95% of the population claim to speak Russian fluently.[2]

Language Endangerment

Almost all of the 130 country's minority languages are endangered, most of them seriously, but the indigenous languages of Arctic and Siberia with a few thousand speakers or even less, face the most immediate threat.[3]

Language rights have been very political in Russian Empire. Already the medieval czars developed a Russification policy in order to standardize culture, religion, and language across their territories. After the Revolution, in the 1920s, Stalin first changed this policy by developing "nationalities policy": languages whose had never had an alphabet before got Latin alphabets along with supplementary instruction programs in certain languages (along with Russian) up to the college level. However, in the 1930s Stalin began imposing harsher restrictions concerned about to lose the control over various nationalities during the economic slowdown.

Today there is no active pro-Russian policy and the right to free choice of the language of communication, education, and creative work is granted by the constitution. On the one hand, many speakers of minority languages want to learn Russian due to fear of being left out of the economy. On the other hand, the educational budget only makes sure the use of Russian in classrooms and significant cuts in the amount of money available for a lot of the smaller languages. As a result, some of those are going to die causing the loss of irretrievable human diversity and potential.[4]

Russian Language

Russian is one of the ten most spoken languages in the world, which is spoken by around 154 million worldwide.[5] It has developed and has been spoken by Slavic folks for many centuries with first written evidence tracing back to the ninth century.

---

[2]Even informative by the census 2010.
[3]http://www.unesco.org/languages-atlas/, retrieved on October 2nd, 2020.
[4]https://www.bostonglobe.com/ideas/2014/02/16/the-amazing-endangered-languages-russia/XkKZcl5TJDOWTIMKvB8jNJ/story.html, retrieved on February 2nd, 2020.
[5]https://www.ethnologue.com/statistics/size retrieved on October 2nd, 2020.

After decades of language development, Russian reached its final and present state in the second half of the nineteenth century.

Slavic languages are divided into three subgroups according to the similarity to each other East, West, and South, which together constitute more than 20 languages. Russian together with Belarusian and Ukrainian is a language of east Slavic folks.

There are several dialects in the Russian language influenced by geographical areas and ethnic groups. Compared to German dialects that are very strong and sometimes incomprehensible, Russian dialects mostly differ only in pronunciation but can easily be understood by others. The Standard Russian dialect (or better to say "accent") which is used in the public media equals the language spoken in Moscow.

Russian Alphabet

The modern Russian alphabet, Cyrillic, was created in the ninth century to translate Eastern Orthodox religious texts into Old Church Slavonic. It is an adaptation of the Greek alphabet into the Slavic language with the inclusion of new letters and some Hebrew letters. It was named after Cyril, the leader of the first religious mission from Byzantium to the Slavic people, the alphabet is used in Russia, Belarus, Bulgaria, Ukraine, and Yugoslavia. The Central Asian republics, Moldova, and Azerbaijan used a modified Cyrillic alphabet in the Soviet period. Most non-Russian languages spoken in Russia also use this alphabet sometimes with different variations and letters.

Foreign Languages

The ability to speak a foreign language is associated in Russia with being highly educated. The school standard is to choose between four foreign languages: English, German, French, and Spanish. Although this foreign language education is mandatory in Russia, only around 10% of the population claim to speak one of these for languages, mostly English (Богоявленский, 2013).

References

Богоявленский, Д. Д. (2013). *Население России 2010–2011. Восемнадцаты-й-девятнадцатый ежегодный демографический доклад*. Издательский дом НИУ ВШЭ.
Российская академия наук. (2008). *Народы России. Атлас культур и религий*. Москва.

Migration 19

Olga Medinskaya and Henk R. Randau

International Migration: Brain Drain and Muscle Inflow

Following the isolation policy under Ivan the Terrible's reign, Russia became open to foreigners. The vast majority of migrants to Russia in the sixteenth and seventeenth century came from the Middle East and Western Europe mostly because of the different wars or for religious reasons. Under Peter the Great, migration into Russia was even guided by a legal framework. In his effort to transform the economy, reform the administrative system, and to improve national education, Peter the Great introduced in the late 1690-ties a policy of openness by inviting foreign professionals, especially for military, shipbuilding, and teachers. These came mainly from countries in Northern and Western Europe with whom he intended to build close economic relations. In addition, he also launched initiatives to send Russians to study in Europe.

Russia's efforts to attract foreigners continued under Catherine the Great, who originally came from a German aristocrat family. Russia even established a specialized State Migration Management Department as early as 1763 with its main objective being to promote further inflow migration from Western Europe to Russia. Foreigners willing to relocate to Russia were granted different privileges (e.g., tax exemptions, land). Consequently, thousands of well-skilled craftsman and experts in different technical fields immigrated, the majority of them being Germans. According to historical data, there were about 1.8 million ethnic Germans living in the Russian Empire at the end of the nineteenth century (total population in 1897:

O. Medinskaya (✉)
Cultural Connectors, Mannheim, Germany
e-mail: info@cultural-connectors.com

H. R. Randau
Weinheim, Germany
e-mail: hrandau@whu.edu

128[1] million) Ivakhnyuk (2009). Immigration outflows were also high in tsarist Russia. From 1828 to 1915, a total of 4.5 million citizens (mainly ethnic minorities such as Jews or Ukrainians) left the country, mostly to the USA, Canada, Argentina, and Brazil (Осинский 1928) (Fig. 19.1).

International migration stopped during Soviet times, especially in the 1960s during the height of the cold war. Migration between Soviet countries and its Western opponents was almost impossible. Highly developed border controls stopped irregular migration altogether and even international travel was very limited. Soviet citizens needed to obtain exit visas to travel abroad (Ivakhnyuk 2009). The exception was the connections to other communist countries, such as Vietnam, North Korea, and China. Exchanges were mostly driven by educational reasons, for example, around 50,000 Vietnamese Students studied in the Soviet Union during the cold war.

In the last decades, the nation has seen several waves of Russian citizens leaving the country (Fig. 19.2).

Nowadays approximately 25–30 million Russian reside abroad, which makes Russians the second-biggest diaspora in the world, after the Chinese (Suslov 2017) (Fig. 19.3).

Had Russia not seen massive immigration inflows from former SSRs, it would have had a sharp population decline.[2] In total, Russia gained approximately an additional 10 million residents due to migration in the period between the censuses of 1992 and the end of 2020.[3] The visa-free travel agreement between most of the CIS members,[4] close economic, social, and cultural ties between the people, as well as knowledge of the Russian language determine the continued persistence of annual migration flows in the multi-millions between the countries (Fig. 19.4).

Due to more stable economic conditions, the emigrational outflow has halved in the 2000–2018 timeframe compared to the 1990s.[5] However, though Russia avoided a decline in population, it found itself at odds with a new problem. While highly skilled Russians leave the country, the inflowing migrants often had lower levels of education compared to the 28%[6] of the native Russian population that have a university degree (Fig. 19.5). The migrants which have come in recent years have been lacking Russian language skills and have had limited vocational qualifications.

---

[1] Rosstat (www.gks.ru) retrieved on October 2nd, 2020.

[2] According to estimates of experts from the Population Division of the United Nations, Russia is on the second place in terms of the number of migrants in the world after the United States.

[3] Demographic Yearbook of Russia, Rosstat (www.gks.ru), retrieved on February 2nd, 2020.

[4] Commonwealth of Independent States is a regional intergovernmental organization post-Soviet republics, including Azerbaijan, Armenia, Belarus, Kazakhstan, Kyrgyzstan, Moldova, Russia, Tajikistan, Uzbekistan, Turkmenistan, Ukraine.

[5] Russian Presidential Academy of National Economy and Public Administration under the President of the Russian Federation 2018, Квалифицированная миграция в россии: баланс потерь и приобретений, Н. Мкртчян, Ю. Флоринская.

[6] According to the 2010 census of people aged over 15. Rosstat (www.gks.ru), retrieved on October 25th, 2020.

Fig. 19.1 Waves of Russian migrations

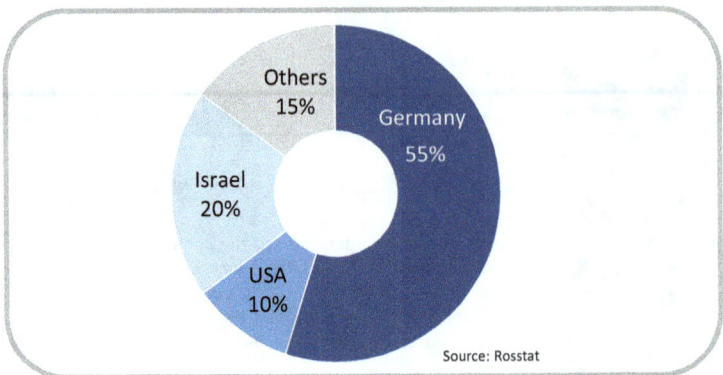

Fig. 19.2 Emigration from Russia to major countries in 1983–2015

Subsequently, the majority of these migrants have found careers in blue-collar work.[7] The continuous outflow of highly skilled Russian professionals abroad, as well as their further concentration in megacities, the major obstacle for the future economic growth of the country[8] (Fig. 19.6).

Internal Migration

Historically, Russia has experienced significant migration within its borders. Before 1861, as peasants were forced into serfdom to the state and aristocrats,[9] migration had two main drivers:

The first was by peasants who sought to start a new life under new, more favorable conditions. Initially, their motivation to migrate into new territories was driven by seemingly unlimited opportunities for resettlement to the East. Locations further from Russia's developed heartland offered an opportunity to escape from governmental pressure, state control and offered freedom and the possibility to start a new life.

The second driver was the Government's own desires to fulfill its plans of strategic expansion. The fact that peasants were bonded through serfdom gave the

---

[7]Russian Presidential Academy of National Economy and Public Administration under the President of the Russian Federation 2018, Квалифицированная миграция в россии: баланс потерь и приобретений, Н. Мкртчян, Ю. Флоринская.

[8]Мониторинг экономической ситуации в россии тенденции и вызовы социально экономического развития 1(62) 2018; https://iep.ru/files/text/crisis_monitoring/2018_1-62_January.pdf; Квалифицированная миграция в России: баланс потерь и приобретений, Н. Мкртчян, Ю. Флоринская, retrieved on February 2nd, 2019.

[9]In 1861, Emperor Alexander II passed the so-called Emancipation Reform, which abolished serfdom and thereby set all peasants free.

Russian Diaspora	in millions of people
Lived outside of USSR (or today's RF) in 1989	25
Left Russia in 1989-2015	4.5*
Ethnic Russians, born abroad and having one or two Russian parents	7
Total Russian diaspora estimated at	25 – 30
Total Chinese diaspora estimated at	> 60

* According to Rosstat, the real number of Russians who emigrate abroad is higher than the official data states. Rosstat classifies an emigrant as one who gives up Russian citizenship. In reality, around 4 million emigrants keep their Russian citizenship while living and working abroad without attempting to return to their home country.

Sources: Mikhail Suslov, "Russian World": Russia's Policy towards its Diaspora", Russie.Nei.Visions, No.10 3, Ifri, 2017,; Савоскул М.С. Эмиграция из России в страны дальнего зарубежья в конце XX - начале XXI века, Вестник Московского Университета, География. 2016, №2, с. 44-54.; South China Morning Post: Overseas Chinese 'have role to play' in building political trust abroad for belt and road, 24 August, 2018, Rosstat, Russian Presidential Academy of National Economy and Public Administration under the President of the Russian Federation 2018, Квалифицированная миграция в россии: баланс потерь и приобретений, Н. Мкртчян, Ю. Флоринская.

Fig. 19.3 Russian diaspora

state the advantage of forced and/or state-sponsored[10] migration/colonization of remote regions (e.g., Siberia) (Sunderland 1993).

In the Soviet era, urbanization and industrialization became the new driver for voluntary migration (Зайончковская 2010), while forced migration/colonization began in 1937 through the large system of forced labor camps (Gulags).

---

[10]Provincial land shortages in central Russia resulted initially in resettlement programs in the eighteenth century and continued throughout the following century. Initial decrees for relocation were given in the 1760s when the state encouraged individual state peasant communities to relocate to borderline provinces. Peasants who agreed to relocate received land and usually received tax privileges for a certain period. In most cases, the obvious factor leading state peasants to resettle was economic misery, like land shortages and poor harvests.

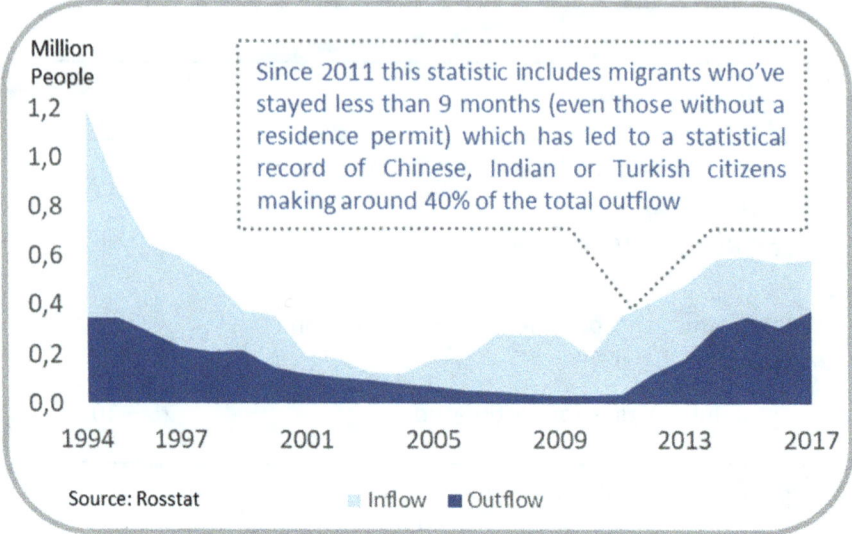

Fig. 19.4 Total international migration: Inflow-outflow

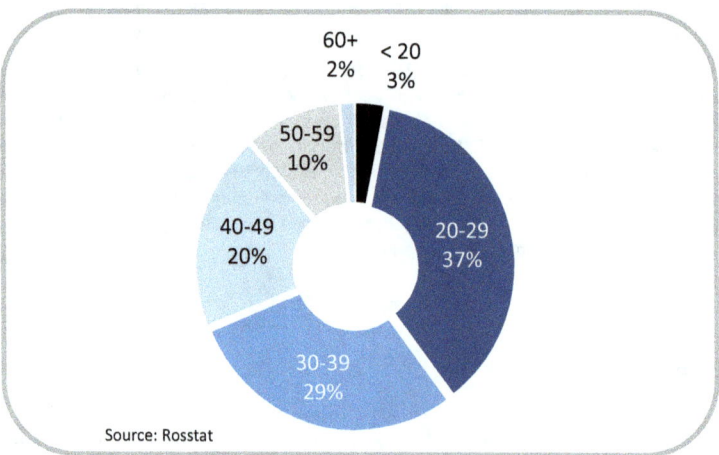

Fig. 19.5 Russian emigrants of 2005–2015 by age

Additionally, it took on a new form of deportation in which entire ethnic groups and minorities were forcibly moved to Siberia or Central Asia (e.g., Germans, Crimean Tatars, Jews). Oftentimes, intellectuals and professionals who were part of these

Top 10 countries with highest migration net outflow by popularity	% of emigrants with an University Degree and/or unfinished University Degree	
Germany	51%	Total net gain (2017) **185 k**
USA	70%	
Israel	50%	
Finland	39%	
Canada	71%	
Australia	72%	Net loss: **2 k**
France	70%	
Norway	64%	
Italy	63%	
Sweden	66%	

Top 10 countries with highest net inflow by popularity	% of emigrants with an University Degree and/or Unfinished University Degree	Russian average 28%
Ukraine	43%	Total net gain from top 10 countries: **178 k**
Tajikistan	15%	
Kazakhstan	43%	
Uzbekistan	18%	
Kyrgystan	11%	
Armenia	28%	
Belarus	24%	
Moldova	35%	
Azerbaijan	16%	
Turkmenistan	44%	

Migrants who indicated their educational level and were older than 14 yrs
Source: Rosstat 2017

Fig. 19.6 Brain drain and muscle inflow

minority groups, part of opposing political ideologies, or even just critical of the regime were also shipped east which led to a brain drain effect.[11]

Today, the main direction of migration in Russia remains the "Western drift." This means people moving to the capital Moscow and the other economic centers in the main cities located in the European part of the Federation. Despite the efforts of the Soviet leadership to redirect the flow of migration to the north and east of the country, in the late 1970s started a process of remigration of ethnic Russian from the southern republics back into central Russian regions. In the 1980ies, the remigration process engulfed nearby (the whole) all republic of the USSR. Then the remigration transubstantiates into evacuation and mass flight from areas of acute ethnic conflicts. Thousand years of migration-colonization came to the end.

Residence Permit: Propiska

In the Soviet Union, the residence permit called *propiska* served as an important part of the Russian migration control policy. Violations were treated as criminal offences. After the collapse of the USSR, the *propiska* system was officially abolished, but a skeletal version of it remains. Officially, its name has been changed to simply "registration," but for most Russians, *propiska* is still the widely used and accepted term. In order to control internal migration, the government demands citizens to officially register with the Ministry of Internal Affairs (Police) should they at any time decide to move to a new place of residence or stay somewhere other than their location of permanent residence for longer than 90 days. Living anywhere in Russia without registration makes one subject to a violation fine. Having one is necessary in order to find anything from legal employment to a slot in a kindergarten or school for one's children.

Today there are two kinds of registration for citizens: permanent and temporary.

- The permanent residence permit appears as a stamp on the internal passport. The document states the citizen's address and those they live in the location permanently.
- The temporary residence permit is a separate document. Every citizen should obtain this if they intend to stay anywhere other than their location of permanent registration for more than 90 days. Unfortunately, it is not always possible for one to find a proprietor who is willing to sanction temporary registration for his tenant as it accrues extra costs since communal payments for the property rise proportionally in relation to the number of residents as well as income taxes. For this reason in large cities and especially in Moscow, where many people from other regions live, the black market service of selling temporary registrations has

---

[11] Миграция в российской истории, А.С. Ахиезер, Опубликовано в журнале "Полития" №4, зима 2004–2005, с. 70–76. http://www.demoscope.ru/weekly/2006/0233/analit08.php, retrieved on February 2nd, 2020.

become very popular. Through this service, a willing property owner register someone as a temporary resident for a charge.

Labor Migration Today

Work permits for migrants seeking employment in Russia varies greatly depending on the visa regulations the Russian government imposes on the specific country of origin.

Foreign workers from the countries with **required visa entry** should apply for a general work permit.[12] Around 65% of the general work permits were issued to citizens of China (28%), North Korea (20%), Vietnam (9%), and Turkey (7%) in 2016.[13]

Foreign workers from countries **with visa-free entry** to Russia may be officially employed, as soon as they receive a so-called *patent*—a work permit from the government. The cost of patents varies from region to region with the most expensive being around USD80 per month for Moscow. The cost of patents is increasing from year to year. According to the authorities, the increase of price should help to restrain migration flows.[14]

Since two decades, illegal migration has developed as a central problem for Russia with all the negative social and economic consequences associated with a black market economy. According to different estimations, 2–5.5 million illegal migrants from abroad are currently working in the country. The majority of them come from the CIS nations and usually are seeking a better life and opportunity.[15] Typically, these migrants come legally under the visa-free regime but stay longer than allowed and work illegally (Гребенюк 2014). Besides the obvious motivation of the employee to stay longer than the legal timeframe, the opportunity to avoid costs associated with patents and income taxes encourages migrants to seek out illegal employment. From the viewpoint of the employer, employing illegal migrants since they will often work more than 8 h a day, have less weekends, and receive 30–50% less salary than an average worker in a particular region. Additionally, an employer avoids the cost of insurance and social benefits.

---

[12]https://мвд.рф/Deljatelnost/emvd/guvm/оформление-разрешения-на-работу retrieved on February 2nd, 2020.

[13]Rosstat, (www.gks.ru), retrieved on February 20th, 2020.

[14]https://rg.ru/2017/10/31/reg-cfo/v-moskve-v-2018-godu-uvelichitsia-stoimost-rabochego-patenta.html retrieved on February 2nd, 2020.

[15]The Commonwealth of Independent States (CIS) was founded on 8 December 1991 by the Republic of Belarus, the Russian Federation and Ukraine. 8 former Soviet Republics—Armenia, Azerbaijan, Kazakhstan, Kyrgyzstan, Moldova, Turkmenistan, Tajikistan and Uzbekistan jointed the CIS 2 weeks after that. Georgia joined two years later, in December 1993 and left CIS after the South Ossetian war. Three former Soviet Republics—Estonia, Latvia and Lithuania have never jointed CIS.

References

Гребенюк, А. А. (2014). Нелегальная трудовая миграция в России: причины и последствия. *Экономика и предпринимательство*.

Ivakhnyuk, I. (2009). *The Russian migration policy and its impact on human* development. *The historical perspective*. Human Development Research Paper.

Осинский, В. В. (1928). *Международные и межконтинентальные миграции в довоенной России и СССР*; Центр. стат. упр. СССР, p. 17.

Sunderland, W. (1993). Peasants on the move: State peasant resettlement in imperial Russia, 1805–1830s. *Russian Review, 52*(4), 472–485.

Suslov, M. (2017). *"Russian world": Russia's policy towards its diaspora*. Russie.Nei.Visions, No.10 3, Ifri.

Зайончковская, Ж. А. (2010). Внутренняя миграция в России и в СССР в ХХ веке как отражение социальной модернизации. *Мир России, 8*(4), 22–34.

Centralization and Urbanization

Olga Medinskaya and Henk R. Randau

Moscow has traditionally been Russia's center of political and economic power for many centuries. Due to rising population in the city's metropolitan area, the city governance incorporated in 2012 some areas of the Moscow Oblast into the city proper, thereby expanding the city's size by 240%.[1] Even after the expansion, it still covers only 1.5% of the Russian territory but is home to about 10% of the RF's population and generates more than 20% of the country's GDP.[2] The official statistics do not even show the full magnitude: the mayor of Moscow estimated in 2017 that up to 25 million people are living in the Moscow city area and the entire Moscow Oblast together—that is about 5 million more than the official statistics document.[3] The excess population is mostly made up of those without a residency permit. Many are illegal residents from former Soviet republics seeking employment in Moscow.

The hyper centralization[4] around Moscow has its historical roots in the fourteenth century when Russians' lands that were divided into dozens of duchies, started to unite (Chap. 15). Moscow's location was geographically favorable due to its

---

[1]Постановление Совета Федерации Федерального Собрания Российской Федерации от 27 декабря 2011 г. N 560-СФ "Об утверждении изменения границы между субъектами Российской Федерации городом федерального значения Москвой и Московской областью".

[2]Rosstat (www.gks.ru) retrieved on February 2nd, 2020.

[3]https://news.rambler.ru/moscow_city/36403230-sobyanin-otsenil-naselenie-moskvy-v-13-15-mln-chelovek/, retrieved on March 4th, 2019.

[4]https://jamestown.org/program/hyper-centralization-russia-threatens-development-survival/, retrieved on October 22nd, 2020.

O. Medinskaya (✉)
Cultural Connectors, Mannheim, Germany
e-mail: info@cultural-connectors.com

H. R. Randau
Weinheim, Germany
e-mail: hrandau@whu.edu

distance from the border, far from dangerous potential enemies. The central location of the city on major trade routes, as well as the leadership qualities of the pre-Tsar Dukes who made the Duchy of Moscow their home, made the city the epicenter of national unity in the years that followed. Even when Peter the Great built St. Petersburg in the eighteenth century and made it to the administrative capital of the State, Moscow remained the economic center of the country. After the revolution of 1917, the Communist government returned the Capital status to Moscow.

Moscow attracts millions of people from all over the country. High-income level (twice as large as the yearly average of the whole of Russia[5]); territorial concentration of functions, as well as the diversity of economic agents and places of employment (due to better potential for business enterprise); the best infrastructure and medicine in the country, and quality of life comparable to western megacities—these factors make the city the prime location for many Russians.

The quality of life in Moscow differs dramatically from the life in the provincial countryside. Oftentimes, one person with just a simple job as a taxi driver or on a construction site in Moscow earns enough cash to cover the cost of living of an entire family living in the provincial countryside.

In many countries, costs are reduced for relevant businesses and consumers because of the "agglomeration effect."[6] High density and diversity of economic agents enhance competition and accelerates innovation, but the agglomeration has many negative consequences for the city and the country as a whole. To name just a few examples with special relevance for the Russian capital:

- Overconcentration in the capital: the headquarters of the largest and most important corporations for the country are situated here, as they need to be close to the Kremlin in order to lobby for their interests.[7] Around 10% of the Russian natural resource extraction industries are based in Moscow, despite there being no oil or gas mines in the capital. Oftentimes, large corporations register in Moscow for tax optimization despite having most of their operations in places like Siberia. As a result, the corresponding tax revenues flow into Moscow rather than the regions of operation.
- Traffic jams: Moscow has the worst traffic in the world after Los Angeles (the USA). Despite the effort of the New Moscow project, the drivers spend an average of 3 working weeks per year (128 h) in traffic.[8]
- It is the largest transport hub of Russia, accounting for 50% of all volume of traffic (passengers and cargo) through the airports of the Moscow aviation hub.[9] The reason for the high ratio is the lack of direct connections to provincial cities.

---

[5]Rosstat (www.gks.ru) retrieved on February 2nd, 2019.
[6]Fujita, Krugman proved by mathematical models.
[7]http://carnegieendowment.org/files/ProEtContra_57_6-18.pdf, retrieved on October 20th, 2020.
[8]http://inrix.com/scorecard/, retrieved on October 26th, 2020.
[9]Federal Air Transport Agency http://www.favt.ru/dejatelnost-ajeroporty-i-ajerodromy-osnovnie-proizvodstvennie-pokazateli-aeroportov-obyom-perevoz/, retrieved on February 2nd, 2019.

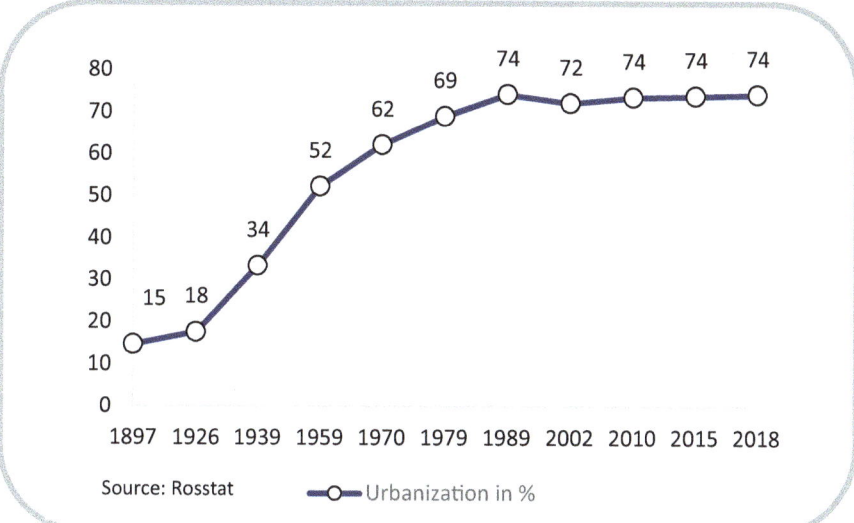

Fig. 20.1 Urbanization

All this affects the quality of life and hinders the development of the country, especially weakening its eastern regions, which have harsh climate conditions, lower standards for quality of life, and constant outflows of people. Russia's best human capital migrate to Moscow, causing a disproportionate concentration of wealthy and successful citizens in the city. A proposed solution to the problem suggests more decentralization by giving regions more political autonomy. This means the right to choose governors without any interference from the capital, as well as a proportionally distributed budget with emphasis on regional priorities.[10]

Urbanization: The "Dying Village"

With 74% of the population living in urban settings, Russia is an urban country (Fig. 20.1). Uniquely, Russian urbanization is characterized by over concentration of the population in the capital; as well as cities separated by great geographical distance, combined with a vast, depopulated periphery territory (Нефедова et al., 2015).

The urbanization rate statistically plateaued in the 1990s and has remained that way ever since. These numbers are misleading partly because of government changes in the classification of some small cities, which were allowed to return to their "rural area" status, thereby distorting what can be considered "rural."

---

[10] https://snob.ru/selected/entry/128172, retrieved on March 3rd, 2020.

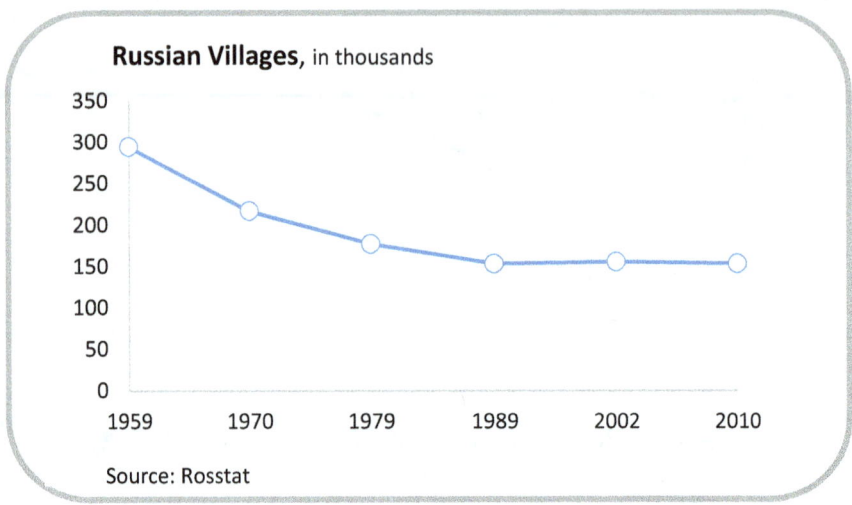

Fig. 20.2 The number of Russian villages

What these numbers also do not reveal is the continuous trend of dying villages. In the last few decades, the rural population has shifted its center to Southern Russia. Regions in Central and Volga Federal Districts, which have had dense rural populations historically, are now emptying. The villages of the north and northwestern regions are depopulating as well, while the southern rural areas have been developing quite actively in recent decades. Almost all federal districts experience rural population decline, with the lowest percentages of the rural population being in the Northwestern Federal District (around 15% of its population), while the North Caucasian Federal District's and South Federal District's populations are 50% and 40% rural respectively.

More than 20,000, or around 12% of all Russian villages commonly found on maps, are entirely abandoned (Fig. 20.2). Up to 30,000 others have fewer than 10 residents each.

The reason for this is that rural populations concentrate in the suburbs around the major agricultural hubs. During the last decade, concentration and monopolization in the agricultural sector has accelerated and forced many small- and medium-size agricultural enterprises out of business. The attached jobs were lost and consequently concentrated in areas around major enterprises. Statistically, this population is still classified as rural, despite being economically and socially tied with cities[11] (Fig. 20.3).

---

[11]Centre for Economic and Political Reforms (CEPR); Россия – страна умирающих деревень, http://cepr.su/wp-content/uploads/2016/12/Россия-страна-умирающих-деревень.pdf, retrieved on February 7th, 2019.

20 Centralization and Urbanization

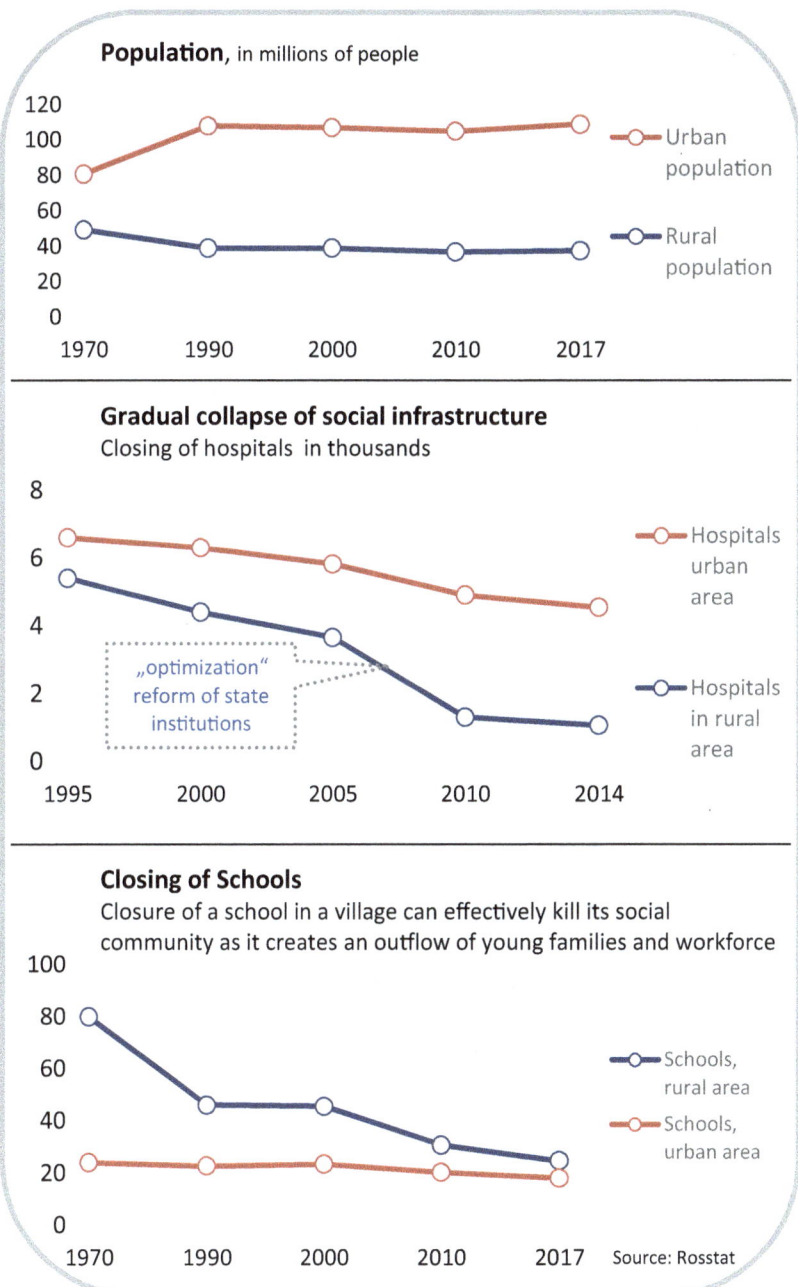

Fig. 20.3 Dying village

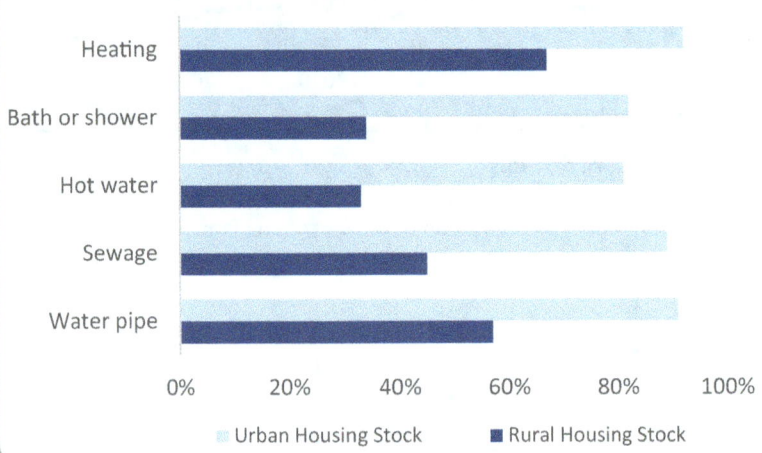

Fig. 20.3 (continued)

Depopulation of rural areas is not a uniquely Russian phenomenon—many urbanized countries experience the same problem. The speed of depopulation is also comparable to what other countries experienced.[12] Yet, it is important to consider the socio-economical background of this tendency. In some countries, depopulation of rural areas may follow the implementation of new technologies in agricultural sectors or the change of the official status of suburbs from rural to urban. Conversely, in Russia, it is an uncontrolled mass migration of the rural population of working age. Due to the geographical and climatic particularities of Russia, the depopulation of huge territories becomes a strategic problem: It makes infrastructure restoration much more difficult and will require much higher investments than in other countries (Fig. 20.3).

Russian authorities are trying to stop the degradation of rural areas through different programs.[13] Such programs include financial aid for farmers, subsidies for buying new homes in rural areas, the building of highways, new schools, and maternity wards. Even though these programs exist, little has been achieved over the past years because these programs are offset by government efforts to "optimize and save cost" combined with the general direction of most state policy that leads to a concentration of finance and jobs in large cities.

Reference

Нефедова, Т. Г., Покровский, Н. Г., & Трейвиш, А. И. (2015). Урбанизация, дезурбанизация и сельско-городские сообщества в условиях роста горизонтальной мобильности. *Социологические исследования*.

---

[12]World Bank (https://www.worldbank.org) retrieved on September 3rd, 2020.

[13]For example: "Устойчивое развитие сельских территорий на 2014–2017 годы и на период до 2020 года"; "Государственной программы развития сельского хозяйства и регулирования рынков сельскохозяйственной продукции, сырья и продовольствия на 2013–2020 годы".

Religion and Philosophy

Olga Medinskaya and Henk R. Randau

History of Russian Christianity

Christianity was first introduced to Russia in 988 AD by Vladimir the Great (Chap. 15). Before the arrival of Christianity, paganism was common in Russia as well as other Slavic countries. In the eleventh century, Slavic churches were separated from Catholicism, as the influence of the Papacy was seen as too strong by the Eastern leaders. They called their belief "orthodox," which derived from Greek and meant "correct belief" or "right thinking." Christian Russian Orthodox is one of several Orthodox denominations. Similar to other forms of Christianity, Orthodoxy postulates that God revealed himself in Jesus Christ and that his crucifixion and resurrection were real events. The Orthodox Church differs from the other Christian Churches in way of life, worship, and in certain aspects of theology.

Orthodoxy remained an important part of peoples' lives through the Czarist era. After the October Revolution, religion was prohibited, as Lenin and his followers viewed religion as supportive of the czarist power and tradition. This was carried out through forced secularization, transforming Communism into a quasi-religion to replace traditional beliefs. The majority of churches were destroyed or served as museums or stores. Clerical books were burned and icons were stored in cellars.

After the dissolution of the Soviet Union, religious freedom was enshrined in the Russian Constitution (Fig. 21.1). The collapse of the USSR became the starting point for the crisis of identity on a national scale. As a result, religion in Russia has become a national tradition once again—however, religion does not play a large role in everyday life. In Russia today, there are essentially three categories of religious

O. Medinskaya (✉)
Cultural Connectors, Mannheim, Germany
e-mail: info@cultural-connectors.com

H. R. Randau
Weinheim, Germany
e-mail: hrandau@whu.edu

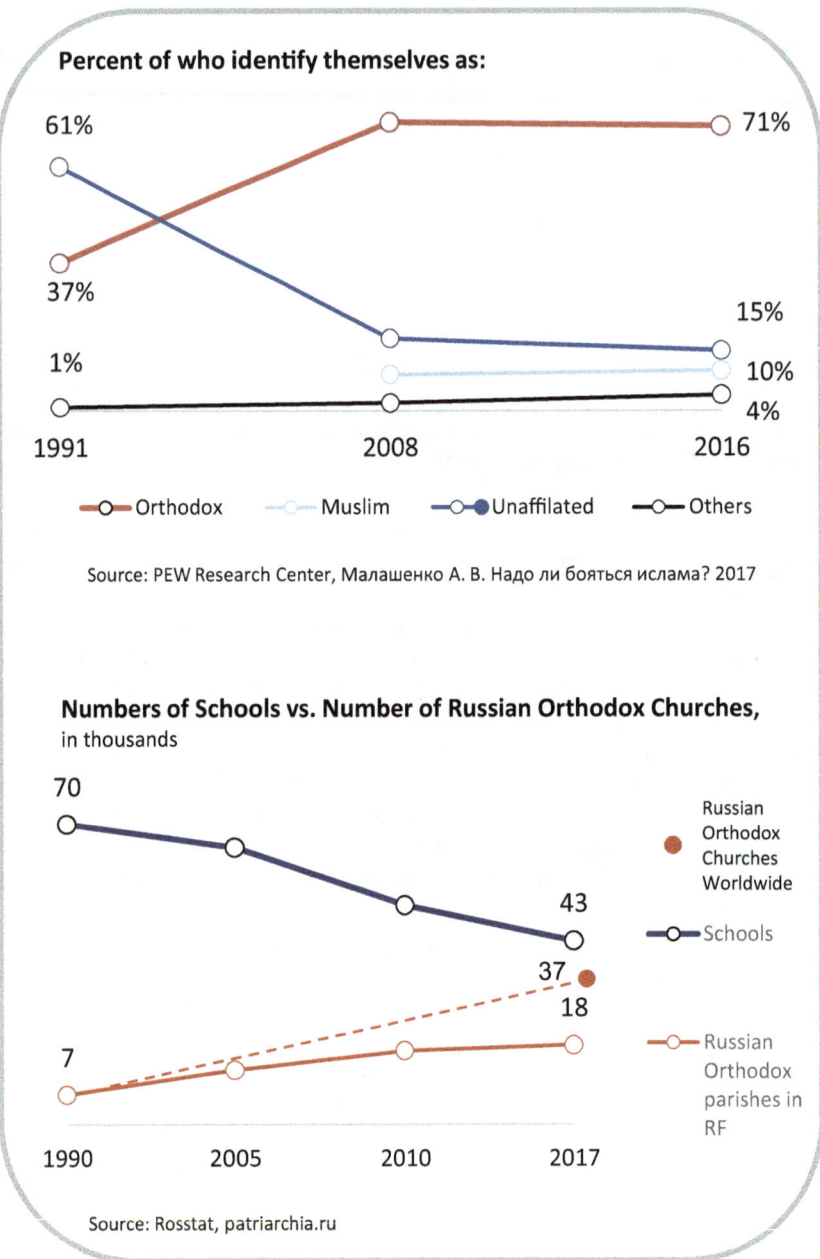

Fig. 21.1 Upraise of religion in Russia

identity: those with faith in major world religions (especially Russian Orthodoxy, Islam, and Buddhism), secular people and esoterics (Arinin, 2005). Presently, around 71% of Russians identify themselves as Russian Orthodox,[1] but only 4–8% of the population falls within the traditional Church's understanding of religiosity (including activities like daily prayer and regular church attendance). The majority visits church only several times a year while 3% of the population visit the church once a week, and 18% do not go to church at all.[2]

Church and State

According to Russian law, Russia is a secular nation. Despite this fact, separation of church and state is still not clearly defined. In recent years, the role of the Russian Orthodox Church has transformed dramatically, now a defining characteristic of Russian identity, the church is actively supported by the Kremlin. For example, when Putin was elected president, the election results were celebrated in a Sunday liturgy in one of the biggest cathedrals in Moscow. Similarly, during the war in Chechnya, the Patriarch of the Russian Orthodox Church blessed the weapons of the Russian troops before they left for battle. Very often, the Patriarch of the church is present in important political meetings. The state uses the church as an instrument of power and as a symbol of the tradition of the nationalist idea. At the same time, other religions and minority beliefs experience social hostilities. Based on the scores of Pew Research Center's *Index on Social Hostilities Involving Religion* and *the Index of **Government Restrictions on Religions*** Russia is ranked together with 8 other countries as "very high" in regards to laws, policies, and actions by officials that restrict religious practices and hostilities.[3]

> **TIPS, OPPORTUNITIES and WARNINGS**
> When visiting an Orthodox Church women should wear a long skirt and a headscarf. Men in contrast are not allowed to wear a hat.

Religion and Sexual Minorities

Since 1999, the constitution has guaranteed moral and cultural pluralism and prohibits any discrimination, including based on sexual orientation. However, after the 2013 Pussy Riot case, the Russian parliament adopted a series of laws that set out

---

[1] Pew Research Center: Russians Return to Religion, But Not to Church (http://www.pewforum.org/2014/02/10/russians-return-to-religion-but-not-to-church/), retrieved on November 2nd, 2020.
[2] https://ria.ru/religion/20170823/1500891796.html, retrieved on February 2nd, 2019.
[3] http://www.pewforum.org/topics/restrictions-on-religion/, retrieved on November 2nd, 2020.

to protect "religious feelings and traditional values." These amendments have escalated the conflict between two sets of values: the traditional values that largely promote the creeds of the historical religious denominations, and the liberal values that prohibit limitations on rights based on discriminatory clauses. Due to their fundamentalist religious beliefs, the traditional denominations (Russian Orthodox Christianity, Islam, Judaism, and Buddhism) are hostile toward sexual minorities, making open or latent conflicts between their believers and sexual minorities routine, especially in sensitive areas such as education, the adoption of children, marriage, etc. (Antonov, 2017). Religious dogma has a strong impact on decision-making in Russian courts, and can sometimes overrule the formal provisions of the Constitution and laws that grant protection and guarantees to sexual minorities. The prevailing social philosophy is characterized by a significant degree of religious conservatism and emphasizing collective interests. This development, historically rooted in religious ideas, still shapes the general conservative attitudes of Russians towards sexual minorities.[4]

Philosophy

"The Karamazovs are not scoundrels but philosophers, because all real Russian people are philosophers." Dmitry Karamazov, in Fyodor Dostoevsky. The Brothers Karamazov.

The first significant works containing philosophical ideas were created during the introduction of Christianity in the Kiev Rus. Prior to the reforms of Peter the Great (1696–1725), philosophical thought was mostly religiously oriented. Peter's reforms (Chap. 15) and the active social development process in the nation, the spread of education, and cultural contacts with Europe gave power for breakthroughs in philosophical thought. Russian philosophical thought for the next 200 years (late eighteenth–nineteenth centuries) was focused on the liberation of the spirit and the desire for a fair and perfect social order. The determination of national identity, historical and religious purpose, as well as defining their relationship with the West, were central problems discussed in the society (mainly between Westernizers and Slavophiles).[5] Westernizers were guided by ideas of personal freedom and equality for all people. They insisted that Russia, for its own good and prosperity, should imitate European practices. Their opponents, *Slavophiles*, promoted an idea of Russian exceptionalism and rejected conformity with the West. In their opinion, Russia should develop its own way and bring Orthodox truth to Europe who they viewed as having fallen into heresy and atheism. They rejected Peter's decision to connect Russia to the west and bring it closer to the bosom of Europe. They believed

---

[4] Also Islam is a part of the Russian tradition: in the North Caucasus Islam has been religion for over 1300 years. In the republics like Kalmykia population represent the ancestors of Mongolia. There the main religion is Buddhism.

[5] in the first half of the nineteenth century.

the country must not go the same way as the West. This problem of the "median" position of Russia (between Asia and Europe) and the search for a distinct historical and cultural path remains relevant today.

Among other western philosophical ideas, Marxist philosophy piqued the interest of some Russian intellectuals who had access to it in the 1840s. During the 1890s, Marxist ideas began to quickly penetrate the minds of the masses. G.V. Plekhanov initiated this process in 1883 as he founded the first Russian Marxist group called "*Emancipation of Labor*" in Switzerland (Geneva). One of the main tasks of this group was to spread the ideas of Marxism. The group's activity made Marxism an ideological trend back in Russia despite being abroad. In 1893, Lenin's views came under the strong influence of Plekhanov's philosophical works and he evolved himself into a social democratic. One year later, he formulated the credo of Leninism: "the Russian worker rising at the head of all the democratic elements will overthrow absolutism and lead the Russian Proletariat (side by side with the proletariat of all countries) along the straight road of open political struggle to the victorious Communist Revolution" (Lenin, 1894). This set the foundations for the rhetoric that inspired the October Revolution.

In the following decades, the zeitgeist was no longer religion, but politics instead. Soviet philosophy was, for the most part, of a restrictive and ideological nature rather than an educational or rationalist one. Official Soviet science viewed the philosophical process as the opposition between "bourgeois" philosophies and "socialist" ideology. "Bourgeois" was the Soviet label for contemporary European thought, branded "Eurocentric" and therefore "decadent."

With the religious and philosophical renaissance of the 1990s, scholars became focused on thoroughly familiarizing themselves with the research and works of foreign colleagues, which had long been banned, and the revival of Russian traditions in the field of history of philosophy (Mesyats & Egorochkin, 2014).

References

Antonov, M. (2017). *Religion, sexual minorities and the rule of law in Russia: mutual challenges.*
Arinin, E. (2005). Science & religion in Russian post-soviet context. *European Journal of Science and Theology, 1*(1), 51–62.
Lenin, V. I. (1894). *What the "friends of the people" are and how they fight the social-democrats. A reply to articles in Russkoye Bogatstvo opposing the marxists.*
Mesyats, S. V., & Egorochkin, M. V. (2014). After the eclipse: History of philosophy in Russia. *Studies in East European Thought, 66*(3/4), 211–226.

Festivals: Knowing the Roots

22

Olga Medinskaya and Henk R. Randau

Similar to other countries, the colorful world of festivals in Russia reflects its cultural heritage. Russians love to celebrate and the times around festivals offer any business professional the great opportunity to strengthen their business relationships, show their generosity and display the ability to celebrate.

The broad festival landscape in Russia includes official public holidays and a large number of festivals (Fig. 22.1). The subjects of the Russian Federation may additionally declare their own holidays and days off. Thus, for example, in regions with large Muslim populations (Bashkortostan, Tatarstan, Adygea, Dagestan, Ingushetia, Kabardino-Balkaria, Karachay-Cherkessia, and Chechnya) the Islamic festivals are non-working days. The following paragraphs detail the most important celebrations.

New Years

The most important, and by far the favorite, the federal holiday is the New Year celebration. As of 2012, the official holiday spans around 10 days (from January 1 to 8 plus the following weekend). New Year's became a principal celebration due to the atheist stance of the government in the Soviet Union era. It is an analogous holiday to Christmas in the West and shares many similar customs, such as decorated trees, gift giving, and celebration with family.

New Year Eve is considered a family festival usually spent at home for a late dinner with loved ones. Some also spend the evening in restaurants, which usually

O. Medinskaya (✉)
Cultural Connectors, Mannheim, Germany
e-mail: info@cultural-connectors.com

H. R. Randau
Weinheim, Germany
e-mail: hrandau@whu.edu

© The Author(s), under exclusive license to Springer Nature Switzerland AG 2021
O. Medinskaya et al. (eds.), *Russia Business*,
https://doi.org/10.1007/978-3-030-64613-4_22

Fig. 22.1 Public holidays

arrange a New Year's show. The evening of December 31 is traditionally a time for gift giving. Children are made to believe Grandfather Frost (Ded Moroz) brings the gifts. Originally the thin and tall Slavic god of winter. He is usually portrayed as an old man with a long, white beard, wearing a blue, white, or red coat. He gets around on a Russian troika (a sleigh) and is usually accompanied by his granddaughter (Snegurochka). Later at night, Russians meet on the city's main square or gather in front of the TV to watch the president's speech. This happens right before the Kremlin's Watch on Spasskaya Tower counts down the last seconds of the year.

> **TIPS, OPPORTUNITIES and WARNINGS**
> It is not advisable to plan business trips a week before, during or a week after major holidays. Especially two weeks before Russia's New Year Eve should be avoided. Besides the public holidays listed above, one might also consider school holidays (1-10 November, 30 December-11 January, the 1-10 May) when planning trips as these periods are often used for family vacations).

Victory Day

The second most popular state holiday is Victory Day, in celebration of the victory of the Soviet Union over Fascism and the end of World War II on May 9, 1945. What started as a calm day of mourning and general happiness about the end of the war's disasters has become a massive public event. Today, military parades and public mourning marches take place nationwide in Russia on this day. The increase in popularity over the last decade is mainly the result of president Putin's efforts to strengthen patriotism by encouraging greater celebrations. Accordingly, the government uses May 9 as a day to display military strength and foster national pride.

Ancient Slavic Festivals

There are many festivals rooted in pre-Christian folk religions and tied with the agricultural cycle. The most famous is the Crepe Week (Maslenitsa). It marks the border between winter and spring and means the start of the new (agricultural) year. The date of the celebration is based on lunisolar calendar what makes it to movable feast. In 2019, it is celebrated from 4.03 to 10.03. This is a non-official festival.

Orthodox Celebrations

Previously banned religious holidays such as Orthodox Easter and Christmas are gaining popularity again. Christmas has become an official day off in Russia since the fall of Communism. The celebration days follow the Julian calendar,[1] as the Orthodox Church observes it instead of the Gregorian calendar, which is used by Catholics, Protestants, and most of the world. The Julian calendar holidays are 13 days later than holidays on the Gregorian calendar.

Accordingly, the Russian Orthodox Christmas is celebrated on January 7, and on January 14, the so-called Old New Year. The date of Orthodox Easter is based on the lunisolar calendar and does not fall on a fixed date. As the calculation is based on the Julian calendar as well, the Orthodox Easter falls later than Catholic and Protestant Easter. It is celebrated in Russia with decorated eggs and cake, which could be sanctified in a church. There are no days off for Easter.

International Women's Day

The International Women's Day is a popular non-labor day that is celebrated on March 8. It became an official holiday in Communist times to remember the massive demonstrations held by women in St. Petersburg in 1913 and 1917 against the Tsarist government. It was observed as a general celebration of women's contribution to Soviet society. Usually, the day focuses on emphasizing the value and beauty all women contribute to society. The holiday also includes more traditional themes such as motherhood, love, and the beginning of the spring.

The government usually holds receptions for accomplished female officials, artists, and social role models. As it is a non-labor day, most companies organize parties for women the day before the holiday. Colleagues congratulate all women with a "Happy 8th of March" and the company director holds speeches about how valuable and appreciated women are at their workspace and in society as a whole. It is also a special occasion to get together with the women of the family.

---

[1]The Julian calendar was established by Julius Ceasar in 46 BC and was widely replaced by the Gregorian calendar, which was created in 1582. Since then, the Orthodox Church has chosen to continue using the Julian calendar as a statement of defiance against the power of Roman Catholic Church.

TIPS, OPPORTUNITIES and WARNINGS
The presents to the women are important on 8th of March

If the business meeting is planned with a woman before this day, it is advisable to take a present like a bouquet of flowers to the meeting and congratulate her. Please be aware that an uneven number of flowers should be given, as the even number of flowers should only be brought to a funeral or to remember someone who has passed. It is important to note that yellow flowers normally represent separation and red roses represent passionate love. Make sure to use it accordingly to avoid misunderstandings.

Professional Days

The last category is so-called professional days (Table 22.1). They are dedicated to specialists of different fields of activity. Most of them were introduced during the Soviet era and remain very popular. For example, February 10 is the day of diplomats, October 5 is the day of teachers, and so on. To remember the professional day of the relevant profession is a good opportunity to strengthen a relationship with Russian partners.

Table 22.1 Professional days

Month	Day	Professional Festival
Jan	12	Day of Prosecutors
	13	Day of Russian Printed Press
	21	Day of Engineering Corps
	25	Students day (Tatiana Day)
	25	Day of Navigator of the Russian Navy
Feb	6	International Bartender's Day
	8	Russian Science Day
	2nd Sunday	Day of Aeroflot
	9	International Dentist's Day
	10	Diplomats' Day
	18	Day of Russian Transport Police
Mar	9	International Day of DJ
	10	International Archives Day
	11	Day of Drug Control Specialists
	2nd Sunday	Day of Geodesy and Cartography
	12	Day of the Penal System of the Ministry of Justice
	18	Federal Tax Police Service' Day
	19	Day of Submariners
	21	World Poetry Day
	25	Day of Russian Culture Specialists
	27	World Theatre Day
	27	Day of Internal Troops of Russia's MIA
	4th Sunday	Day of Trade, Consumer Services, and Utilities
	29	Day of legal service specialist in the Armed Forces
Apr	1st Sunday	Geologists Day
	6	Day of the investigating authorities of MIA
	8	Day of Members of the Military Commissioners
	12	Cosmonautics Day
	2nd Sunday	Day of the Air Defense Forces
	15	Day of a specialist in electronic warfare
	last Wednesday	Secretaries Day
	30	Day of Firemen
May	5	Day of Cypher
	5	Diver's Day
	7	World Radio Day
	13	Black Sea Fleet's Day
	18	International Museum Day
	18	Day of the Baltic Fleet
	21	Day of the military translator
	21	Day of the Pacific Fleet
	24	Day of HR Specialist
	26	Day of Russian Entrepreneurship
	27	All-Russian Library Day

(continued)

Table 22.1 (continued)

Month	Day	Professional Festival
	28	Day of the Border Guards
	29	Day of The Veterans of the Customs Service
	31	Day of Advocacy
	4th Sunday	Chimist's day
Jun	1	Day of Irrigator
	8	Day of Social Worker
	2nd Saturday	International Beer Day
	2nd Sunday	Day of Light Industry
	14	Day of the worker of the Migration Service
	3rd Sunday	Medical Workers' Day
	21	Day of canine units of MIA
	27	Fisherman's Day
	4th Saturday	Inventors' Day
Jul	1st Sunday	Day of Sea and River Fleet of Russia
	2	World Sports Journalists Day
	3	Day of traffic police of MIA
	2nd Sunday	Day of the Russian Post
	3rd Sunday	Day of Metallurgist
	17	Day of Naval Aviation
	last Friday	System Administrator Appreciation Day
	28	Day of PR Specialist
	Last Sunday	Day of trade, consumer services, and utilities
	Last Sunday	Neptune Day
Aug	1	Day of Collector
	2	Day of Airborne Forces
	1st Sunday	Day of Railways
	6	Railway Troops Day
	12	Day of Builder
	15	Day of Archaeologist
	27	Day of Russian Cinema
	Last Sunday	Coal Miner's Day
	Last Sunday	Day of Air Fleet of Russia
Sep	1	Knowledge Day
	2	National Guard Forces Command's Day
	4	Day of Nuclear Specialist
	1st Sunday	Day of the Oil, Gas, and Fuel industry
	8	Financier's Day
	8	International Day of Journalists' Solidarity
	9	Day of Tester
	2nd Sunday	Tankman's Day
	12	Day of the Programmer
	3rd Sunday	Day of Foresters

(continued)

Table 22.1 (continued)

Month	Day	Professional Festival
	19	National Secretaries Day
	27	Day of pre-school teacher and all pre-school staff
	27	World Tourism Day
	Last Sunday	Day of the machine builder
Oct	1	Ground Forces Day
	4	Day of Space Forces
	4	Day of Civil Defense Emergency
	5	World Teachers' Day
	5	Day of the criminal investigation
	6	Day of Russian insurer
	6	Archives Day
	1st Monday	International Doctor's Day
	1st Monday	World Architecture Day
	9	World Post Day
	2nd Sunday	Day of Agriculture and Processing Industry Workers
	12	Day of HR Specialist
	16	World Food Day
	16	Boss' Day
	20	Day of Military Communications Specialists
	20	Navy Day
	3rd Sunday	Day of Food Industry Workers
	3rd Sunday	Day of Roads Workers
	23	Day of Advertising Specialists
	24	Day of Special Forces
	25	Day of Russian Customs Officers
	Last Sunday	Day of Automotive Transport Workers (professional holiday)
	28	Day of Army aviation
	29	Day of private security of MIA
	30	Day of Mechanical Engineer
	31	Day of Sign Language Interpreter
	31	Day of Jail and Prison Workers
Nov	5	Day of military intelligence officer
	6	Day of Bailiff
	8	Day of Journalists
	10	Police and Internal Affairs Servicemen's Day
	12	Day of Security Specialist
	13	Day of Chemical Corps
	14	Day of Sociologist
	17	Day of Precinct
	19	Day of Glass Industry workers
	19	Day of Missile Forces and Artillery
	21	Day of the Tax Authorities

(continued)

Table 22.1 (continued)

Month	Day	Professional Festival
	21	World Television Day
	21	Accountants Day
	27	Marine Corps Day
	27	Day of Appraiser
Dec	2	Day of Banker
	3	Lawyer's Day
	7	International Civil Aviation Day
	First Sunday	Day MLM
	8	Day of Russian Treasury
	3rd Saturday	Day of Realtor
	22	Day of Energy Industry Workers

Corruption and Fraud Risks

23

Henk R. Randau

Corruption poses an enormous challenge to all domestic and foreign enterprises operating in Russia (Bremmer 2020). The Association of Chartered Certified Accountants (ACCA) estimated the Russian "shadow" economy to be around 40% of nominal GDP. This makes it the fourth largest in the world, behind Azerbaijan, Nigeria, and Ukraine. Transparency International (TI), in its corruption perception index, ranked Russia as low as the 138 least corrupt country in 2018 out of the 180 countries in the world. This is much higher than other major developing economies, the worst amongst BRICS member states (Table 23.1, Fig. 23.1).

Systematic corruption is the result of the fundamental problem Russia is facing: the close nexus between political power and property. Ever since the Soviet era, political and economic order stayed closely intertwined. In the business-to-business environment, it is led by oil and gas kickbacks. Within the state apparatus, neither the police, the military, nor the legislature can honestly claim that they have escaped the maw of corruption. Wages in these institutions tend to be low and for this reason, individuals in middle to lower ranking positions in these institutions highly engage in "survival" corruption.

The Russian economy is estimated to be losing between US$300 to US$500 bn each year to corruption. One of its notable problems is illicit financial outflows, according to the *Global Financial Integrity (GFI)* report on illicit financial flows. Additionally, it was ranked as the country with the third highest level of illegal capital flight in the world between 2008 and 2017.[1] Interestingly enough, the 2013 GFI report found that the island nation of Cyprus was a preferred money-laundering destination for Russians.

---

[1] Global Financial Integrity: Illicit Financial Flows, at https://gfintegrity.org/report/trade-related-illicit-financial-flows-in-135-developing-countries-2008-2017/, retrieved on October 27th, 2020.

H. R. Randau (✉)
Weinheim, Germany
e-mail: hrandau@whu.edu

Table 23.1 Transparency International Corruption Index: Major economies

Country	Rank out of 180 countries	Transparency International Corruption Index 2018
Germany	11	80
UK	11	80
Japan	18	73
USA	22	71
Lithuania	38	59
India	78	41
China	87	39
Brazil	105	35
Ukraine	120	32
Russia	138	28

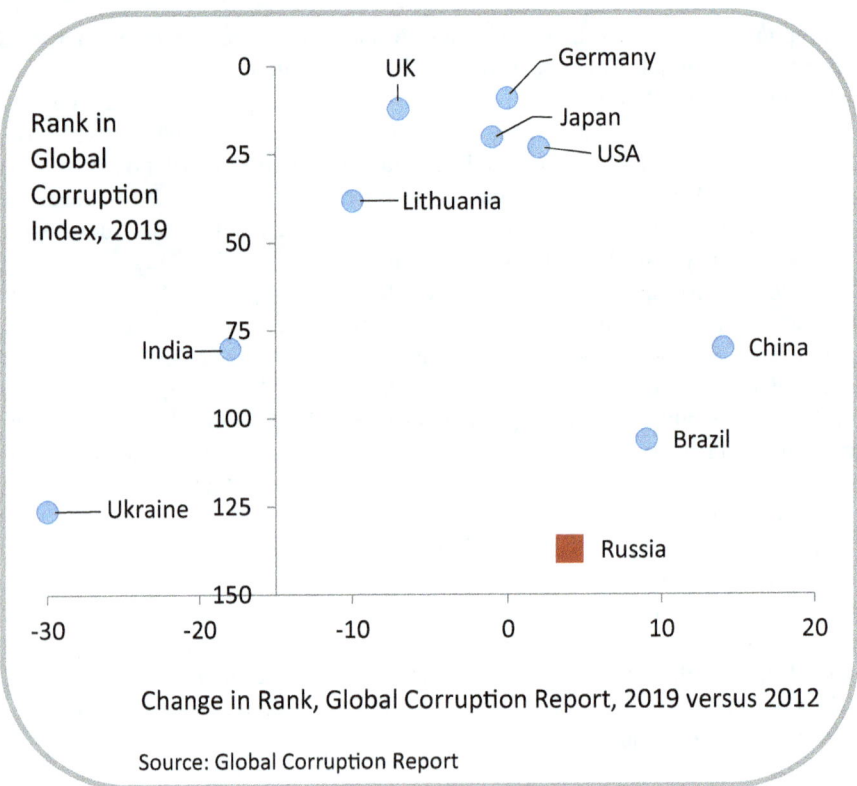

Fig. 23.1 Corruption in major economies according to Transparency International

Everywhere in Daily Life

It can be said that the effects of corruption extend beyond business and government, as ordinary citizens are also adapting to it in their daily lives. Sometimes it seems like Russians have grown so accustomed to the corruption that they have come to view it as "Russia's own special way."

Corruption has a long legacy in Russia; it was an integral part of the Gulags, which were created in 1919. Administrators of Gulags engaged in bribery, theft of state and prisoner property, participation in illegal markets, and embezzlement. Moreover, prisoners would bribe administrators to receive better food or better work assignments. Since prisoners had predetermined working quotas, they would falsify logs to show that they had fulfilled their quotas as failure to do so could mean death. After Stalin's death in 1953, the Gulags were either closed or turned into public companies. Some prisoners chose to stay in the areas and to continue to work in the industries that the Gulags had participated in.

Furthermore, corruption blossomed in the Brezhnev era, with those in power enjoying better food, clothes, apartments, and other privileges. Still, corruption and crime were, overall, under better control in the Soviet times in light of the years to come. During Gorbachev's perestroika, through the 1990s, corruption, and crime spiked (Ciravegna et al. 2016).

However, President Putin brought this to an initial stop; but like his predecessors, he has his own "inner circle" of loyal followers and supporters. These individuals enjoy many privileges, as some have become very rich. Especially considering his second term in office starting in 2012, it seems as if he, himself, is a perpetuator of corruption. Take for example his spokesperson, *Dmitry Peskov*, who shocked Russian and international media by wearing a watch with a 565,000 € retail value at his wedding in 2015. The problem with this was that on a 132,000 € annual salary, he could not afford this Swiss luxury watch from *Richard Mill*. However, he justified it as a gift from his bride, Olympic gold medal holder Tatjana Nawka.

Anti-Corruption Efforts

Even though the government has called for tighter control, previous anti-corruption campaigns have been largely ineffective. This is especially when compared to initiatives taken by China in recent years, which questions the seriousness of the Russian anti-corruption drive. Constitutionally, Russia disposes of an independent judiciary that entails a court of arbitration of similar nature.

Russia's Federal Anti-Corruption Law adopted in 2010, criminalizes bribery, abuse of power, and conflicts of interest. It restricts gifts to government officials worth more than RUB 3000. Government officials and heads of government-owned companies are also required to publicly declare their assets, including those of their spouses and children. Additionally, in 2007, Russia adopted the 1999 Council of Europe Criminal Law Convention on Corruption and ratified the OECD Anti Bribery Convention in 2012. As well, it is a member of the Council of Europe

Group of States against Corruption. These actions show the government's resolve to bring its corruption legislation up to pare with internationally recognized legislation.

Violations of Russian anti bribery rules by business and government personalities can result in severe fines, occupational bans, and imprisonment. Violation by companies or organizations is punishable by fines based on the size of the bribe. For example, a company can end up paying a fine of US$1.7 mill. for a US$350,000 bribe. The degree of willingness to cooperate with government officials in a corruption investigation can influence the resulting penalty (Lubitzsch 2018).

When it comes to dispute settlement, court rulings on company-to-company cases are perceived to be fair while, cases involving state entities tend to be biased. However, Russia has ratified the New York Convention on the Recognition and Enforcement of Foreign Arbitral Awards. Equally, the Convention on the Settlement of Investment Disputes between States and Nationals of Other States. This means companies can include foreign arbitration clauses in contracts so as to reduce reliance on the Russian legal system should the need arise.

Russia is one of the few countries in the world that requires companies to have an anti-corruption compliance program by law. This shows that at least on the surface how serious the government is about tackling this problem. Failure to adhere to this law can result in severe fines, the size of which also depends on the company's willingness to cooperate. Below are the six required measures for a compliance program according to GAN Integrity word for word:

- Designate responsibility for the prevention of bribery offences
- Adopt procedures for cooperating with authorities
- Implement procedures to ensure ethical business conduct
- Adopt a code of conduct for all employees
- Create policies for conflicts of interest
- Prevent the use of false documents

A criticism of Russian dispute settlement law is that it changes too often, resulting in conflicts of practice. Equally as concerning, is the overarching influence of political figures on the judicial system, which can negatively affect the application of the law. It is generally believed that businesses can obtain government favoritism and leniency thanks to close ties with politicians.

However, starting a business in Russia only takes about 11 days, which is very efficient when compared to other countries in the region. As well, paying taxes is much easier when compared to neighboring countries. This is due to the ability to file tax declarations online that also reduces the possibilities for bribery. Therefore, it can be said that the Russian system has its weaknesses but comparatively, it is improving and there is a drive for change (Fig. 23.2)

23 Corruption and Fraud Risks

Fraud Risks			
Integrity	**Corruption**	**Financial Statements**	**Misappropriation of assets**
Background and Reputation • Political ties • Organized crime / terrorist group • Criminal record / involvement in unethical activities	Offshore accounts	Asset/Revenue over- or understatement	Payments made for fictitious goods or services (billing)
	Designated agents	Recording fictitious revenues	Misuse of non-cash resources
	Kickbacks	Concealing liabilities or expenses	Expense reimbursements
Capital: Origin of companies seed capital	Diverted rebates	Improper disclosures	Cash stolen before recording in books & records (skimming)
	Dummy companies	Improper asset valuations	
Ownership • Hidden shareholders • Hidden beneficial owners	Fraudulent reimbursements		Cash stolen after recording in books & records (cash larceny)
	Side letters		
	Slush funds		Cash on hand
Relationships • Related parties • Non-arms lengths transactions • Relationships of other conflicts of interest	Sham sales at prices lower than market value		
	Consumable gifts		
	Travel & Entertainment on demand		
	Sham purchases at higher prices than market value		

Source: Based on an overview of fraud risks provided by Deloitte

Fig. 23.2 Samples of fraud risks. Source: Based on an overview of fraud risks provided by Deloitte

Suggestions for Further Reading

Transparency International: Corruption Perceptions Index	www.transparency.org
The Association of Chartered Certified Accountants: Emerging from the shadows The shadow economy to 2025.	https://secure.accaglobal.com/content/dam/ACCA_Global/Technical/Future/pi-shadow-economy.pdf
Business anti corruption portal	https://www.business-anti-corruption.com/

References

Bremmer, I. *Here's why Russia's economy is cratering*, at: http://time.com/3998248/these-5-facts-explain-russias-economic-decline/, retrieved on February 7, 2020.

Ciravegna, L., Toews, G. & Vezina, P. (2016). *Corruption: The long shadow of the Gulag*, at: https://lagv2017.sciencesconf.org/file/323591, retrieved on September 7, 2020.

Lubitzsch, H. (2018). *Anti-corruption and bribery penalties in Russia*, at: https://www.lexology.com/library/detail.aspx?g=dc31f326-a062-4ec0-8d32-abf47e2417e1, retrieved on March 7, 2020.

Health and Healthcare

Olga Medinskaya and Henk R. Randau

Health Status

Life expectancy at birth (LEB)[1] has risen rapidly around the world over the last century due to a number of factors such as reductions in infant mortality, rising living standards, improved lifestyles, and better education, as well as advances in healthcare and medicine. Although Russia ranks 11th in the world for overall GDP according to the IMF,[2] it ranks as low as 110th in the WHO's latest World Life Expectancy ranking (2015). The current LEB of 71.8 years is about 8 years lower than the OECD average (80.2 years) and significantly lower than economically well-developed countries, such as the United States, Japan, or Germany, or compared with countries with similar income levels[3] such as Turkey or Mexico. In spite of recent gains, Russia even trails behind countries with much lower per capita incomes levels, such as Brazil (74.8 years) and China (76 years)[4] (Fig. 24.1)

The main reason for this low ranking can be contributed to the fact that life expectancy at birth for males is as low as 64.7 years while females have an

---

[1]Life expectancy at birth (LEB) is a statistical measure of the average time a human being is expected to live and one of the key indicators used to analyze and compare mortality patterns in different countries and regions. It is one of the most important demographic indicators used to compare different population groups.

[2]International Monetary Fund: Ranking by Gross domestic product, current prices, U.S. dollars, (https://www.imf.org/), 2020, retrieved on November 7th, 2020.

[3]The World Bank national accounts data: GNI per capita, (https://datacatalog.worldbank.org/), 2017.

[4]OECD (http://www.oecd.org/), retrieved on October 9th, 2020.

O. Medinskaya
Cultural Connectors, Mannheim, Germany

H. R. Randau (✉)
Weinheim, Germany
e-mail: info@cultural-connectors.com

© The Author(s), under exclusive license to Springer Nature Switzerland AG 2021
O. Medinskaya et al. (eds.), *Russia Business*,
https://doi.org/10.1007/978-3-030-64613-4_24

Fig. 24.1 Health status

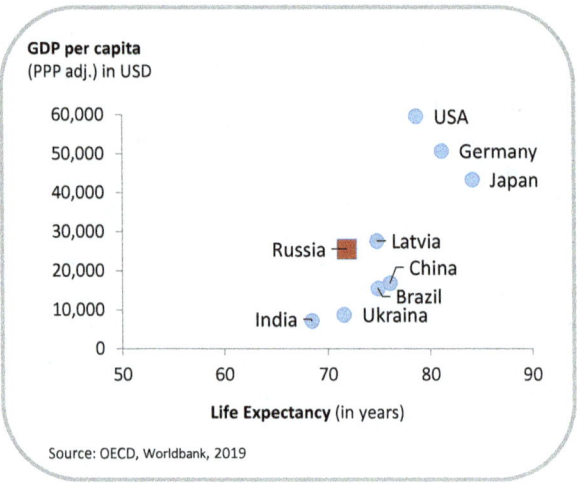

Fig. 24.2 Comparable life expectancy

expectancy of 76.3 years—this is one of the biggest gaps in the world. Yet, the general rise in income and reduction in poverty has undoubtedly helped to reduce mortality. Since the early 1950s, male life expectancy has gone up by only 10 years in Russia, compared to 32 years in China and 21 years in Brazil (Fig. 24.2 and Table 24.1)

Some positive news to be noted is that some health-related indicators have improved in Russia in recent years: mortality rates have been steadily decreasing since 2004.[5] The infant mortality rate in the RF has been cut by more than half over the past two decades, from 17.3 deaths per 1000 live births in 1990 to 5.5 deaths in

---

[5]Federal State Statistic Service of Russian Federation (www.gks.ru), retrieved on February 7th, 2020.

Table 24.1 Russia's health in comparison

	Russia	China	Germany	USA
Under-five mortality rate (deaths per 1000 live births, 2018)	7	9	4	6
Probability of dying between 15 and 60 years (deaths per 1000 population, 2016)	Male: 294 Female: 111	Male: 93 Female: 67	Male: 88 Female: 49	Male: 142 Female: 86
Current health expenditure per capita (current US$, 2018, 2019)	1.529	688	6.646	11.072
Current health expenditure (percent of GDP, 2019)	5	5	12	17

https://www.unicef.org/publications/files/Child_Mortality_Report_2015_Web_9_Sept_15.pdf), retrieved on February 9th, 2019; http://apps.who.int/gho/data/view.main.1360?lang=en), retrieved on June 17th, 2020; https://data.worldbank.org, retrieved on June 7th, 2020

2017.[6] Nonetheless, it remains higher than the OECD average of 4.0 deaths per 1000 births).[7]

The reason why Russia displays such short LEBs is that the nation leads the world in certain categories of cause of death. Non-communicable diseases (NCDs), in particular cardiovascular diseases and cancer, are major reasons for premature mortality in Russia. These can be linked to high levels of alcohol and tobacco abuse. Other main contributors to premature mortality are AIDS, suicide, as well as external causes, such as road traffic accidents (Russians are four times more likely to die from traffic accidents than Germans[8]), murder (murder in Russia is 10 times more common than in Germany[9]), pollution, and the corrupt healthcare system.

Suicide Rate

Russia topped the list of the *WHO Mortality Database* with more than 26 suicides per 100,000 population and men 6 times more likely than women to commit suicide.[10] The suicide rate is not uniform across the country. In some parts of the country, the rates reach about 100 or 200 suicides per 100,000 people. Risk multiplies in rural areas and in the northern and far eastern regions—places where

---

[6]Ministry of Health of the Russian Federation (www.rosminzdrav.ru/en) retrieved on February 7th, 2019.

[7]OECD (http://www.oecd.org/) retrieved on February 16th, 2019.

[8]WHO Global status report on road safety at https://www.who.int/violence_injury_prevention/road_safety_status/2018/en/), retrieved on February 7th, 2019.

[9]UN Office on Drugs and Crime's: International Homicide Statistics database (https://www.unodc.org/gsh), retrieved on February 7th, 2020.

[10]World Health Organization, Global Health Observatory Data Repository, (https://www.who.int/gho/en/), Age-standardized mortality rate (per 100,000 population), last date available—2016, retrieved on November 7th, 2020.

the social and economic situation is worse. The lowest suicide rates are in Moscow, St. Petersburg, several areas of the South, and the Republic of the North Caucasus.[11]

Several studies highlighted a significant aggregate level association between alcohol consumption and suicide in Russia.[12] At the same time, alcohol consumption is a result and an indicator of stress in society. Past decades have shown that in years of economic and social crisis, the consumption of alcohol is exceptionally high while in periods when social optimism increases, alcohol consumption decreases.[13]

Regional Disparities

The RF displays large differences in LEB and mortality rate outcomes between regions and socioeconomic groups. These differences may reflect factors such as diet and lifestyle but they are certainly also driven by access to medical care. In general, urban communities tend to have much better health indicators than rural. Life expectancy in far northeast Chukotka is 64.2 years (59.4 for men), but in Moscow city, it is 76.8 years (73 for men).[14] Between the regions with the best and poorest healthcare, there are also huge disparities in the infant mortality rate (2.4 in Tambov Oblast versus 10.6 Jewish autonomous region[15]). Additionally; there are huge gaps in life expectancy between the better off and the disadvantaged, who have a much higher burden of cardiovascular disease. Both total mortality rates and deaths due to cardiovascular disease among 55- to 69 year olds have been found to be higher for groups with less education[16] (Fig. 24.3)

---

[11] https://themoscowtimes.com/articles/suicide-watch-why-russian-teens-are-killing-themselves-53017), retrieved on February 19th, 2020.

[12] For example: Pridemore (2006).

[13] Розанов Всеволод Анатолиевич, Самоубийства, психо-социальный стресс и потребление алкоголя в странах бывшего СССР, Суицидология, 2012, No 4. - С. 28–40.

[14] Russian Federal State Statistics Service (www.gks.ru), last date available—2016, retrieved on February 7th, 2020.

[15] Russian Federal State Statistics Service (www.gks.ru), last date available—2017, retrieved on February 7th, 2020.

[16] Russian Federation Systematic Country Diagnostic p. 104. (http://www.worldbank.org/en/country/russia/publication/systematic-country-diagnostic-for-the-russian-federation-pathways-to-inclusive-growth), retrieved on June 15th, 2020.

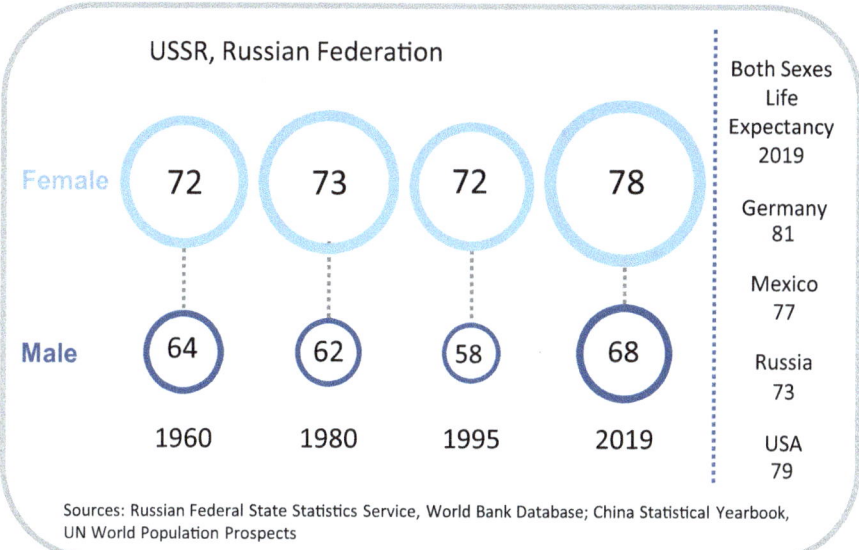

Fig. 24.3 Change in life expectancy at birth

Unhealthy Lifestyle

Russians' taste for strong spirits is well known in the world and remains one of the main health-related problems for the Russian Federation. Excessive alcohol consumption is a major factor for the high mortality rates, mostly leading to deaths from heart disease and violence. Many men begin drinking around 13 and alcohol use is deeply rooted in society. In addition, Russia has one of the highest levels of tobacco use in the world. The Global Adult Tobacco Survey from 2009 found that 39% of adults in Russia use any tobacco product, smoking or smokeless every day; 61% of all men and almost 22% of women[17] (Fig. 24.4) Up to half a million people die in Russia every year from tobacco-related diseases. The need to take action was obvious, and accordingly, the government introduced rigorous laws to control tobacco use in 2013. The new legislation bans smoking and tobacco advertising in public places. It has increased taxes and set fixed retail prices for tobacco products, and mandated public information campaigns on the harmful effects of tobacco on health. In addition, the government launched an alliance of smoke-free cities, e.g., smoking was forbidden during the Sochi Olympic Games. The Russian Ministry of Health reported that the various measures under the Tobacco Act helped to cut the number of smokers in Russia: by the end of 2017, only 45% of all men and 15% of women continued to smoke.[18]

---

[17]Global Adult Tobacco Survey at http://gatsatlas.org/, retrieved on February 7th, 2019.

[18]https://iz.ru/736238/2018-04-25/minzdrav-rasskazal-o-sokrashchenii-doli-vzroslykh-kurilshchikov-v-rossii, retrieved on February 7th, 2020.

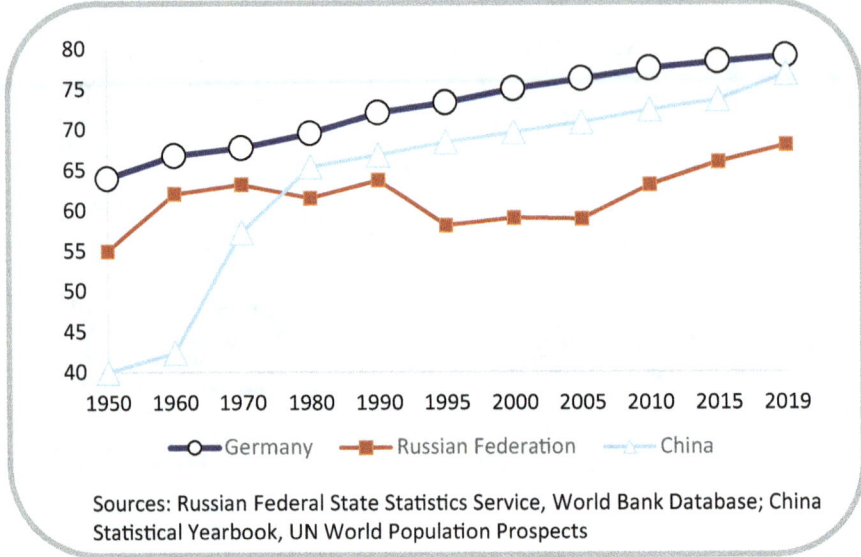

Fig. 24.4 Life expectancy at birth, male

A result of an unhealthy lifestyle is reflected by sharply increasing levels of obesity in Russia. The obesity rate among adults women—based on self-reported data—is higher in Russia by 16% than the average found across OECD countries in 2017.[19] The growing prevalence of obesity foreshadows increases in the occurrence of health problems such as diabetes and cardiovascular diseases, which consequently leads to higher health care costs in the future.

AIDS and HIV

Another factor that negatively affects life expectancy is the rising number of AIDS related deaths. In recent years, Russia has been challenged by a rapidly broadening HIV epidemic (Fig. 24.7) The RF has the largest number of HIV-infected citizens in Europe (UNAIDS 2016) and is ranked third in the number of newly registered HIV infections. With more than 1 million actual infections diagnosed (and the fact that the real number is undoubtedly higher due to undiagnosed and/or unreported cases),[20] HIV has become a problem for all Russians. Contrary to global trends, infection and

---

[19] According to OECD Statistic, the obesity rate in the Russian Federation was 14.5% for men and 23.2% for women. This is lower than the average of 19% for men and higher than the average of 20% for women among adults across OECD countries in 2017.

[20] https://www.economist.com/europe/2016/09/29/immune-to-reason, accessed September 29th, 2020.

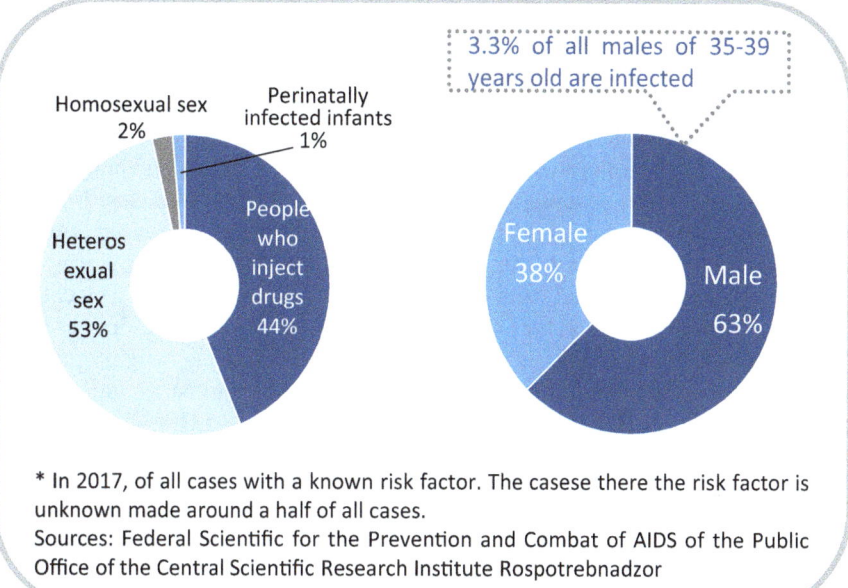

Fig. 24.5 Everyone is at risk: new HIV diagnoses

death rates from HIV/Aids continue to expand significantly.[21] Even more worrying is that the epidemic is moving into a new phase, reaching the broader population: already half of all new cases in Russia are now from heterosexual contact and not vulnerable groups like homosexuals and intravenous drug users[22] (who made until 2008 up to 80% of new cases)[23] (Fig. 24.5)

It is apparent that this dramatic health crisis is caused by the failure of public policy and neglect of state prevention programs. For many years, Russian authorities refused to acknowledge the problem and made no or very limited efforts to use internationally recognized policies to combat HIV infections, such as health and safe sex education or drug substitution programs. The main reason lies in the Russian conservative political ideology, which is based on adherence to "traditional values"

---

[21]"Reference on HIV infection in the Russian Federation as of June 30, 2018"; Perm Krai Public Health Office, Perm Krai Center for the Prevention and Combat of AIDS and Infectious Diseases 2018.

[22]Federal Scientific for the Prevention and Combat of AIDS of the Public Office of the Central Scientific Research Institute Rospotrebnadzor: The latest epidemiological data on HIV in the Russian Federation. Available on http://www.hivrussia.ru/stat/bulletin.shtml#40, accessed November 4th, 2020; European Centre for Disease Prevention and Control, WHO Regional Office for Europe. HIV/AIDS surveillance in Europe 2017 surveillance report. Stockholm: ECDC, 2017. Available on https://ecdc.europa.eu/en/publications-data/hivaids-surveillance-europe-2017-2016-data, accessed January 23rd, 2020.

[23]http://www.afew.org/ru/novosti/hiv-epidemic-russia-ru/, retrieved on June 7th, 2020.

and stigmatizes drug users, sex workers, and homosexuals. In the past, the Russian government has not focused on the organization of preventive measures like the use of condoms and sex education. Instead, it has chosen to campaign for a "healthy lifestyle:" traditional family values—heterosexual marriage, marital fidelity, and faith are promoted as the best way to protect against HIV infections.[24] Accordingly, clean needle distribution programs have been rejected as sinful. The promotion of the use of condoms is believed to be a cause of dangerous behavior and is seen as only exacerbating the problems of HIV.[25] The growing alliance between Putin and the conservative Russian Orthodox Church has even created conditions in which sex education in schools is prohibited—the parents are expected to educate their children themselves by telling them about the dangers of unprotected sex and drug use.

Recently, the government has increased its efforts and funding to fight against the rapidly spreading disease.[26] Unfortunately, this might prove to be too little too late. According to the WHO's Global Health Sector Strategy for HIV 2016–2021, in order to stop the HIV epidemic, it is necessary to identify at least 90% of all HIV-infected people and provide antiretroviral therapy to at least to 90% of all discovered HIV-infected people. This is because the infected people who have not received medical care may continue to spread the virus for many years before eventually succumbing to the disease. Unfortunately, only 35% of all HIV-infected people in Russia have access to treatment. (Brazil: 64%, UK: 98%). The main reason for this is also the lack of funding given for HIV prevention and control, with some sources reporting that the state budget is the only 1/5th of what is needed.[27] To increase the treatment coverage, the Russian Ministry of Health is trying to reduce the cost of treatment by purchasing outdated generic medication. Patients need to take about 12 pills daily, compared to Europeans who take only one pill of the contemporary version. As a result, some of those who start treatment stop it after a while. Another cost-saving measure was a recommendation from the Ministry of Health in 2017 to not give medications to psychiatrics and "hard addicts" until they recover[28] (Fig. 24.6)

---

[24]Head of the Federal Center for the Prevention and Control of the Spread of AIDS, Vadim Pokrovsky by www.dw.com, retrieved on February. 7th, 2019.

[25]Russian Institute for Strategic Studies (RISS).

[26]Veronika Skvortsova, Russia's health minister, reported that measures taken under the program had helped slow growth of new infections but other Russian and global health experts believe the government is doing too little, too late. https://www.ft.com/content/d34662fc-d5ea-11e7-a303-9060cb1e5f44, retrieved on November 7th, 2020.

[27]In 2013, the World Bank reclassified Russia as a high-income country. As a result, international support for HIV programs decreased and domestic funding for HIV prevention did not fill the funding gap. According to Clark, the state budget was about a fifth of what was needed to address the problem (Clark 2016).

[28]Ministry of Health of the Russian Federation: Clinical recommendations. HIV infection by adults, at https://arvt.ru/sites/default/files/rf-2017-protokol-vich-vzroslie.pdf, retrieved on November 3rd, 2020.

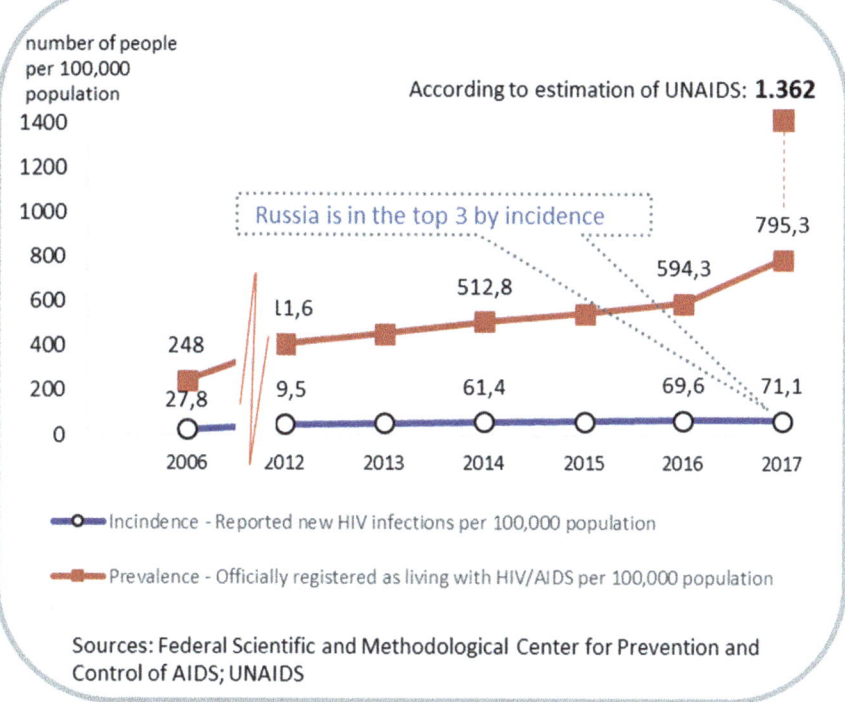

Fig. 24.6 Estimated prevalence and incidence of HIV

The comparably low treatment rate is also the result of the fact that many HIV-infected people refuse to take medication, as they believe that HIV is a myth. Shockingly, some social media networks exist, made up of thousands of participants, who do not believe in the existence of this disease. HIV is called the "greatest myth of the 21st century" created to ensure a huge profit for pharmaceutical corporations and members of these groups exchange information on how to avoid treatment[29] (Fig. 24.7)

Healthcare System

Total spending on health in the RF trended slightly above 5% of GDP in recent years (Fig. 24.8) This is low compared to other developed nations and significantly lower than the OECD average.[30] The picture does not change when health expenditure per

---

[29]"Do never get tested for HIV. No testing—no diagnosis—no problem", accompanying message to a popular video posted in such a group. "As soon as we got 1 million follower the "epidemic" will stop. Invite your friends!" A slogan of a popular group in a social network.

[30]OECD Health Statistics, at http://www.oecd.org/els/health-systems/health-data.htm, retrieved on October 27th, 2020.

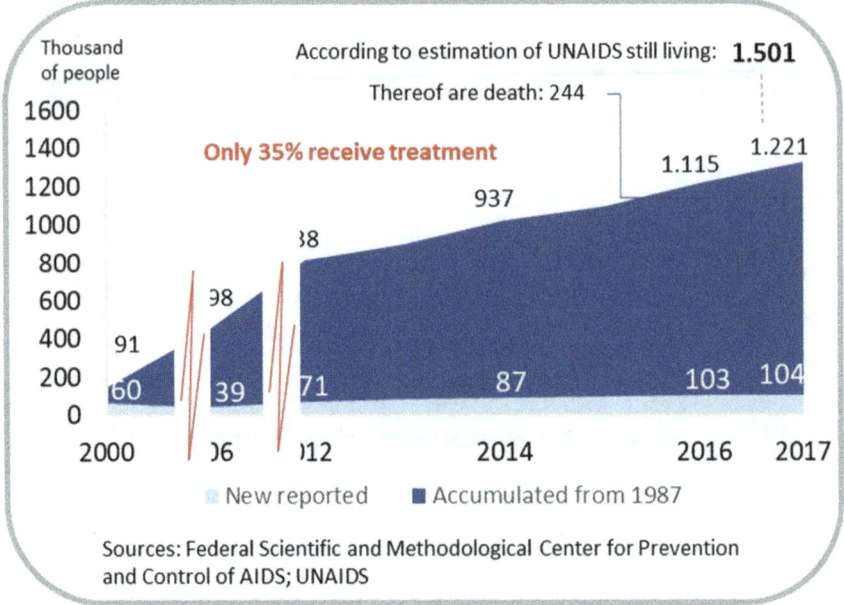

Fig. 24.7 Cumulative number of registered HIV cases

capita is taken into consideration as Russia spends roughly 1/3 of the OECD average per capita.[31] Given the rapid aging society and a rising number of patients with multiple chronic diseases, the healthcare system is challenged against a backdrop of already stretched budgets. Russia needs to find cost-effective approaches to addressing NCDs along with reducing out-of-pocket cost of key outpatient care and strengthening access to good-quality outpatient care for the disadvantaged (The World Bank 2016).

Efficiency and Reform

Compared internationally, Russia placed last out of 55 developed nations in the last *Bloomberg report* on the efficiency of the national health care systems.[32] The last two decades saw a range of healthcare reforms aimed to optimize costs by closing inefficient hospitals and expanding the use of high-tech medical facilities. As a result, by 2017, the number of hospitals dropped below the number that existed in the county in 1932.[33] The government explains this cut was necessary in order to

---

[31] OECD Health Statistics, at http://www.oecd.org/els/health-systems/health-data.htm, retrieved on October 27th, 2020; Calculation based on purchasing power parity.

[32] Bloomberg at https://www.bloomberg.com, retrieved on October 7th, 2020.

[33] It were 5.962 hospitals in Russia in 1932, https://inosmi.ru/social/20171222/241068724.html, retrieved on October 25th, 2020.

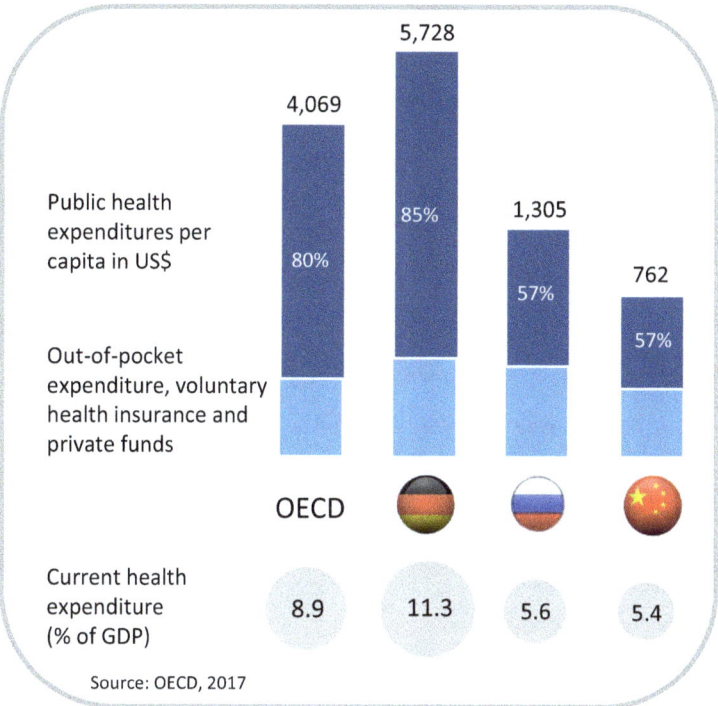

Fig. 24.8 Health spending

secure high capacity usage of hospital facilities. It claimed that high-tech medical facilities and outpatient medical centers would improve efficiency. Since the number of outpatient clinics (Fig. 24.9) did not change much in recent years, this policy has had negative side effects: in 2015 17,000 communities were left without any medical infrastructure whatsoever. It is not surprising that in the minds of citizens healthcare reform has become associated with the reduction of medical organizations, personnel, and a general reduction in the volume of medical care.[34]

Obligatory Medical System

Since the Soviet era, the idea that healthcare and education should be free for all citizens has been a widely held belief amongst Russians. This is manifested through the Federal Obligatory Medical Insurance Fund (FOMIF) created as a nation-wide system by the government in 1993. The obligatory insurance scheme ensures free medical care for all Russian citizens (whether they are employed or not) which is a right incorporated in the Russian Constitution.

---

[34]https://inosmi.ru/social/20171222/241068724.html retrieved on September 17th, 2020.

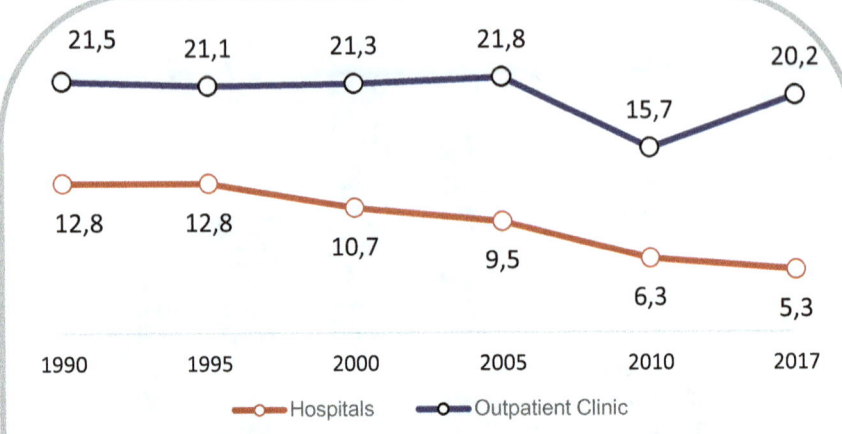

Fig. 24.9 Health care: organizations and HR

FOMIF applies to treatments at all state-run hospitals but not private hospitals. The treatment and procedures offered under the FOMIF plan are limited, mainly covering emergency medical attention. It does not include denture treatment, some expensive drugs, and access to treatment for some significant diseases.

This FOMIF plan is funded mostly by the direct contribution from salaries.[35] The reasons for underfunding come from some challenges with collecting social insurance contributions as well as growing expenses. This will cause the risk of a further

---

[35] Федеральный фонд обязательного медицинского страхования at http://www.ffoms.ru/system-oms/about-fund/formation-of-income/ retrieved on September 15th, 2020.

decrease in the quality and accessibility of free medical care in the coming years.[36] This means that in reality, citizens often have to pay additional fees for quite ordinary treatments that should be included in the FOMIF insurance plan.[37] For a more comprehensive care, Russians need to either purchase private medical insurance or one would have to pay out of pocket for each provided medical service or procedure.

Because of the very limited services FOMIF offers, the expenditure on private healthcare amongst individuals has risen ten-fold in the past 15 years. Today, out-of-pocket expenditure is as high as 43%[38] of the total healthcare budget (The World Bank 2016). Since the share of out-of-pocket spending in total health expenditures is an indicator of the degree of financial barriers to access to healthcare services. Internationally, Russia ranks 23rd out of 60 countries in healthcare accessibility.[39]

Private Medical Insurance

Since many vital treatments and procedures are not covered by the compulsory FOMIF, a myriad of private medical insurances exist. These insurance plans are acquired by an individual ('legal' commercial healthcare) or his employer (voluntary health insurance). In Russia, it is customary that large or mid-sized companies purchase voluntary health insurance plans as an employment perk. Typically, these plans only cover basic medical services. The desire of enterprises to save money in recent years has led to the effect that employers choose insurance programs with less coverage. The declining availability of medical care in the obligatory health insurance segment and the decrease in insurance cover under corporate voluntary medical insurance policies has led to the growth of "legal" commercial healthcare, private health insurance held by individuals. Primarily the lower-priced segment will continue to grow and could be positively affected by the plans of the Russian Ministry of Labor, which is considering limiting the access of self-employed individuals (who

---

[36]Private Healthcare Market in Russia: Outlook for 2017–2019, KPMG Russia, at https://home.kpmg/ru/en/home/insights/2017/03/private-medical-services-market-in-russia.html, retrieved on October 12th, 2020.

[37]https://www.dw.com/ru/пять-фактов-о-системе-здравоохранения-россии/a-18856366, retrieved on October 14th, 2020.

[38]The World Bank. Twice as high as the 20% OECD at http://stats.oecd.org/Index.aspx?DataSetCode=SHA, retrieved on October 5th, 2020.

[39]The Economist Intelligence Unit has launched a Global Access to Healthcare Index in partnership with Gilead Sciences, to demonstrate how healthcare systems across 60 countries are working to solutions to the most pressing healthcare needs of their populations. This is done by assessing countries on a total of 23 sub-indicators, https://eiuperspectives.economist.com/healthcare/global-access-healthcare, retrieved on October 16th, 2020.

currently evade taxation, yet enjoy social benefits) to the obligatory medical system.[40]

Russians also can visit private clinics without any policy and simply pay directly for services. Some Russians choose to use the basic government plan or their work-provided plans to cover basic medical services and to find a doctor with whom they can strike a deal with over what to be done in the case of emergency. This is so they can pay this doctor under the table in order to save money and ensure that they receive proper care. A medical shadow economy exists where under the table payments are made by patients to their medical care providers, typically made directly in cash to the practitioner, in order to receive more or better quality services.

> **INSIGHT: CoVid-19 and Russia**
>
> Russia's society and the economy were struck, as so many other countries, heavily by the corona virus in 2020. Initially, in March 2020, when infections in many other countries reached already significant levels, it seemed as Russia could escape the epidemic due to its overall low infection rates. In the first week of March 2020, the country had only seven official corona cases. National newspapers and social media claimed at the time that the virus would mainly hit Asian people and could hardly infect Russians. The pictures changed dramatically within the following weeks as infection numbers shot up. Consequently, President Putin was forced to introduce a strict curfew and self-isolation policy for senior citizens and people returning from foreign countries. A few days later, the Russian government closed all borders and the president declared the entire month of April as a national full paid vacation month. Later he extended the non-working period until 31 May.
>
> As figures were rising rapidly in Moscow City and the Moscow region, a digital tracking system was introduced in the capital to enforce the lockdown. Citizens were only allowed to leave their homes with an electronic QR code that served as an official governmental permit. Police was allowed to check the code of citizens in public areas and to sanction offenders. Despite these strict measures, Russia was in 2020 the nation with the fourth most Covid-19 infections worldwide behind the USA, Brazil, and India. Even several political leaders, such as Dimitrij Peskow, Speaker of Russian President, Aleksandr Drozdenko, Governor of Leningrad Region, or Prime Minister Michail Mischustin were diagnosed with the virus. Accordingly, the corona outbreak got full media attention at the time.
>
> Over the summer period of 2020 when number of daily infections slowed down, the government started to introduce social and economical plans to
>
> (continued)

---

[40]Private Healthcare Market in Russia: Outlook for 2017–2019, KPMG Russia, at https://home.kpmg/ru/en/home/insights/2017/03/private-medical-services-market-in-russia.html, retrieved on October 18th, 2020.

support struggling businesses. President Putin faced the challenge that metropolitan regions were heavily hit by the virus while others had seen only a small number of cases. Consequently, governors were requested by the president to evaluate the situation in their region and take individually suitable measures. Moscow continued to ask people to wear masks and gloves in public space and left restaurants, business center and parks closed whereas other regions lifted the lockdown and restrictive measures much faster.

Economy in Corona Modus

During the lockdown of the economy from March until May, only businesses in sectors for basic supply were allowed to continue operation. The government made also some exceptions for the automotive and chemical industry where a cut of the supply chains would lead to irreparable damages. Accordingly, the crisis hit those companies the hardest, which had to discontinue their business without alternative options. They lost all their revenues and at the same time had to pay full salary to everyone on their payroll.

In order to avoid a total breakdown and a deep recession, President Putin introduced at the beginning of May a 3-stage reopening plan combined with support packages for business and employees. In a first stage, people would be allowed to leave their houses freely. Small shops and service providers such as haircutter, beauty shops a. o. could gradually start to operate. In a next step, schools and bigger shops would get a chance to open again before in a third and last step even hotels, restaurants, fitness center, etc. were allowed to start their business. Parks and fairgrounds would be the last once to open. Putin left the decision when and how to introduce lifting measures to the regional governors as long as their decisions would be transparently based on key parameters such as infection rates, test results and hospital capacities. However, most of the regions were quite cautious and until mid of May 2020 only 15 regions were in the first stage and lifted restrictions significantly. Only in June, several regions lifted restrictions but most of them made wearing masks and gloves in public transport or shops mandatory.

President Putin introduced during his 6 corona speeches key measures to support the affected group of people. As part of the package, he gave increased compensation and benefits for medical staff, granted a one-time payment for children between 3–15 years, and increased minimum benefits and payments for people who lost their jobs during the crisis. Companies were allowed tax and social contribution deferrals in order to stabilize their cash flow. Import duties on pharmaceuticals and medical equipment were waived.

In a final support initiative, small and middle-sized companies (SMU) were separately supported as they were the most affected and fragile sector of the economy. They got financial support for paying their office rent, got suitable conditions for company loans and tax referrals.

(continued)

The measures were designed to reach a widespread of affected people and business owners. However, the total amount of the package reached roughly 10 Bio Euro and remained on a low level compared to countries of the European Union.

The government was careful in granting more substantial financial benefits as the fiscal situation of the country was tense. Russia had to face extremely low oil and gas prices in the first half of 2020. Oil prices plunged to 20 USD for Brent crude per barrel and recovered slowly. Even Russia's agreement with Saudi Arabia to reduce oil production was not able to stabilize prices as the demand for oil during the corona crisis was extremely low. As a consequence of the corona crisis, Russia's GDP fell dramatically in the second quarter of 2020 and experts forecast an overall drop of GDP by approximately -5% in 2020.

Political and Social Aspects

The sudden outbreak of the corona virus had an impact on the political agenda of the government. It forced the president to postpone the referendum on a new constitution as it was initially planned for 22nd April 2020, a peak time of corona outbreak. The new constitution would have allowed President Putin to extend his presidency for another two terms until 2034. A few weeks later the epidemic forced political leaders to change planned celebrations of May 9 and cancel the parade even though Victory Day had special importance for Russia in 2020 as it marked the same time 75th anniversary of the end of World War II.

The government had been quite fast in implementing restrictive measure and canceled all flights from and to China when there was only single corona cases in Moscow. However, it took almost two months before these measures showed first positive results. Mid May saw still 10.000 new infections per day. Official statements from the administration explained that delayed slow-down of corona cases was consequence of a high activity level of the population, which did not stay home as requested. At the same time, a heavily crowded public transport posed a permanent high infection risk to commuters. It is also fair to mention that with an increasing number of corona tests a higher number of documented cases came along. Until mid of 2020 more than 6 million people were tested in Russia, more than in all other European countries.

Like most the other governments all over the world, Putin took the opportunity to make additional affords to strengthen Russia's health care sector. The outbreak of the virus showed again that in particular, the regions needed investments into hospital infrastructure, medical equipment, and human resources. Special funds went into e-health solutions. In future medical consultations, ordering of drugs, or communication with medical administration should be available as online services.

(continued)

Outlook

Many experts point out that there are good reasons why Russia should be able to absorb the economic impact of corona virus much better than other European countries.

They claim that the Russian economy of 2020 is in a much stronger position than it was after 2014 when multiple sanctions have been imposed. Sanctions forced the country to build up more regional supply chains, to stimulate local production, and to get more independent from international products. Russian corporates were forced to finance their business with local banks as they lost access to external financing. Therefore, they are now significantly less reliant on international funding and fluctuating foreign currency rates. The ruble has been allowed to a certain extend to float freely since 2014. This helped to keep Russia's foreign exchange reserves on a high level, they are the second highest after China. External borrowing of the country is rather small and Russian foreign exchange reserves remain on an extremely high level.

On the microeconomic side of the crisis governmental restrictions let to a higher acceptance of e-services in all sectors. Requests for social distancing and self-isolation let e-commerce in the country grow by almost 30%. E-health services were supported through governmental funding in order to provide better medical services in less populated regions of the country. As one of only a few countries in the world, Russia used geolocation techniques and cellphone apps to monitor the movements of their citizens in certain regions. Online work, online trainings and e learning became quite quickly part of daily life. It still has to be seen to which extend these trends will actually lead to higher quality of life after lifting of corona restrictions.

However, it would be naïve to believe that Russia will get away without any negative impact on economy and society. Many indicators lead to the conclusion that the crisis will have a long-term impact on the country.

Main Trade associations in Russia like *Opora Rossii* and *Delowaja Rossija* forecast that more than 1 mill. SMU`s have to discontinue their operations and close business as their financial reserves are not sufficient to survive a long-term crisis. At least three mill. employees of SMU`s are in danger to lose their jobs by the end of 2020. The Head of Russia`s Accounts Chamber, Alexej Kudrin, warned that end of the year unemployment rate could double to almost 10%. High unemployment rates would inevitably lead to an internal migration from less developed regions like Tschuwaschien, Samara, Omsk, or Nishnij Nivgorod into economical strong regions like Moscow and St. Petersburg. The performance of the Russian economy will depend on the question whether the country is able to use funds of the corona crisis for development of services and products that are able to compete on a regional or even global market. As the country cannot exclusively rely on export of oil and gas, it needs a clear strategy to develop products, which will create demand beyond its limited national market.

Suggestions for Further Reading

European Center for Disease Prevention and Control (ECDC) www.ecdc.europa.eu/en
Germany Trade and Invest (GTAI) https://www.gtai.de/gtai-en
Eberhard Schneider: Das politische System der Russischen Föderation, 2. Auflage, 2001.

References

Clark, F. (2016). World report: Gaps remain in Russia's response to HIV/AIDS. *The Lancet, 388* (10047), 857–858.
Pridemore, W. A. (2006). Heavy drinking and suicide in Russia. *Social Forces, 85*, 413–430.
The World Bank. (2016). *Russian federation: systematic country diagnostic. Pathways to inclusive growth*, pp. 105–106
UNAIDS. (2016). *Gap report*. Geneva: UNAIDS., at http://www.unaids.org/sites/default/files/media_asset/2016-prevention-gap-report_en.pdf, retrieved on February 7th, 2019

Snapshot of Mass Media

Olga Medinskaya and Henk R. Randau

These days the Russian mass media landscape is just as diverse as in most other countries, with a wide range of broadcasting and print outlets. As is the case with the rest of the world, this landscape is rapidly changing thanks to the Internet and an explosion of new mobile services.

Not unlike other countries, Russian media outlets have both state-owned and private corporate media outlets. Despite this, the Russian media landscape sets itself apart from others due to the central role that the state plays:

- All key media is mostly owned directly, or via a third party, by the state.
- Since 2016 a law caps foreign ownership of media outlets at 20%.
- All Russian media, whether state owned or privately owned, is limited by the de facto political order: the media mostly provides information which does not conflict with the official narrative of the state, nor are they allowed to provide information that is imposed from the top.

Print Media

In December 1991, any attempt to obstruct the independent creation of media by citizens and organizations was officially abolished. Following this, the number of printed media outlets in the nation exploded exponentially (Петрунина and Калужский 2020). By the end of 2019, more than 18,000 newspapers (Out of which 20 can be described as national titles) and around 27,000 magazines were

---

O. Medinskaya
Cultural Connectors, Mannheim, Germany

H. R. Randau (✉)
Weinheim, Germany
e-mail: info@cultural-connectors.com

registered within Russia.[1] However, only about 45% of the registered printed media is in constant market turnover and it is estimated that only 30% of publications are profitable.[2]

The established newspapers with the largest amount of readers are usually supportive of Kremlin policies, and moguls with direct Kremlin connections own some of the most influential papers.[3] Thus, the sector is best described as "closed" and therefore it is unsurprising that only a few companies publish their financial records and ownership structure.

Like elsewhere in the world, print media is under huge competitive pressure due to the availability of free alternative news media on the Internet. Print media has lost approximately 60% of its advertising market in the recent past due to different legislative initiatives and prohibitions adopted in the last 3 years.[4] In addition, the industry faces huge challenges due to the weakness of the ruble. This is because the industry relies on imported printing materials, technology, equipment, and paper. Following the trend of recent years, the traditional news industry in Russia will likely continue to demonstrate negative rates of growth in the near future.[5] This will probably lead to a further consolidation of the industry, with only those media outlets that service through multiple mediums having the best chance of surviving and retaining some portion of their audience.[6]

TV and Radio

Similar to print media, the number of radio and TV broadcasting stations has risen exponentially since the early 1990s (Кириллова 2005) after the legalization of various forms of ownership and freedom of speech. Today, Russia has 2400 public and commercial radio stations (The three main state networks are *Radio Rossii*, *Mayak*, and *Vesti FM*), 13 national stations, and approximately 3300 regional or local TV stations.[7]

---

[1] Roskomnadzor (https://rkn.gov.ru/), accessed on October 8th, 2020.

[2] Federal Agency on Press and Mass Communications of the Russian Federation, Российская периодическая печать. Состояние, тенденции и перспективы развития, 2018.

[3] BBC, Russia profile—Media, at http://www.bbc.com/news/world-europe-17840134, retrieved on October 8th, 2020.

[4] Federal Agency on Press and Mass Communications of the Russian Federation, Российская периодическая печать. Состояние, тенденции и перспективы развития, 2018, at http://www.fapmc.ru/rospechat/activities/reports/2018/pechat1.html retrieved on November 3rd, 2020.

[5] Global Entertainment and Media Outlook 2018–2022, https://www.pwc.com/gx/en/industries/tmt/media/outlook.htmlr, retrieved on October 9th, 2020.

[6] Russian Public Opinion Research Center, 2018 (https://www.wciom.com), accessed on October 8th, 2020.

[7] CIA, The World Factbook: Russia, at https://www.cia.gov/library/publications/the-world-factbook/geos/rs.html, retrieved on October 28th, 2020.

Television is a popular source for news and entertainment with a penetration rate close to 100%.[8] The Russians spend an average of 4 h per day watching TV, with the older generations spending almost 6 h a day in front of the screen.[9] The most popular news provider is *Channel One*. This outlet is mostly government-owned and is watched by roughly half of the entire nation's population every day.[10] Foreign broadcasters wishing to air programs in Russia must receive a license by media watchdog *Roskomnadzor*. As of January 2016, Russian law dictates that foreign ownership in media companies in Russia is limited to 20% of the media outlet.

Internet and Social Networking

Internet usage is soaring in Russia. The authorities are keen to curb the influence of major international internet companies. The so-called Sovereign Internet Law, which came into effect in November 2019, paves the way for making the Russian internet an autonomous entity separate from the World Wide Web.

Two companies stand out on the internet market in Russia: *Yandex*, which runs the top search engine; and the Mail.ru Group, which owns two of the most popular social networks, *VKontakte* and *Odnoklassniki*

Russians use the Internet predominantly for researching, reading news, and connecting with others. Social media networks are not only used to connect, but also to spread and comment on political events, to watch movies, and to listen to music. Some popular social media networks include the Russian platforms *Vkontakte, Odnoklassniki*, western networks like *Instagram* and *Facebook*, followed by *Moi Mir*. The penetration of the various social networks is geographically not uniform: *VKontakte, Instagram,* and *Twitter* are predominately in Moscow and St. Petersburg, while *Odnoklassniki* and *Moi Mir* are more popular in provincial Russia (Figs. 25.1 and 25.2)

Due to the efforts of state propaganda, Russian social networks are filled with stories and photographs spread from hundreds of fake accounts belonging to the state's "troll army". It is also common government practice to use social media posts to drive the public opinion in a desired direction. Social media is the third most used source of news (compared to the USA where it is the fourth), after official news sites and television.[11]

---

[8]Rosstat: Russia in figures, 2018, at http://www.gks.ru/free_doc/doc_2018/rusfig/rus18.pdf, retrieved on February 16th, 2020.

[9]Mediascope (https://mediascope.net/).

[10]FOM, at https://fom.ru/SMI-i-internet/14029 retrieved on January 13th, 2020.

[11]Pew Research Center (www.pewresearch.org).

	🇷🇺	🇨🇳	🇺🇸	🇯🇵	🇧🇷
Time spent on social networks daily, average	2h 19m	2h 0 m	2h 01m	48m	3h 39m
E-commerce penetration*, in % of population	46%	45%	69%	63%	45%
Internet penetration, in % of population	76%	53%	88%	93%	66%

* Percentage of the population who bought something online via any device in the past month [survey-based]. Source: Globalwebindex 2018

Fig. 25.1 Internet penetration and use

Control and Censorship

The Russian Federation's constitution guarantees freedom of speech and prohibits censorship, which means that officially the government cannot filter the Web, like China or Iran. Despite this, in recent years, the freedom of media in society has undergone significant changes. Mass media is under stronger supervision from the state and as a result, the Russian Federation has steeply declined in all rankings on press freedom. The organization *Reporters Without Boarders* ranked Russia as low as 148th out of 180 countries in its worldwide 2018 report index of press freedom.[12] *Freedom house*, another organization that compiles a similar ranking, placed Russia at number 176 out of 197 countries.

Journalists often face the threat of physical violence or trumped-up charges in Russia. *The Committee to Protect Journalists* states that 26 journalists have been killed under suspicious circumstances since the beginning of 2000. Russia is the country with the tenth largest number of journalists killed in suspicious circumstances since 1992.

Because the Russian Federation claims to be a "sovereign democracy," the Russian government must officially guarantee and visibly protect freedom of speech. In order to maintain the status quo, the Russian autocracy needs to control the flow of information that goes to the electorate's head. In order to gain and maintain this control, the government has built a network of directly and indirectly owned (e.g.,

---

[12] Reporters without boarders (https://rsf.org/en/russia).

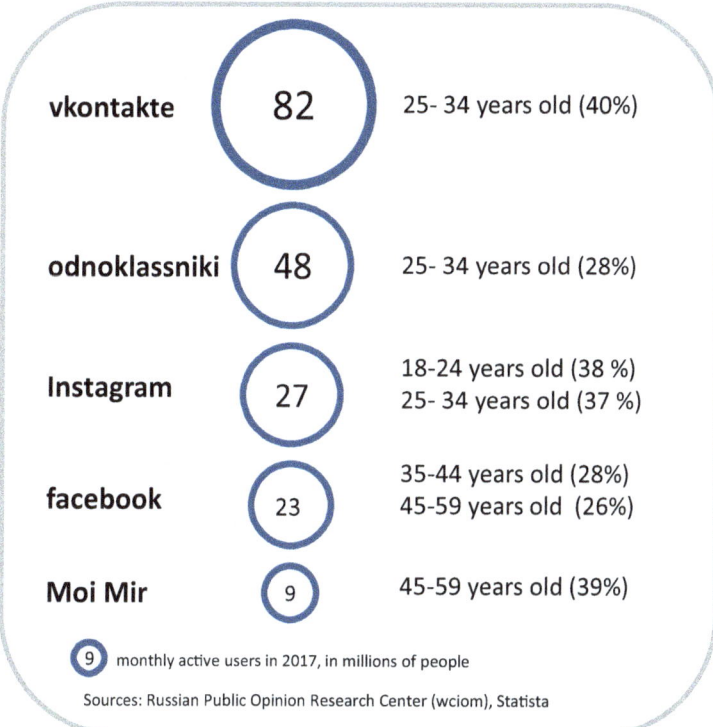

Fig. 25.2 Active users by age of the most popular social networks

through companies such as *Gazprom Media*) mass media outlets. The fully state-owned media empire includes currently six national TV networks, two national radio networks, two news agencies, and over 60% of the remaining press.[13]

Two factors make it particularly difficult for independent journalists to work in Russia: One is an increasingly restrictive legislature, which is continuously drafting new legislation to limit the freedom of the press further, and the other is vaguely worded judicial principles that can be interpreted and used by the politicized judiciary system to silence wayward media outlets as they please. "Inciting extremism or public disorder, publishing offensive content, defamation, insulting a state official in public" and "violating the Russian Federation's territorial integrity" have all been made crimes. Over the past years, the list of such offences has expanded, and fines have sharply increased—by a factor of ten.

---

[13] http://www.europarl.europa.eu/RegData/etudes/ATAG/2015/559467/EPRS_ATA%282015%29559467_EN.pdf, retrieved on January 17th, 2020.

Lately, legislative powers have specifically targeted the Internet to increase control on content distribution: since 2014, bloggers with more than 3,000 daily readers must register as media outlets[14] (And may not therefore remain anonymous). Social media networks (including foreign operators such as *Google* or *Facebook*) must keep six months' data on users, stored on Russia-based servers to facilitate government access.[15] New legislation has also made it much easier for the authorities to clamp down on the Internet. Media regulator *Roskomnadzor* added 28,000[16] URLs to the Registry of banned websites, including those of opposition activists and news portals sympathetic to the opposition.

Russian citizens and representatives of mass media may report whatever they want, especially through the Internet, but the state controls the distribution of the information, and more importantly, they often ignore or deny information that is undesirable for the sake of maintaining the narrative. Data supporting this can be found in the investigative documentary published in December of 2015 by the *Anti-Corruption Foundation (FBK)*[17] on the current Prosecutor General of Russia *Yuri Chaika* and his family. The Report came with a 40-min film, which could be found on *youtube*. The film resonated in mass media and on the Internet. In response, the Kremlin's press secretary claimed that the Kremlin "had no time" for this and that "the investigation did not catch their interest".[18]

Propaganda

Now with the availability of the internet, Russians have access to news outlets from abroad and Russians are becoming exposed to viewpoints and perspectives outside of the Russian mainstream media. However, the information on the internet is still manipulated. The government actively tries to shape information to suit its needs and canvasses for pro-government sentiments via cyberspace. The "Internet Research Agency," based in Saint Petersburg, is known as "trolls from *Olgino*." The main task of this agency is purely to manipulate opinions on the Internet on behalf of the Kremlin. An army of freelance agents supports the Agency. Some of these agents act as PR-professionals and work to discredit opposition internet and/or social media posts or opinions. Oftentimes, the Kremlin sanctioned, anti-opposition, counter-arguments put forth by these agents are elevated to be the most liked or discussed posts across social media platforms via bots, fake accounts, and manipulation of the

---

[14] https://www.vedomosti.ru/opinion/articles/2015/04/24/kak-gosudarstvo-razrushaet-rinok-smir, retrieved on October 7th, 2020.

[15] http://www.bbc.com/news/world-europe-17840134, retrieved on January 7th, 2019.

[16] Roskomsvoboda, http://reestr.rublacklist.net/, accessed on October 25, 2020.

[17] The FBK have been established by Alexey Navalny, who is a political and social activist, the leader of the political party Progress Party. Since December 2014 he is placed under house arrest for embezzlement and restricted from communicating with anyone but his family for 3.5 years.

[18] http://www.interfax.ru/russia/483587, retrieved on January 7th, 2020.

social media "trending" mechanics. The agency analyzes data, which profiles and categorizes people based on age, political views, activity times and they pay close attention to what kind of posts or comments bring the most success on different internet-portals.[19] Some agents escape detection by creating multiple social media profiles that at first glance appear to belong to private individuals. However, the profiles will often spam Kremlin talking points-en-masse to maximize impressions while also avoiding being identified as government propaganda. They often influence public opinion through completely fabricated news. This is always done in order to support a narrative through using shocking photographs from movies or past historical events presented in such a way that they appear to come from contemporary reality. There were many examples of this during the Ukrainian conflict.[20]

Despite these tactics, the general trust in the media remains high, with 70% believing that coverage of events in Ukraine by state TV channels is fully or mostly objective. Belief in the need for pluralism is declining and a mere 5% believing that media censorship should be abolished.[21]

Even though a growing percentage of Russians regularly go online (79% in 2020)[22] and the trust in TV news is eroding, TV remains the dominant source of news for most Russians. Currently, only 21% use the Internet to keep up to date with current affairs (TV: 85%).[23]

References

Петрунина, А. И., & Калужский, М. Л. *Общая ситуация на российском рынке печатных СМИ: тенденции и перспективы развития*, at http://www.aup.ru/articles/marketing/46.htm#_ftnref8, retrieved on October 8th, 2020.

Кириллова, Н.Б. (2005). *Медиасреда российской модернизации*, Академический проект.

---

[19]http://www.sueddeutsche.de/politik/propaganda-aus-russland-putins-trolle-1.1997470-3, retrieved on January 17th, 2020.

[20]http://www.watson.ch/Best%20of%20watson/watson-Leser%20empfehlen/332133461-So-arbeitet-das-geheime-Netzwerk-der-Russland-Propaganda; http://www.faz.net/aktuell/feuilleton/debatten/russische-propaganda-putins-botschaft-fuer-jeden-14097884.html, retrieved on January 7th, 2019.

[21]http://www.europarl.europa.eu/RegData/etudes/ATAG/2015/559467/EPRS_ATA%282015%29559467_EN.pdf, according to surveys by independent pollsters, Levada Centre, retrieved on January 7th, 2020.

[22]Russian Public Opinion Research Center (http://wciom.com), retrieved on October 26th, 2020.

[23]http://mresearcher.com/2015/12/levada-centr-doverie-rossiyan-k-novostnym-istochnikam.html, retrieved on January 7th, 2020.

Part III

Doing the Business

Legal Forms for Business Activity in Russia

Alex Stolarsky

Overview of the Legal Forms

Russian law offers the following legal forms for entrepreneurial activity:

- **Representative Offices/Branches/Subdivisions** (*predstawitelstwo/filial/ obosoblenoe podrazdelenie*): dependent branches of a foreign company in Russia that represent its interests or partially carry out its duties. They especially play a role in the initial phase of engagement or for temporary projects in Russia.
- **Partnerships: a full partnership** (*polnoje towarischtschestwo*), in which the partners assume liability for the company's liabilities with their own assets or a trust partnership (*towarischtschestwo na were*), in which at least one partner is personally liable and at least one other partner is liable only for the amount of their contributions.
- **Limited Liability Company** (*OOO or obschtschestwo s ogranitschennoi otwetstwennostju*) is a company in which the partners are liable only for the amount of their contribution to the share capital of the company (this corresponds to a GmbH).
- **Joint Stock Company** (*AO or akzionernoje obschtschestwo*) is a company whose share capital is divided into a specific number of shares. The shareholders are liable only for the value of their shares.
- **Investment Partnership** (*investizionnoje towarischtschestwo*) is a simple partnership created by the merger of deposits through a notarized contract and is intended to be a joint investment activity for profit without forming a legal entity.
- **Economic Partnership** (*chozajstwennoje partnjorstwo*) is a commercial organization that can be formed by at least two natural persons or legal entities that are liable only for the amount of their contributions.

A. Stolarsky (✉)
Schneider Group, Moscow, Russia
e-mail: stolarskya@schneider-group.com

- **Cooperative** (*proiswodstwennyi kooperatiw*) is an association of natural persons to perform joint production or other business activity based on membership and personal labor or participation.
- **Peasant Farming** (*krestianskoe (fermerskoe) khosiaistvo*) is a voluntary association of persons for joint production or other economic activity in the field of agriculture.
- **Individual Entrepreneur** (*indiwidualnyi predprinimatel*) is a natural person who has been registered as economically active on a register.
- **State Enterprises**, such as the unitary enterprise (*gosudarstwennoje unitarnoje predprijatije*), are legal forms for state and municipal enterprises.

For economic activity and especially for foreign investment some legal forms have proved to be particularly suitable. These are the subdivision, representative office, branch, Limited Liability Company, and Joint Stock Company. They are therefore presented in detail below.

Representative Office

- Often suitable for the achievement of short-term goals, in exceptional cases a long-term solution for a solid business in Russia.
- Not a legal entity, but rather represents the interests of a foreign legal entity, acts on behalf of a foreign company; it is justified and compelled by the acts of representation, so there is no liability limitation umbrella.
- Subject to Russian law; legal bases for their establishment and activity: "On Foreign Investment in the Russian Federation" Law and a series of orders by the Federal Tax Service of Russia (FTS).

Opening a Representative Office

For taking up the activity, the representative office has to be accredited by the Federal Tax Service of Russia. Therefore, a corresponding application along with associated documents must be submitted to the authorities. These include, but are not limited to, a certificate of incorporation, the statutes of the foreign company and of the representative office, the decision regarding the opening of the representative office in Russia, power of attorney for the head of the representative office, the certificate of registration of the foreign company as a domestic taxpayer, proof of a registered office in Russia and some others.

Documents not produced in Russia must be legalized. In the relationship between Russia and Germany or Austria (and many other countries), a so-called apostille is sufficient. Legalized document must then be translated into Russian with the further certification of the translator's signature by a Russian notary.

The accreditation as well as the entry into the register of accredited representative offices takes place within 30 business days. The state accreditation fee is 120,000 rubles.

Before submitting the application to the FTS, a so-called documentary expertise for foreign legal entities with the establishment and certification of the number of foreign employees in the representative offices or branches in Russia must be applied for with the Chamber of Commerce and Industry of the Russian Federation (RF CCI). A fee for this procedure is 18,000 rubles. The entire process takes about 3 months to be completed, including preparation and completion of the required documents. After tax registration of the representative office, the registration with the state social insurance funds and the opening of a bank account takes place.

Activities of the Representative Office

The legal basis of the activity of a representative office is its statutes. The statutes must regulate the following issues:

- Trade name of the foreign company and of the representative office
- Legal form of the foreign company
- Address of the foreign company
- Status of the representative office
- Documents, that define the activity of the representative office
- Registered office of the representative office
- Objectives for opening and areas of activity of the representative office
- Administrative bodies of the representative office
- Information on the assets of the representative office
- Procedure for hiring employees and procedures for the conclusion of temporary employment contracts
- Procedure for filing reports by the representative office to the authorized relevant authorities of the Russian Federation
- Procedure for suspension of activity of the representative office

The primary figure is the head of the representative office, who conducts the business of the representative office based on the power of attorney granted by the foreign legal entity and in accordance with the competences specified in the statutes of the representative office.

The representative office is entitled to hire employees. However, the foreign company acts as an employer. A foreign employee needs a work permit before starting work in the representative office, which is granted for the term of their employment contract, but for a maximum of 3 years (with possible prolongations). Changes in the number of foreign employees in the representative office must be entered in the state register.

Regarding the tax liability, the Russian taxation laws are subsidiary to double taxation treaties (DTT) that Russia has concluded with other states. According to these DTT, a representative office is not taxed unless it is a subdivision of the foreign company in Russia. When exactly such a subdivision arises depends on the DTT's provisions and on each individual case. No subdivision is established by merely preparatory or auxiliary activities.

The representative office is subject to foreign exchange control in business relationships with Russian clients so that for some transactions between the representative office and its Russian clients, a transaction certificate must be filed with the bank. This rule also applies to branches as well as subdivisions of foreign companies.

Special Case: Branch

The most important difference from the representative office is that a branch can act fully on behalf of the company, while the representative office acts exclusively in a representative capacity. The establishment of a branch is therefore expedient if the foreign company intends to have active business (commercial) operations in Russia. The accreditation of a branch is similar to the procedure for a representative office.

Subdivision

A subdivision is a dependent subsidiary of a foreign company and one of the simplest legal forms used especially for temporary projects. The registration of a subdivision is similar to the procedure for representative offices, but instead of accreditation, a simple tax statement is sufficient.

Limited Liability Company

The LLC (*OOO obschtschestwo s ogranitschennoi otwetstwennostju*)

- The most common legal form in Russian business.
- General legal basis: Civil Code and Law for the LLC.
- Nominal capital divided into shares ("participatory interests").
- It is a separate legal entity, can have rights and obligations; obtains its legal capacity only after state registration (a "pre-LLC" does not exist in Russia as compared with Germany, for example).
- Liability affects all assets of the LLC; the participants are liable for the liabilities of the LLC only if they have not fully paid their contribution into the charter capital.
- In some cases a parent company shall be liable as a joint debtor by way of lifting the corporate veil.
- LLC is subject to foreign exchange control (in business relations with foreign companies).

Founding Procedures

One or more persons or legal entities can found the LLC. However, when establishing a 100% fully owned LLC, the founder may not itself consist of only one participant. A subsequent two-time 100% participation is thus precluded.

The founding takes place at a foundation meeting, where the founding partners make a decision regarding the formation of the LLC and approve the charter for the company. Although no longer submitted for registration, the founding contract is recommended to be concluded when LLC is founded by more than one participant.

Mandatory information to be included in the charter of an LLC is regulated in Art. 12 of Law for the LLC. A creation of a company stamp is not obligatory, but recommended, because it is still formally required not by the legislation, but by several documents' forms to be submitted to the tax authorities.

The tax authorities at the registered office of the legal entity to be established are responsible for the registration of the LLC according to the registration law. Registration of the LLC is carried out by registry in the "Uniform State Register of Legal Entities" ("EGRUL"). The application for state registration must be submitted in the prescribed form and with the notarized signature of the applicant(s) along with the necessary documentation (minutes of the founding meeting, charter of the LLC, certificate of registration of the parent company, proof of a registered office and some others).

The process of registration takes place within three business days following the submission of the application. The entire procedure including all steps of preparation and registration usually takes 2–3 months. Upon completion of registration, the LLC receives a registration certificate.

The charter capital of an LLC must be paid within 4 months of its official registration.

Creation of the Charter

Although the law only requires a few items to be included into the Charter, the registration authority often expects repetition of the legislative provisions in the charter.

The share capital of an LLC must be at least 10,000 Rubles and can be provided in cash or in-kind contributions. If an in-kind contribution exceeds the value 20,000 rubles, an independent appraisal must be obtained.

The supreme body of the LLC is the participant's general meeting. The fundamental decisions and important administrative and control rights fall under its exclusive jurisdiction. Once a year an ordinary participants' meeting must be held. Further extraordinary meetings of the participants may be convened. The voting rights of the participants depend on their capital participation. A simple majority of votes by all participants generally passes resolutions unless otherwise provided for by the legislation or the charter.

The management body of the LLC can be an individual (General Director, CEO) or a collegial executive body (called "directorate" or "executive board"), both to be appointed by the general meeting. Such management body has exclusive powers of representation; the other representatives' act only based on the power of attorney. However, the charter of the LLC may provide that the power to represent the LLC may be delegated to several persons acting jointly or individually (multiple Directors option), which is subject to registration.

The CEO runs the business and acts without power of attorney on behalf of the company. However, the charter may limit the scope of the power of representation. In case the General Director acts outside the power of representation a transaction may be, under certain circumstances, declared invalid by the action of a participant of the LLC. In addition, the General Director is responsible for the management of the list of participants.

The charter of the LLC may provide for the formation of a Board of Directors as a supervisory body as well as provide for an audit commission. For an LLC with more than 15 participants, an audit commission (an auditor) is mandatory.

Change in Ownership

A participant of an LLC may dispose of its participation interest in the charter capital even to third parties without the consent of the company or the other participants, if not forbidden by the charter of the LLC. Current participants have a legal pre-emptive right for purchasing a participatory interest in proportion to the size of their own participation.

If the transfer of a participatory interest to third parties cannot take place due to the lack of consent, the LLC shall pay the affected participant or heirs the actual value of the participatory interest determined based on the accounting reports. The transfer of participatory interest requires notarial form.

An LLC participant furthermore has the right to declare his withdrawal from the LLC, if the charter explicitly provides for this right. The withdrawing participant must then be paid the actual value of the share within 6 months after the end of the fiscal year in which the withdrawal was declared.

Finally, a participant may face expulsion from the company if he/she grossly violates his/her obligations or significantly impedes or prevents the activities of the LLC.

Joint Stock Company

The joint stock company exists in Russia in two legal forms: public (shares and convertible bonds are publicly placed or publicly traded) and non-public (shares and convertible bonds may not be publicly issued or otherwise offered for sale to an unlimited group of persons).

The joint stock company is liable for its assets. Shareholders, on the other hand, are liable for commitments of the joint stock company only within the amount of their shares. In rare cases, for example, if the parent company issues binding instructions to the subsidiary, the corporate veil may be lifted.

Issuance of Shares

Rights to shares only arise when they are indicated in the register of shareholders. Public joint stock companies with less than 50 shareholders may independently manage their shareholders' register. With 50 or beyond shareholders, an expert registrar is required.

The issuance of shares by a joint stock company is mandatory in order to register with the Russian Central Bank. Otherwise, shares may not be transferred to third parties. Subsequently, the shares are registered by issuing a state registration number for the respective share issuance. Then the Russian Central Bank issues a formal notification to the joint stock company about the share registration and the decision on the issuance of shares, the issue prospectus, and the emission report, accompanied by an official note on its registration.

Bodies of the Joint Stock Company

Shareholders' meeting (general meeting): solely responsible for amendments to the statutes, the appointment of the Board of Directors (the Supervisory Board), the decision on dividend payment, conversion measures, and the liquidation of the company. Once a year, an ordinary shareholders' meeting must take place.

In general, the shareholders' meeting passes its resolutions with a simple majority of votes of the participating shareholders. Amendments to the statutes or a resolution to liquidate the company require a three-quarters majority. Other majority requirements cannot be prescribed in the statutes.

Board of Directors: elected and dismissed by the shareholders' meeting; supervisory tasks, responsible for basic issues of corporate governance that do not fall within the authority of the shareholders' meeting.

General Director: manages the company's day-to-day business, represents it, the scope of the power of representation may be limited by the statutes. A collegial management body ("directorate" or "executive board") may be set up; the chairperson is the General Director.

Audit Commission (the auditor): controlling body, type of internal auditor who audits the financial and economic activity.

Tips, Opportunities, and Warnings
Selecting the Right Legal Form for Your Russian Business Activities

In a typical evolutionary manner many western companies start their Russian business with pure export from their home country (if speaking e.g., about supply of goods), often paired with advance payments and EXW delivery clauses to avoid "Russian-related risks."

Once a significant volume of contracts and clientele has been reached, many companies tend to establish a representative office first to promote their products directly on Russian soil, participate in network events and trade fairs with one or several representatives permanently present in Russia, conduct client seminars and activate structured client acquisition and marketing activities. However, all commercial terms and final contracts are still negotiated and signed by the headquarters in Western home countries.

Once business gained sufficient traction, the seemingly logical next step is to either continue business with a trusted network of distributors or decide to perpetuate the market by their own and establish a commercial branch or a real independent legal entity (mostly in form of an *OOO*, the Russian *LLC*) which allows for full commercial activity under Russian law. While this evolutionary approach seems consistent, one should note the following when selecting the right legal form for an engagement in Russia:

- In general, setting up a representative office, a branch or legal entity in Russia tends to be more time and cost intensive as compared to Western Europe jurisdictions.
- Medium and long-term goals should be considered when establishing a permanent Russian presence because restructuring in Russia takes more time and is often associated with greater effort than in western jurisdictions.
- It is not possible to "convert" a representative office or a branch to a LLC at a later stage. Either these two will co-exist once a decision to establish a real commercial entity has been made or the representative office or branch will be liquidated. Liquidation procedures in Russia are even costlier and take more time than the incorporation procedures in the first place.
- The chosen corporate structure must be suitable for future developments in accordance with the real business goals and financial planning.
- LLC is flexible in the formation of its statutes and simple in its management, allows at the same time for a functioning corporate governance.
- A joint stock company is more complex in its governance than an LLC, but shareholders are more closely tied to one another.
- The decision for the right legal form in order to establish a Russian business case in my opinion shall not be bound by evolutionary phases of business activity only and driven by costs and estimated effort. Especially the start-up phase requires significant financial, time and human resources for a proper set up, so a dedicated team of professionals shall accompany this venture to streamline the processes most efficiently.
- A thought through business case for Russia with enough space for variables and unexpected delays shall serve as the base and then one shall build on that. In many cases, the right decision will be to go directly for establishing a full commercial legal entity, despite the initial costs and administrative efforts. In other cases, the representative office may serve as the right choice of a Russian presence for a decade or more and headquarter still are happy with profits gained from a stable Russian business.
- Many other important aspects such as taxes, financial management, employment and customs law to name just a few fields that require as well diligent analysis and professional knowledge have not been touched in this article (due to format) and should be taken into consideration when deciding on the right legal form.

The Russian Taxation System

Tanja Galander and Ekaterina Cherkasova

Russian tax law is relatively new, though fast developing. It is based on the Russian Tax Code (hereafter Tax Code RF) which consists of two parts. The first part came into force on January 1, 1999. It governs the general tax system and provides for common provisions for all types of taxes, as well as tax administration procedures. The second part came into force on January 1, 2001. It contains particular regulations for each type of tax (including necessary elements: object of taxation, taxpayers, tax base, tax rate, reporting and payment requirements, etc.).

As mentioned above, the Tax Code RF is subject to frequent changes. However, there are still certain "gray areas" requiring further improvement by both the jurisdiction and the financial authorities.

Double Tax Treaties (DTT) concluded by the Russian Federation with other states prevail over national tax laws, according to Art. 7 Sec. 1 Tax Code RF.

The Russian tax and fiscal authorities issue official clarifications on particular uncertain tax matters, which affect the position of the tax authorities towards the respective issues; however, they are not binding. In addition, the position of the fiscal authorities is impacted by court practice on tax matters, which develops rapidly and may significantly vary from one region to another.

In this article, we would like to draw your attention to selected aspects of the Russian tax law, which appear to be of utmost importance for foreign investors entering and/or expanding their business activities at the Russian market based on the common Russian tax law.

T. Galander (✉) · E. Cherkasova
PwC, Frankfurt, Germany
e-mail: tanja.galander@pwc.com; cherkasova.ekaterina@pwc.com

Basics of the Russian Tax System

Types of Taxes

Federal taxes—which are regulated and administrated on the federal level:

- Personal income tax (PIT).
- Corporate income tax (CIT).
- Value added tax VAT, and.
- Certain other types of taxes applicable to specific activities, such as excise tax, taxes on natural resources (for example, mineral extraction tax), etc.

Regional and local taxes—which are regulated and administrated on regional and local level accordingly are:

- Property tax
- Transport tax, and
- other types of taxes, such as land tax, etc.

In addition, Russian employers as well as freelancers have to contribute towards social security. Although such contributions do not represent taxes as such, the tax authorities administer most of them.

The Russian tax law also provides for special simplified taxation regimes aimed at supporting small businesses and/or particular industries.

Tax Administration—Selected Aspects

Compulsory Tax Registration for Legal Entities

According to Art. 83 Sec. 1 Tax Code RF a company is subject to compulsory tax registration at the place of its activities, or at the place of activities of the company's separate subdivisions, or at the location of company-owned real estate and vehicles. Based on the provisions of Art. 83 Sec. 4 in connection with Art. 11 Tax Code RF, tax registration is in fact compulsory for every foreign company exercising its business in Russia for more than 30 (not necessarily consecutive) days in one year. This information is especially important for foreign companies providing services and/or conducting other activities, which imply the physical presence of their representatives in Russian territory. This obligation applies independently from whether the activities of such foreign companies lead to the creation of a permanent establishment (PE) in Russia or not.

A point to note is that activities in different regions of Russia require separate tax registrations.

Tax Return and Tax Payment

Unlike European jurisdiction (for example, Germany), the Russian tax authorities are not obliged to provide the taxpayers with a tax assessment upon submission of the tax return. Although the submitted tax returns are subject to a desktop audit on the side of the tax authorities, there might be no significant adjustments until the on-site tax audit for the respective period is initiated. A taxpayer in Russia is, as a rule, subject to self-assessment of tax, and has to determine the tax amount due, and, upon declaration in a tax return, has to pay it to the Russian budget. This generally includes foreign taxpayers conducting business activities in Russia (unless Russian tax agents are responsible for remittance of the respective tax).

The taxation period for both individuals as well as legal entities is the respective calendar year. However, the tax period for particular taxes (like VAT) is every quarter of a year.

Depending on the respective type of tax, tax returns are to be declared monthly or quarterly. The deadlines for submission of tax returns and provision of tax payments are established by the Tax Code RF and are generally not subject to prolongation. However, the taxpayers have a right to submit amended tax returns and, respectively, adjust their self-assessments within a period of 3 years.

Statute of Limitation and Tax Audits

As mentioned above, tax returns submitted by a taxpayer are subject to desktop tax audits within 3 months from the submission date. Such audits can be quite intensive and could lead to the necessity of provision of additional documentation and clarifications in case the taxpayer applies for a refund or declares losses.

In addition, the tax authorities conduct regular on-site tax audits covering particular types of or all taxes. Such audits provide for a deeper analysis of the taxpayers' activities and direct access of the tax authorities to the relevant documents and responsible employees. The general statute of limitation applicable to tax liabilities is 3 calendar years. Accordingly, the tax authorities may initiate an on-site tax audit of the past 3 calendar years.

Taxpayers may appeal against the results of tax audits at the higher tax authority (as the first step) and in court (upon the decision of the higher tax authority).

Corporate Income Tax

Taxation of Income from Business Activities in Russia

Russian legal entities as well as PEs of foreign legal entities in Russia are subject to CIT on profits gained in Russia. The general tax rate is 20%.

Although the corporate income tax is a federal tax, only 3% enter the federal budget whereas up to 17% enter regional budgets. The federal subjects may reduce the regional tax rate in order to attract investors; however, the law has limited such purely regional incentives. Reduced regional rates introduced before January 1, 2018, will apply until the date of their expiry but not later than January 1, 2023.

In addition, specific reduced tax rates may be applicable to particular activities (e.g., 0% rate applicable to agricultural manufacturers, disposal of shares in Russian subsidiaries under particular conditions, etc.). Numerous investment programs also provide for reduced CIT rates.

The taxable basis is the total amount of income reduced by deductible expenses and, as a rule, is determined on an accrual basis. Expenses are deductible if they are:

- Economically justified.
- Supported by relevant and sufficient documents (if applicable—in the legally prescribed form).
- Incurred with profit generating intention, and.
- Not declared as non-deductible by law, see Art. 270 Tax Code RF.

Particular types of expenses are limited for the deduction. For example, certain advertisement costs are deductible for profit tax purposes as such, but only within the amount of 1% of revenue. In addition, loan interest costs may be limited to deduction based on (1) cap interest rates and (2) thin capitalization rules applicable to particular intercompany loans (acceptable debt/equity ratio is 3/1).

Certain types of income qualify as non-taxable by law (for example, contributions into assets from parent companies, if provided in compliance with Russian civil law).

Tax-deductible losses may be generally carried forward within an unlimited period. However, the current tax law provides for a minimum taxation requirement for the period until December 31, 2021, which constitutes that prior years' tax losses may be offset against the current year taxable profits in the amount not exceeding 50% of the current taxable profit, whereas the remaining amount is carried forward. In comparison to other jurisdictions (including Germany), the Russian legislation does not provide for any restriction on carrying forward tax losses in case of shareholders change of the respective legal entity (unless such change is caused by a merger with the main purpose of offset of accumulated tax losses of the merged entity).

Permanent Establishment

A PE is defined in the Tax Code RF as "a branch, division, office, bureau, agency, or any other place through which a foreign legal entity regularly carries out its business activities in Russia." The Russian tax legislation also provides for a number of exemptions not leading to the creation of a PE (e.g., conduction of mere preparatory and auxiliary activities for the benefit of the head office).

As mentioned above, foreign legal entities pay tax on profits attributable to a PE. The profits of a PE are calculated primarily on the same basis as Russian legal entities, including the composition of tax-deductible expenses, wherein the allocation of risks, assets, and functions between the head office and the Russian PE has to be considered. Special profit allocation mechanism is provided for PEs conducting preparatory and auxiliary activities for the benefit of third parties.

In general, the Russian provisions on PE taxation are in line with international practices. Additional exemptions, as well as other special conditions, might apply under a respective double tax treaty (DTT).

Withholding Tax

Withholding tax (WHT) is a profit tax, which applies to certain types of income from Russian sources (including dividends, royalties, interest on loans, particular capital gains, etc.) gained by foreign entities and individuals not conducting their activities in Russia through a PE and not being so-called Russian tax residents respectively.

Dividends from Russian companies payable to foreign shareholders are taxed in Russia at a rate of 15%, interest income, and license fees at a rate of 20%, and other income at a rate of 10% up to 20% depending on the specific type of income. For example, sales of stocks and shares of Russian or foreign companies, if the respective company's assets consist (directly or indirectly) of Russian real estate by more than 50% are subject to WHT at 20% rate.

Domestic WHT rates may be reduced (and certain types of income could be completely exempted from taxation) under DTT provisions. In order to benefit from a reduced WHT rate/WHT exemption, the foreign income recipient should provide the Russian payer with (1) a certificate of residence for the respective financial year as well as (2) a written confirmation (since 1 January 2017) that it qualifies as the beneficial owner of the payments in question under the DTT. The documents must be available to the Russian payer before the payments are actually made.

The Russian legislative regulations on a written confirmation to be provided by the beneficial owner are relatively new, and the tax authorities are currently closely monitoring whether the characteristics of a beneficial owner are met. Based on available clarifications, an economic beneficiary needs to (1) prove a certain degree of substance (activities, personnel, etc.) in the country of residence; (2) have the power of control over the income from Russian sources; and (2) needs to be able to use the Russian source of income in the course of its business activity. Further characteristics, such as number of employees, possible contractual restrictions of power of control over the income, etc. are also considered.

Russia recently started a campaign aimed at strengthening the conditions of DTTs with so-called "transit countries" (e.g., Cyprus, Malta, etc.) resulting in an increase of the treaty WHT rates.

Personal Income Tax and Social Security Contributions

Personal Income Tax

Individuals that are subject to unlimited taxation in Russia are so-called "tax residents." These tax residents are spending not less than 183 calendar days p.a. in Russia and are paying taxes on their worldwide income, which may originate from Russian or foreign sources. Individuals that are subject to limited taxation in Russia are so-called "tax non-residents." This means they are subject to Russian income tax on their income from Russian sources only.

For the year 2020, there is a possibility to opt for unlimited tax liability in Russia also in case the respective individual spent less than 183 days in Russia. The PIT rate for tax residents is 13% for almost all types of income according to Art. 224 Sec. 1 Tax Code RF. For tax non-residents it is 30%. However, the Russian tax law provides for a few exemptions, especially for highly qualified foreign specialists (having a particular residential status in accordance with Russian migration law), which provide for the application of 13% PIT rate to non-residents.

It needs to be noted that in response to COVID-19, the government intends to increase the PIT rate up to 15% for income exceeding 5 million rubles starting from 2021.[1]

Social Security Contributions

Unlike in Germany, only the employer has to pay social security contributions (not the employee). Therefore, social security contributions in fact represent additional payroll costs for the employers. Social security comprises statutory pension insurance, health insurance, and social insurance for accidents, occupational illnesses, and maternity leave.

Individual contribution rates are determined by the individual remuneration (income) and limited to a yearly-adjusted threshold. The maximum overall social security burden equals to 30% (excluding social insurance for accidents and occupational illnesses charged based on the flat rate from 0.2% to 8.5% depending on the types of activities).

Value Added Tax (VAT)

There is no separate VAT registration procedure in Russia (with an exception of separate VAT registration for foreign providers of electronic services).

---

[1] https://www.pwc.ru/en/services/tax-consulting-services/legislation/tax-flash-report-2020-48.html, retrieved on November 27, 2020.

VAT usually applies to the sale of goods, work, services, or property rights provided in Russia. The current standard VAT rate equals to 20%. Reduced rates (10% and 0%) are applicable to certain types of goods/works/services. The VAT rates (applicable to domestic supplies) also apply to the import of goods into Russia.

Exports of goods, international transportation, and other services related to the export of goods from Russia, international passenger transfer, and other supplies are zero-rated with the right of input VAT recovery.

The Russian tax law provides for certain VAT exemptions. For example, most accredited representative offices and branches of foreign legal entities in Russia (as well as their accredited employees) may be exempt from VAT on property rental payments, provided the same exemptions apply for Russian representative offices and branches in the respective foreign country.

The Russian VAT place of supply rules (determining the location of services especially for cross-border services and thus, the application of Russian VAT) contain certain specifics. For example, certain services are deemed to have been supplied where they are performed, whereas some are deemed to have been supplied where the 'buyer' of the services carried out its activity, some, where the relevant movable or immovable property is located, and others where the 'seller' has its place of activity. Reverse-charge mechanism applies to VATable sale of goods/works/services by a foreign entity not registered for Russian tax purposes (however, specific rules apply to foreign providers of electronic services).

Taxpayers are usually eligible to recover "input VAT" associated with the purchase of goods, work, services, or property rights, provided that they adhere to the set of rules established by the VAT legislation.

Each taxpayer performing VATable supplies of goods, work, services, or property rights must issue special VAT invoices and submit them to customers.

Other Types of Taxes

Other types of taxes, such as property tax, real estate tax, or transportation tax as well as special tax regimes will not be further explained in this article since they are rather specific to particular activities and/or properties. However, it is important to note that Russia has not introduced a real estate transfer tax.

Recent Trends in Russian Tax Law

Below we outline the most significant and recent developments in Russian tax legislation, which are mostly impacted by international tax practices.

Transfer Pricing

Russian transfer pricing legislation on the control of prices under transactions between related parties is essentially based on Organization for Economic Co-operation and Development (OECD) principles, with certain important deviations. This legislation establishes criteria for related parties and controlled transactions, transfer pricing methods for determining arm's-length prices/profitability, a list of permitted information sources, and compliance requirements.

The introduction of transfer pricing rules represents one of the most significant developments in the Russian tax law over the last 15 years.

The concept of country-by-country reporting under the OECD Base Erosion and Profit Shifting plan has been also recently implemented in Russia.

"De-Offshorization" Developments

Russian tax law has been significantly modified in 2015. The respective measures were aimed at the return of capital into Russia and limitation of unjustified international tax optimization benefits. The respective developments cover: (1) introduction of the definition of the beneficial owner of income into the Russian Tax Code (relevant for the application of reduced WHT rates and WHT exemptions—see above), (2) introduction of tax residency for legal entities for CIT purposes based on their place of management and (3) taxation of profits of controlled foreign companies (CFC) at the level of their Russian shareholders/controlling parties.

As mentioned above, Russia announced the intention to modify the existing DTTs with so-called "transit" countries in order to increase the respective WHT rates. As of today, Russia managed to reach an agreement at least with Cyprus and Malta in this respect.

Anti-Abuse Provisions

Since the end of 2017, the Russian tax legislation contains a definition of unjustified tax benefit (Art. 54.1 Tax Code RF), which significantly deviates from the prior understanding of the respective concept based on available court practice. In accordance with the new rules, a taxpayer is not allowed to benefit from the reduction of tax base (for example, as a result of the deduction of costs and/or input VAT) if inter alia the facts regarding the respective transactions are distorted and/or if the main purpose of transactions is tax underpayment.

The new provisions are basically focused on transactions aimed solely at tax avoidance. However, it is expected that also bona fide taxpayers may face additional claims from tax authorities as the new rules provide for a rather universal instrument for re-classification of arrangements in tax-driven ones.

COVID-19

Russia has also introduced supporting measures addressed mainly to small and middle-sized businesses and covering tax reliefs as well as deferrals due to the Corona crisis.

Tax Incentives and Tax Opportunities

Tanja Galander

The Russian Federation provides deductions for several tax, customs duties, and other incentives for producers in Russia. Such support can be received both, on the federal as well as regional level.

Therefore, the intended place of conducting business in the Russian Federation and establishing a subsidiary should be selected considering regional or local support. It is useful to get in contact with local decision-makers at an early stage.

Subsequent tax incentives, as well as tax benefits for an investor in Russia, depend on a variety of factors. The most important of these is the nature of the planned activity as well as the willingness to make a certain amount of investment, some of which is legally stipulated. The Association of Clusters and Technology Parks maintains an overview on Russian regions and the attractiveness for investors.[1] In addition, the Russian state agency for strategic initiatives provides information on Russian regions.[2]

Special Economic Zones (SEZ)

The following types of SEZ have been established in Russia:

- Technology Innovative SEZ
- Industrial Production SEZ

---

[1] https://akitrf.ru/upload/Russian_Special_Economic_Zones._Business_Navigator_2019_eng.pdf, retrieved on September 13th, 2020.

[2] Investment Potential of Russian Regions. Project of the Foundation "Roskongress" and the Agency for Strategic Initiatives at www.investinregions.ru/en/, retrieved on October 15th, 2020

T. Galander (✉)
PwC, Frankfurt, Germany
e-mail: tanja.galander@pwc.com

- Tourism and Recreational SEZ
- Port SEZ and
- Other (geographical) SEZ

As special laws apply to geographical special economic zones, they are shown separately below (Fig. 28.1).

Benefits for Residents in an SEZ

Residents of an SEZ enjoy a number of benefits, such as,

- Tax benefits (reduced regional part of CIT rate up to 0% for the first 5 years and further reduced CIT rates for the following years, reduced property and land tax up to 0% for several years, 0% transport tax rate) as well as
- Reduced social security contributions (21% in 2019 and 28% in 2020 instead of 30%).

The tax differences between business activities within and outside an SEZ are provided in Table 28.1 as an example for the SEZ Alabuga.

In addition, companies located in an SEZ are provided with a guarantee, such that changes in Russian tax law leading to less favorable conditions compared with the time of investment agreement conclusion do not apply to residents of special economic zones (grandfathering right).

Furthermore, simplified rules apply for the recruitment of foreign employees. When hiring a highly qualified specialist for whom a work permit can be obtained in a simplified procedure, the salary requirements are reduced. These amount to 83,500 rubles per month when working in an Industrial Production SEZ instead of the minimum salary of at least 167,000 Rubles per month.

Finally, the administrative burden for investors is reduced in SEZs. Contact with all state authorities is facilitated by one-window systems with a contact person who is responsible for all questions. Land plots are provided under favorable conditions including infrastructure facilities (Table 28.2 gives an overview on tax preferences in the SEZ).

Legal Basis and Prerequisite for Becoming an SEZ Resident

The state-owned company *AO Osobye Ekonomičeskie Zony (OEZ)* serves as a central point of contact for interested investors. It operates the Technology Innovative SEZ, Industrial Production SEZ, Tourism, and Recreational SEZ as well as Port SEZ.

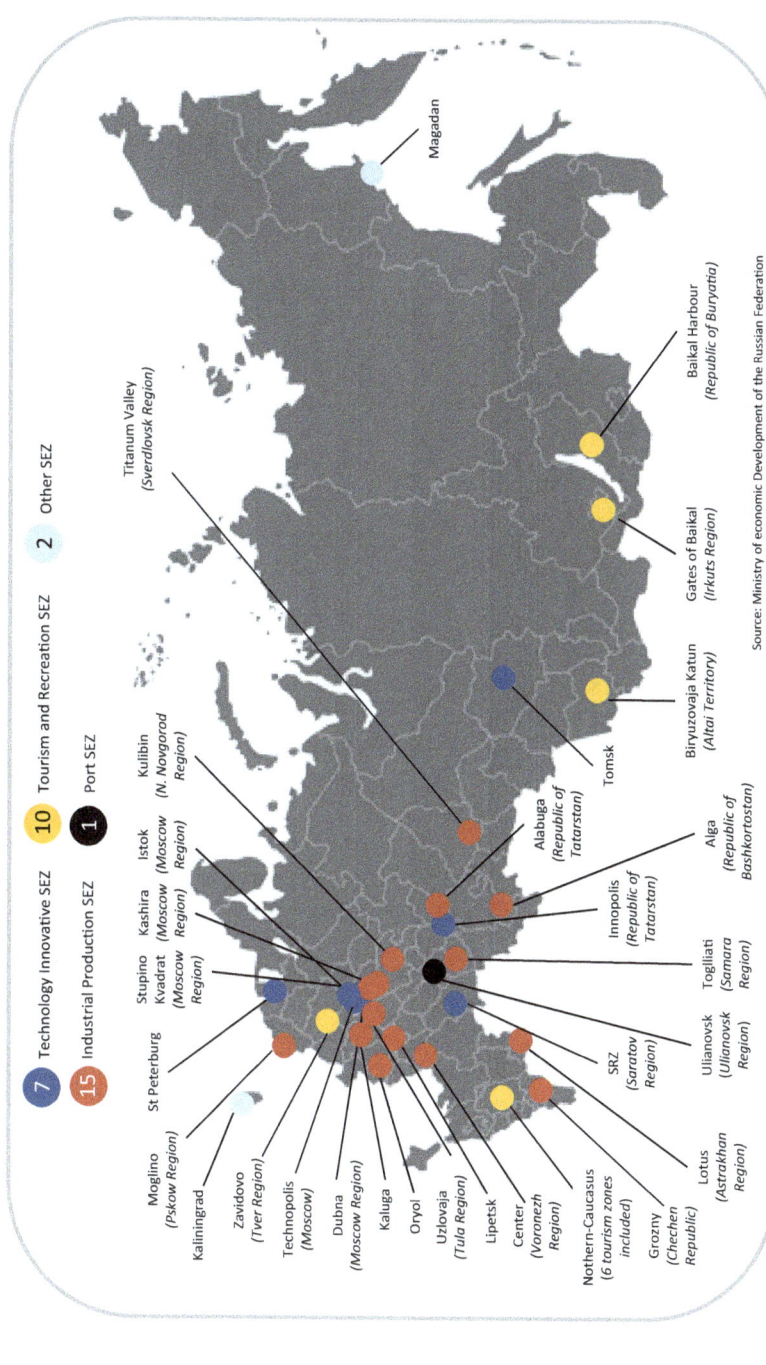

Fig. 28.1 Special economic zones

Table 28.1 The tax differences between business activities within and outside an SEZ

Tax	Russian Federation	SEZ Alabuga
Profit tax	Federal tax: 2% (3% from 2017 until the end of 2020); Regional tax 18% (17% from 2017 until the end of 2020)	Federal tax: 2% Regional tax: 0% within the first 5 years; 5% within the following 5 years (years 6–10); 13.5% from the following years, i.e., starting in year 11 (12.5% in 2017 until the end of 2020).
Property tax	2.2%	0% within the first 10 years
Land tax	1.5%	0% within the first 10 years
Import VAT	Depends on the concrete product, the general rate is 18%, from 2019: 20%	0% (SEZ Alabuga operates as free customs zone)
Transportation tax	Tax rates vary in different regions and for different vehicles.	None, within the first 10 years from vehicle registration
Social security contributions	30%	2018: 21% 2019: 28% (including statutory pension, health, and social insurance)

The most important legal basis for special economic zones is the Special Economic Zone Law RF[3] that covers all SEZs except for the geographical SEZs Kaliningrad and Magadan, for which specific laws apply.

The SEZs are established for a term of (except for geographical SEZs) 49 years. Starting a business in an SEZ requires the respective company to be included in the register of SEZ residents. Only legal entities established in accordance with Russian law and located in the respective SEZ can be accepted as SEZ residents. To qualify for resident status, a request must be submitted to the OEZ or the Ministry of Economic Development together with a business plan and the founding documents. After examining and approving the application and signing an investment agreement, the investor is added to the register of SEZ residents.

Technology Innovative SEZ

In Technology Innovative SEZ, high-tech projects are realized which means development, production, and distribution of high-tech products, such as software, databases, or integral microcircuits. In addition, industrial production is allowed in a Technology Innovative SEZ upon a separate permit.

---

[3]Federal Law as of 22 July 2005 No. 116-FZ 'On Federal Economic Zones in the Russian Federation' (Федеральный закон от 22 июля 2005 г. N 116-ФЗ "Об особых экономических зонах в Российской Федерации").

Table 28.2 Preferences in Special Economic Zones (SEZ)

Tax rates outside SEZ

	Corporate income tax (CIT)	Property tax	Land tax	Transport tax	Social contribution
	2% federal part (3% from 2017 until 2020) 18% regional part (17% from 2017 until 2020)	2.2%	1.5%	Rate depends on region and vehicle	30%

Tax rates outside SEZ

Type of SEZ	SEZ	Corporate income tax (CIT)	Property tax	Land tax	Transport tax	Social contribution
Technology Innovative SEZ	Tomsk	2% federal part from 2018 13.5% regional part for 10 years (12.5% from 2017 until 2020)	0% for 10 years	0% for 5 years	0 RUB for 10 years	2018: **21%** 2019: **28%**
	Moscow, Technopolis (Zelenograd)	2% federal part 0% regional part since 2018 5% from 2028 12.5% from 2033		0% for 10 years	0 RUB for 10 years	
	Moscow Region, Dubna	2% federal part 0% regional part within the first 8 years 5% within the following 6 years 13.5% after 14 years		0% for 5 years	0 RUB for 5 years	
	St. Petersburg	2% federal part from 2018 13.5% regional part (**12.5%** from 2017 until 2020) during the existence of SEZ			0 RUB for 5 years	
	Republic Tatarstan, Innopolis	2% federal part from 2018 0% regional part within the			0 RUB for 10 years	

(continued)

Table 28.2 (continued)

	Moscow Region, Istok	first 5 years 5% from 6th until 10th year 13.5% from the 11th year 2% federal part from 2018 0% regional part within the first 8 years 5% for the next 6 years 13.5% after 14 years		0 RUB for 5 years	
Industrial Production SEZ	Republic Tatarstan Alabuga	2% federal part 0% regional part within the first 5 years 5% from 6th until 10th year 13.5% from the 11th year (12.5% from 2017 until 2020)	0% for 10 years	0 RUB for 10 years	2018: 21% 2019: 28%
	Lipezk	2% federal part 0% regional part within the first 5 years (from the moment of profit gaining) 5% from 6th until 10th year 13.5% from the 11th year (12.5% from 2017 until 2020)	0% for 5 years		
	Samara Region, Tolatti	2% federal part 0% regional part within the first 5 years (from the moment of profit gaining) 5% from 6th until 10th year 13.5% from the 11th year		0 RUB for 10 years	
	Sverdlovsk Region, Titanovaya Dolina	2% federal part 0% regional part from first	0% for 10 years	0 RUB for 12 years	

Pskov, Moglino	until 15th year **13.5%** from 16th year **2%** federal part **0%** regional part within the first 5 years **5%** from 6th until the 10th year **13.5%** from the 11th year	**0 %** for 5 years	**0 RUB** for 10 years
Kaluga, Ludinovo	Federal Part: **2%** **Regional Part:** **For Business Activities:** **0%** within the first 5 years **3%** within the next 4 years **5%** within the next 2 years **8%** within the next 2 years **10%** within the next 2 years **13.5%** from 16th year **For other activities:** **5%** within the first 5 years, **9%** within the next 5 years **13.5%** from 16th year		**0 RUB** for 10 years for trucks and self-propelling vehicles as well as for vehicles using on pneumatic chains and crawlers if they have been obtained by SEZ resident
Tula Uslovaya	**2%** federal part **0%** regional part within the first 5 years (from the moment of profit gaining) **5%** from 6th until 10th year **13.5%** from the 11th year		**0 RUB** for 10 years
Astrahan, Lotos	**2%** federal part **0%** regional part for the first	**0 RUB** for 12 years	**0 RUB** for 12 years

(continued)

Table 28.2 (continued)

	Mocow Region, Stupino Kvadrat	10 years 10% for the following 10 years 2% federal part 0% regional part for the first 8 years 5% for the next 6 years 13.5% after 14 years	0 RUB for 10 years	
	Altai, Birûzovaâ Katun	2% federal part 12.5% regional part	No special legal provisions	
	Irkutsk, Vorota Baykala	2% federal part 13.5% regional part		
	Republic Buryatia Baykalskaâ Gavan	2% federal part 13.5% regional part (2018 until 2020—12.5%) for 10 years		
	Tver, Zavidovo	2% federal part 12.5% regional part since 2018 13.5% from 2021		
Tourism and Recreational SEZ	Republic Kabardino-Balkarya, Elbrus-Bezengi Republic Karatshay-Tsherkessya, Arhyz Republic Dagestan, Matlas Republic Ingushetia, Armhi i Zori Chechen Republic, Veduči	2% federal part until 2022 Up to 13.5% regional part (12.5% until 2020)	0 RUB for 10 year	0% for 5 years
			No special legal provisions	2018: **21%** 2019: **28%**

0 RUB for 5 years appears in the Mocow Region row at the far right.

Port SEZ	Ulyanovsk, airport Ulyanovsk East	2% federal part 0% regional part for 10 years	0 percent for 5 years	0% for 10 years	0% for 10 years	30%
Geographical	Kaliningrad	0% federal part 0% regional part for the first 6 years 50% of the general regional part for the next 5 years	0% for the first 6 years	0% for 5 years	depends on type of transport, no special benefits for SEZ residents	7.6% from 2018 until 2022
	Magadan	0% federal part maximum 13.5% federal part	0% for 10 years	0% for 5 years		30%

Industrial Production SEZ

Both, industrial production and logistics can be performed in an Industrial Production SEZ. Industrial production includes the production in itself, further processing, and distribution. Logistics means to transport and storage of goods. For the development and application of new technologies in an Industrial Production SEZ, a special permit is required.

One of the essential legal requirements of an investment agreement for residents of an Industrial Production SEZ is the obligation of a minimum investment. The minimum amount is RUB 120 million within the first 3 years from the date of obtaining resident status.

Tourism and Recreational SEZ

These SEZs promote and operate tourism, which includes construction, operation, and renovation of tourist facilities, medical rehabilitation and disease prevention services, operation of spa and holiday resorts, expansion of thermal sources as well as the industrial bottling of mineral water.

Port SEZ

Companies based in such SEZs do not only carry out logistical activities but are also involved in the expansion of port infrastructure. Other permitted activities are storage and safekeeping of goods, supplies, equipment, repair and maintenance of ships and aircrafts, packaging and product labeling, wholesale and production activities (the latter upon special permit).

Residents of a Port SEZ that have taken over the construction, reconstruction, or rehabilitation of a port under an investment agreement are required to make the following investments:

- RUB 400 million in 3 years from the date of receipt of a resident status in a Port SEZ in cases of construction of port facilities.
- RUB 120 million in case of reconstruction.

Furthermore, residents of a Port SEZ are obliged to provide security in the event of receiving customs benefits within a duty-free zone, in the following amount:

- RUB 30 million for warehousing and storage of goods, wholesale and trading in commodities and mineral raw materials.
- RUB 10 million for storage, wholesale, and exchange of trading of goods that are not subject to consumer taxation.
- RUB 2.5 million for other port-related activities.

Geographical SEZs Kaliningrad and Magadan

These SEZs promote economic development in a given area and are not limited to activities. SEZ in the Kaliningrad region has been established until 31 December 2045. SEZ in Magadan has been established until 31 December 2025. Both SEZs provide tax and customs duties benefits for Kaliningrad and Magadan territorial areas. In contrast to a general SEZ, in the Kaliningrad and Magadan SEZs, a duty-free zone has been established by law.

Special Investment Contract (SPIC)

A new regulation to support investments in the industrial sector is the federal Law "On industrial policy in the Russian Federation", which came into force in 2015.[4] It provides a framework for investment projects and allows investors to sign special investment contracts (SPIC) that grant them state subsidies or tax benefits. On August 2, 2019, No. 290-FZ "On Amendments to the Federal Law On Industrial Policy in the Russian Federation" reformed the laws regulating the use of SPIC into a so-called SPIC 2.0.

SPIC 2.0, is an agreement between an investor and the Russian government. The investor must implement an investment project for the introduction or development and implementation of technology with the purpose of mass production of industrial products in Russia upon investing its own funds and (or) raised funds within the period stipulated in the SPIC. The Russian Federation (jointly with a federal unit of the Russian Federation and/or a municipal entity) secures the stability of the investor's business environment and provides the investor with tax incentives. In addition, it grants the status of "Made in Russia" (which facilitates access to state tenders provided that certain production localization requirements are met), offers administrative support (e.g., regarding real estate), and may grant grandfathering rights over the duration of the SPIC that protect investors from unfavorable amendments of Russian tax and investment laws.

The SPIC period is limited to 15 years for projects with investments of up to 50 billion rubles, and for 20 years for projects with investments of 50 billion rubles or more.

It is noteworthy that SPIC 2.0 is only intended for investors who will develop and/or implement modern technologies and thereby promote the production of globally competitive industrial products (so-called high-tech products). The government has decided to publish a list of modern technologies that fall under this

---

[4]Federal Law as of 31 December 2014 N 488-FZ 'On industrial policy in the Russian Federation' (Федеральный закон от 31 декабря 2014 г. N 488-ФЗ "О промышленной политике в Российской Федерации").

mechanism and it invited companies and associations to submit applications for technology to be included on the list.

Incentives on Activities

For taxpayers in Russia incentives with respect to business activities are available, such as currently reduced CIT rates for IT companies in several regions. From 2021 onwards, generally CIT for IT companies will amount to 3% rather than the standard 20%. In addition, the social contribution rate will be lowered up to 7.6%. In order to enjoy these benefits, companies need to obtain a state accreditation certificate as an entity engaged in IT business. Revenues from IT activities by the end of the calendar year must not be less than 90% of total company revenues and the average number of employees needs to equal or exceed seven people. It must be noted that with the introduction of these incentives for IT companies go along with limitations for VAT exemption on software and databases. Transactions regarding the transfer of exclusive rights to software and databases or their use will remain exempt from VAT only if they are included in the Unified Register of Russian Software and Databases. All other current existing tax benefits for IT companies will become unavailable from January 1, 2021.

Some R&D services and R&D service-related expenses are also exempt from VAT. For agricultural producers, the CIT rate on activities related to the sale of produced agricultural products is 0%. Moreover, agricultural producers are entitled to apply a single agricultural tax at a rate of 6% from the difference between income and expenditure, instead of income tax, property tax that is used for agricultural activities, and VAT. Small- and medium-sized companies with low annual revenues may apply for similar single flat taxes, provided they meet the respective legal requirements.

Lastly, local producers exporting their goods can receive export loans at reduced interest rates and may be provided with export insurances by the *Russian Agency for Export Credit and Investment Insurance (EXIAR)*[5] or state guarantees. Russian exporters may also receive assistance from the Russian export center,[6] such as consulting, marketing or information services and other support.

Customs Duties Incentives for Foreign Investors

Goods being imported as contributions into the charter capital of Russian legal entities by foreign shareholders are exempted from customs duties if such goods are:

---

[5] At www.exiar.ru retrieved on October 14th, 2020.

[6] At www.exportcenter.ru retrieved on September 24th, 2020.

- Non-excisable goods in accordance with Article 181 Tax Code RF[7]
- Fixed capital assets and
- Imported within the agreed terms in accordance with the respective statutory documents of the legal entity[8]

Benefits and State Support on Regional Level

In addition to the federally created SEZ, the federal subjects[9] of the Russian Federation also support foreign investors. The respective funding measures as well as administrative support vary from region to region and include, for example, preferential settlement conditions, provision of infrastructure, reduced regional taxes, and preferential loans or free leasing of land. Thus, most regions provide their own incentives with respect to CIT and transport tax. However, such regional incentives are now limited by law. Any reduced regional rates that were introduced before January 1, 2018, will only apply until the date of their expiry but not beyond January 1, 2023.

Reduced social contribution rates are available for residents of industrial zones if they are engaged in R&D. Many regions establish so-called industrial parks as a special territory with support and convenient conditions for investors.

For providing such benefits, respective regions typically require that the project fits in with regional business priorities and a minimum amount of investment will be contributed.

Regional authorities, such as obligations to employ individuals residing in the region, to invest in infrastructure development or social projects, may establish additional conditions.

Each subject of the Russian Federation, due to regional investment laws, must offer at least the same investment conditions as at the federal level, but may also offer conditions that are more favorable. A comparison of investment conditions and investment preferences between a federal SEZ and a regional industrial park is recommended. You may gain additional information from the Russian Association of Industrial Parks.[10]

---

[7]E.g. are not alcohol or tobacco products or other as listed in Article 181 Tax Code RF.

[8]Decision of the Government of the Russian Federation dated 23 July 1996 No. 883 'On incentives for payment of import customs duties and VAT with respect to products imported by foreign investors as contribution into the statutory capital of legal entities with foreign investments' (Постановление Правительства РФ от 23 июля 1996 г. N 883 "О льготах по уплате ввозной таможенной пошлины и налога на добавленную стоимость в отношении товаров, ввозимых иностранными инвесторами в качестве вклада в уставный (складочный) капитал предприятий с иностранными инвестициями").

[9]A federal subject is similar to a federal state.

[10]www.indparks.ru/en/, retrieved on September 24th, 2020.

Other Areas with Special Conditions

In addition to SEZ, there are a number of other areas in the Russian Federation that provide incentives and benefits for investors. In August 2018, the Russian President signed new laws creating the so-called Special Administrative Zones (SAR) on the Russian island "*Ostrov Russky*" in the Primorsky region and on October Island in the Kaliningrad region in order to create new "offshore" zones in Russia.

Advanced Development Zones (ADZ)

In March 2015,[11] new laws became effective which allow the establishment ADZs in the Russian Far East.[12] They offer special terms for companies operating in various industries (e.g., agriculture, textiles, chemicals, pharmaceuticals, furniture, telecommunications, education, science, technology, etc.), including CIT and property tax incentives, free customs zones, project financing and simplified rules for hiring foreign employees. ADZ can be established for up to 70 years.

Free Port of Vladivostok

Residents of the port enjoy tax incentives, such as a zero rate on the federal portion of CIT for a 5-year period, a reduced regional portion of CIT (maximum 5% during the first 5 years of profitable sales and at least 10% during the subsequent 5 years) as well as reduced social contributions (7.6% instead of the standard 30%) during a 10-year period.

Republic of Crimea and Sevastopol City Incentives

An SEZ has been established in Crimea and Sevastopol by special law. However, since Crimea and Sevastopol are not recognized as a part of the Russian Federation by other countries and are subject to EU as well as US-Sanctions, its preferred tax regime is not be described herein detail.

---

[11] Federal Law 'On territories with advanced social-economic development in the Russian Federation' N 473-FZ as of 29 December 2014 (Федеральный закон от 29 декабря 2014 г. N 473-ФЗ "О территориях опережающего социально-экономического развития в Российской Федерации").

[12] E.g. Nadeždensky and und Michailovksy in Primorsky region.

Skolkovo Incentives

A Russian legal entity can become a participant in the *Skolkovo* project in the Moscow Region, provided it is established exclusively for carrying out research in the following areas:

- Energy efficiency and energy saving, including the development of innovative energy technologies
- Nuclear technology
- Space technologies—especially in the field of telecommunications and navigation systems
- Medical technologies (development of equipment, medicines)
- Strategic computer technologies and software
- Biotechnology in agriculture and industry

A legal entity may receive a status of a participant in the Skolkovo project for a period of 10 years and enjoys the following incentives such as:

- CIT exemption within the first 10 years from the date of becoming a participant of the Skolkovo project, provided that its revenues do not exceed RUB 1 billion.
- Exemption from companies' property tax provided that its annual revenues from the sale of goods (work, services, property rights) do not exceed RUB 1 billion.
- Exemption from land tax.
- Exemption from VAT within the first 10 years from the date of becoming a participant of the Skolkovo project (provided that the amount of the profit does not exceed the established amount).
- Reduced social contribution rates (e.g., only 14% payment obligation of the mandatory pension insurance).
- Reimbursement of paid customs duties and VAT, upon the importation of goods.
- Application of simplified accounting methods and simplified reporting.
- Exemption from the payment of state duties for the issuance of work permits, invitations, and visas for foreign employees.

Table 28.2 shows tax preferences and benefits in the various SEZs.[13]

Summary

Russia provides a wide range of incentives for foreign and local investors. It is strongly recommendable to make use of incentive mechanisms for any investments and to get in contact with local authorities at an early stage in the planning process.

---

[13] Original source: Barski/Kast/Prokopyeva in Galander 'Russisches Wirtschaftsrecht' Berlin 2016, pp. 524–529 (Russian economical law), updated and adjusted by author.

Unfortunately, there is little alignment of incentives on federal and regional levels and the preconditions for applications may differ from the case by case. In addition, the SPIC provided on the federal level seems not to be very effective for small and medium businesses.

In any case, incentives and benefits, especially on the regional level may support your investment plans in Russia and help to decrease costs. Many regions provide very reliable and effective measures to decrease the administrative burden. Thus, we recommend comparing regional offers prior to any investment decision. For small- and medium-sized businesses, this means in particular tax reliefs as well and tax deferrals due to the Corona crisis.

Protection of Intellectual Property in Russia

Yulia Leonova and Christian Altmann

Intellectual property (IP), e.g., certain results of intellectual activities of companies and individuals, can enjoy legal protection in Russia. IP is protected by law in the Civil Code of the Russian Federation and covers areas such as copyright protection, trademark protection, or computer programs.

Any IP needs to be registered with *Rospatent*, the Federal Agency for Intellectual Property, Patents, and Trademarks in order to be protected.[1] In case of disputes with *Rospatent* the Russian Intellectual Property Court, established in 2013, would be responsible for the review. However, not every intellectual activity can be lawfully protected in Russia and it may not always be necessary for a company to register intellectual property rights.

The Russian Federation cooperates with the *World Intellectual Property Organization (WIPO)* since 1970 and joined the *World Trade Organization (WTO)* in 2012. Being integrated into these organizations means that the Russian Federation has confirmed their standards and aims to implement international legal rules. Accordingly, the RF has developed a legal framework that protects IPR owners and it has entered into a number of most important treaties and international agreements, which helped to meet most international standards of IPR.[2] However, certain national conditions and traditions have to be considered in order to avoid infringements of IP rights.

---

[1] Russian Federal Service for Intellectual Property (https://rupto.ru/en) retrieved, July 29th, 2020.

[2] Thomson Reuters Practical Law (https://uk.practicallaw.thomsonreuters.com) retrieved, July 29th, 2020.

Y. Leonova (✉)
Cliff Legal Service, Moscow, Russian Federation

C. Altmann
OOO German House, St. Petersburg, Russian Federation

© The Author(s), under exclusive license to Springer Nature Switzerland AG 2021
O. Medinskaya et al. (eds.), *Russia Business*,
https://doi.org/10.1007/978-3-030-64613-4_29

What Can Be Protected?

IP rights reach from patentable inventions, industrial design, and utility models to certain means of individualization such as copyrights, company names, trademarks, and commercial names. All of them can enjoy legal protection, although the duration of protection may differ.[3]

Copyright Law in Russia

Literature, works of art or scientific work can enjoy copyright protection in Russia for a period up to 70 years after the author's death. The intention is to establish high and far-reaching standards as public and even unreleased work is protected. The law covers oral creations, interviews, speeches, or modern poetry slam among other creative art. The Russian Copyright Law offers moral and economic rights to its owner. This can include recognition as author and the right to decide whether the work or parts of the work should be disclosed to the public. Adjusted according to the Berne Convention and copyright law formally meets international standards.

Patent Law in Russia

Civil Code (Part IV) of the RF that protects the use of utility models and industrial property governs patent protection in Russia. The Russian Federation is a signatory member of the Patent Cooperation Treaty. Russia has made it clear that it is committed to meet international legal standards. Accordingly, the *WIPO (World Intellectual Property Organization)* opened an office in Moscow in 2014. Foreign companies can seek patent protection and patents can get legal protection up to 20 years.

Trademark Law

Russia is a signatory member of the Madrid Agreement on International Registration of Trade Marks. Thus, the Russian Federation offers legal protection on trademarks and service marks for companies and other organizations. Legal protection requires the registration of a trademark or a service mark in the RF. The initial duration of a trademark protection is 10 years and can be theoretically renewed an unlimited number of times. It is important to note that legal protection will only be given to those trademarks that are actively used in the respective market.

---

[3]Lawyers Russia (https://www.lawyersrussia.com/intellectual-property-in-russia) retrieved, July 29th, 2020.

Protection of a Company's Intellectual Assets

Computer programs, databases, or business-related algorithms are gaining importance for many industries and therefore require special legal attention. In the RF, they are legally protected and belong to a special intellectual protection category: the protection of the company's intellectual assets. Protection is mainly granted through the Trademark Law. Other protected areas cover company assets such as software, database, or industrial design. Russian law protects even domain names and website content.

Protection of High-Tech IP Rights

Programming and software can also fall under the jurisdiction of the Intellectual Property Law in Russia. IT companies can protect the rights related to their software and programs. Beyond their software, they can protect certain kinds of knowledge (for example, new programming methods or process steps) which they developed. Like all other companies, IT firms can register their trademarks related to their creative work.

Should a Company Always Protect and Register Its IPR in Russia?

Even when a company owns a certain IPR it is difficult for the management to decide whether it is strategically prudent to legally protect its respective IPR. Most international companies have an IP-strategy that defines how to deal with certain inventions or trademarks under specific national conditions. Still most small and medium-sized companies deal with IPR on a market-to-market basis. Important considerations during the decision-making process are:

- Are the respective IPRs entitled to enjoy legal protection?
- How relevant is the market for the company and which legal costs occur by registering the IPR?
- What are the risks of not registering IPR?
- How easy would it be to execute a legal claim?

Some respective national chambers of commerce or law firms in Russia offer an initial free consultation.[4] Specialized law firms in all relevant Russian cities help to register IP. Fees start as low as 100 US Dollars but may increase to ten thousand US Dollar depending on the complexity of the respective case and rights to be protected.

---

[4] AHK Russland: https://russland.ahk.de/, retrieved, July 29th, 2020.

Most companies register their trademark at least in the respective market. Roughly, 180.000 trademarks are registered every year in Russia. Here are some of the most important rules to remember when registering a trademark:

- One should take care to assure their mark is not in conflict with prior rights of other companies.
- One should be concerned with making their mark distinctive (fanciful, arbitrary, or suggestive) in order to be registered by *Rospatent*.
- One will need proof that their mark is strongly associated with specific goods or services as a result of extensive use prior to the filing date.
- One should take careful consideration of the mark's spelling in both Latin and Cyrillic letters and register for both spellings. If the mark has a specific meaning or connotation, the Russian translation thereof must be registered as well.

Please note that in Russia—as in other countries—some agencies are specialized in finding companies that did not properly register their trademark or patent. These "Patent Trolls" register a trademark before the regular owner and user of the mark was able to register its mark safely. A company will be able to reclaim its trademark. However, it would take time and money to reclaim a respective trademark. Going through the invalidity procedure at the patent office may cost up to USD 10,000. Infringement proceedings cause expenses between USD 20,000 and USD 30,000 on average. Complicated cases may lead to even higher costs.[5]

Obtaining Protection and Enforcement

The Russian law offers various mechanisms to enforce intellectual property rights, e.g., through administrative, civil, or criminal enforcement. The answer to the question "Which way is the best way to defend my rights?" is not that simple because it depends on the type of infringement and the damage it may cause.

The key institution in intellectual property regulation in Russia is *Rostpatent*. It is an agency under the Ministry of economic development where property rights and license agreements can be registered. In case of disputes over these rights, the Russian Intellectual Property Court will preside. The creation of the IP Court in 2013 remains the only specialist civil court in Russia. This innovation has provided with the intention to create a sound legal basis for judgments in this area of law. The Intellectual Property Court, as part of the Russian commercial court system, reviews cases as a court of the first instance. It has the right to review legal acts of *Rospatent* such as the issuance of protective legal titles given by the agency. As a court of the first instance, the court hears all kind of disputes and questions of intellectual property rights and intellectual property rights. As a court of the third instance (i.e., a court of second appeal or cassation), it hears cases concerning the

---

[5]http://www.gorodissky.com, retrieved, July 29th, 2020.

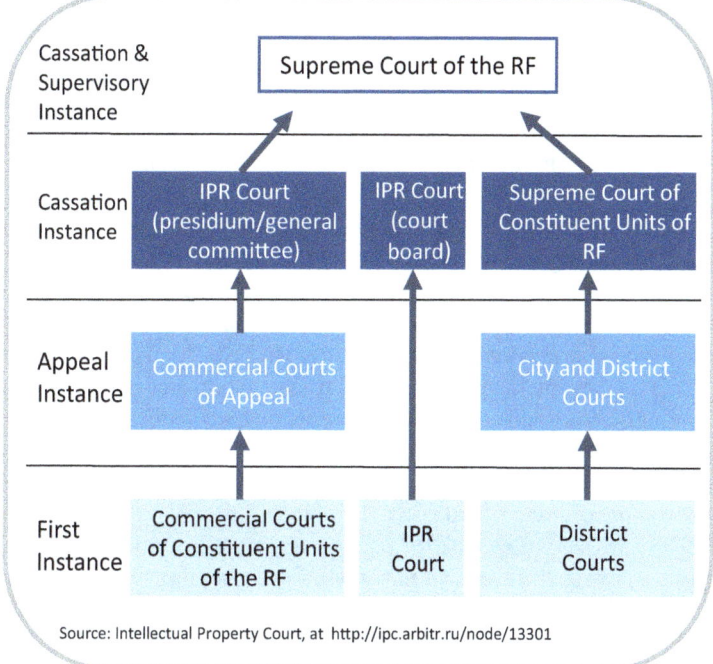

Fig. 29.1 Courts having exclusive authority to hear IP disputes or a particular kind of IP dispute

infringement of intellectual property rights between legal entities and individual entrepreneurs. The cassation rulings of the IP Court can be further appealed to the Supreme Court of Russia. Other rulings are appealed to the presidium of the same Intellectual Property Court. The growing number of crucial rulings since 2013 indicates the need and importance of the Intellectual Property Court and the development in Russian intellectual property practice (Bankovskiy and Danshina 2020) (Fig. 29.1)

Not every dispute leads to a court case, as there are alternative solutions. If both parties agree, a mediation process might be helpful in finding alternative solutions and avoiding higher costs.

Some international companies feel more comfortable avoiding the Russian court system and agree on international arbitration courts in Stockholm or Helsinki. A reason for this could be that all relevant information remains confidential in said courts.

Outlook and Challenges

The protection of intellectual property is important because innovations and creative activities are the source of socio-economic progress. In recent years, the protection and enforcement of IPR have notably improved since the country joined world organizations. Russian law meets today international standards. Accordingly, violators of IPR may face administrative and criminal charges (Bankovskiy and Entyakova 2020). This development demonstrates the rising importance of intellectual property in the legal system of the Russian Federation.

As the field of IP Protection is quite young in Russia, the respective legal framework is continuously amended and continues to evolve. With the establishment of the *Eurasian Economic Union*, the Russian Federation even tried to transfer its standards on an international level. However, compared to other developed nations the number of annual registered patents or trademarks is comparably low. Given the short history of IPR in Russia, these figures do not really come as a surprise. It is alarming though, that the registrations of patents in Russia have not grown substantially in the past decade. The *World Economic Forum* focuses in its *Global Competitiveness Report 2019* on an emerging set of drivers of productivity and long-term growth and evaluates the capability of a country to produce innovative results. Out of 141 countries, Russia´s ranking for Innovation capability is 32, certain subcategories such as number of trademark registration (Ranking 77) or patent application (Ranking 48) are even lower.[6] Entrepreneurs and creators often claim that an ineffective legal framework and varying interpretation of legal norms make it difficult for them to register and protect their IPR in Russia. For the future, it is crucial that the administration develops competent specialists in the responsible organization to increase the trust of companies, entrepreneurs, and creators in the system.

References

Bankovskiy, A. & Danshina, K.. *The intellectual property review* (9th Edn). https://thelawreviews.co.uk/edition/the-intellectual-property-review-edition-9/1226908/russia, retrieved on July 29th, 2020.

Bankovskiy, A. & Entyakova, A. *CMS Russia, in The intellectual property review*, at https://thelawreviews.co.uk/edition/1001177/the-intellectual-property-review-edition-7, retrieved on July 24th, 2020.

---

[6]http://www3.weforum.org/docs/WEF_TheGlobalCompetitivenessReport2019.pdf

Etiquette: Do's and Don'ts

30

Olga Medinskaya and Henk R. Randau

It is a challenge to describe Russian business etiquette as it is rapidly developing and continues to be influenced by traditional, Soviet and Western practices. A major factor that influences business etiquette is the location. Business partners in rural areas tend to be more traditional than those who reside in the metropolitan environments of Moscow or St. Petersburg. Etiquette also differs depending on whom one deals with. The Russian business mentality can be very diverse and ranges from Western-influenced "new-style entrepreneur" to "old-school soviet bureaucrat."

In general, the younger generation of Russian entrepreneurs is comparably easier to deal with because their business practice reflects Westerner practices, or at least reflect some level of acquaintance with these practices. A much larger challenge is conducting business with those who have strong ties to the government or the "*old-guard*," military officers, chiefs of police, or former government officials from the Soviet Era. Having achieved a high level of competence in administrative roles, these businesspersons have developed the flexibility necessary to conform to new standards and lead their firms to success. However, trust and familiarity still play a crucial role for them. Thus, conducting business with them takes time and patience since things can only be moved forward when mutual trust is established.

Another group are representatives of the *intelligentsia*. Typically, these are graduates of the country's leading institutions of higher education who have taken up business either due to the desire for economic stability, or simply because it is their passion. For foreigners, contact with this group is noticeably more straightforward than dealings with the old guard. The Russian intellectual is fairly

---

O. Medinskaya (✉)
Cultural Connectors, Mannheim, Germany
e-mail: info@cultural-connectors.com

H. R. Randau
Weinheim, Germany
e-mail: henk.randau@whu.edu

cosmopolitan in his views, well educated, speaks foreign languages, and is likely familiar with the perspectives of the western world.

Then there are the businesspersons whom Russians refer to as *New Russians*. These persons are seen as keen on clinching deals to make quick "easy" money and then spending it just as quickly and easily. Their extravagant personages, with the tendency to show off wealth, have heavily influenced how the West pictures Russian businesspersons in general. It is certainly worthwhile to invest time in learning about these different groups and to understand where their wealth comes from and their background before entering any business relationship (Pavlovskaya 2011).

Regardless of whom one deals with, being neutral and polite until achieving more familiarity with the business partner is usually the best approach. One should also be prepared for the highly intertwined nature of professional and social/private life in Russian society. Russians give out invitations to private social gatherings to their business colleagues quite frequently. Declining such invitations are viewed as being impolite and passing up the opportunity to become more acquainted with Russian culture.

Typically, Russians meet their business partners by inviting them out to a casual, social space. It is normal to go to a restaurant for lunch or dinner and to eat and drink in a relaxed atmosphere. Apart from business lunches and dinners, the Russians like organizing what they refer to as "cultural programs." Usually this includes outings to more traditional cultural outlets such as the theater or ballet. Invitations involving a trip to the countryside are also very common, especially in the summer. These are usually in the form of outdoor excursions or trips to *Dacha* (summer home).

Business Meetings and Banquets

Punctuality is highly valued in Russia because it signals reliability that fosters trust. However, too much emphasis on punctuality can be seen as obsessive and rude when it interferes with building personal relationships. If the delay is unavoidable, excuses like being stuck in traffic or being lost in the Russian metro system are acceptable. If one mentions the metro system as an excuse for being late, they must not forget to mention how beautiful the metro is. Russians are proud of their metro system and see it as a patriotic symbol in their culture. Delays should not extend 15 min.

The office dress code is formal as a rule and can be rather chic. Russian businesspersons predominately wear dark business suits. For women, business suits, dresses, skirts, or pants are acceptable. In general, Russians tend to show off their wealth and often add to their wardrobe expensive accessories such as luxury watches, jewelry, or expensive handbags.

Meeting and Greeting

It is customary to shake hands when greeting someone in Russia (Mary Murray Bosrock 2006). One should make eye contact, shake hands firmly, and always take

Table 30.1 Titles and honorifics

Respectful	Formal	First Name
Addressing one's business partner by their surname followed by the given and father's name is very respectful (but also distant). Used only in formal situations like at work or in an office and more likely to be used with older people.	Addressing a person as Mrs. or Mr. combined with their respective surname. Common in international companies	Russians often do also shorten the first name, a diminutive that connotes more familiarity. Typically, only close friends and children are addressed in this way.

off gloves during winter months. One should give out handshakes to every man in the room each time they meet a person, even if a negotiation continues for several days. Shaking hands with a woman is always at her discretion. For this reason, it is perfectly normal for men to exchange handshakes while passing over the female coworkers with just a verbal greeting. It is important to pay attention to body language and not be culturally ignorant.

Some may remember when, in Soviet times, high-ranking politicians were accustomed to the Slavic tradition of greeting another man with bear hugs and kisses. Today this is only reserved for good friends and family members after not seeing one another for a long time.[1]

Names can pose a challenge in Russia because sometimes foreigners mistake the father's name for the last name. The reason is that Russian names generally consist of three parts: the first or given name, a patronymic (father's) name and the surname, e.g., Olga Vladimirovna Medinskaya. Russian patronymics are formed by combining the father's given name with the appropriate suffix. The suffix means "son" or "daughter of." For men this is -ovich or -evich and -ovna or –evna for women. It is quite common that Russians greet and refer to one another using their first and middle names, which shows a sign of respect. In a business setting one should avoid addressing their business partners by the first name and do so only when one is invited to do so (Table 30.1)

During the Business Meeting

In general, it is recommended to show a respectful and formal attitude towards one's Russian business partners. Russians are happy when foreigners acknowledge their hospitality. Brief feedbacks when thanking the host for offering drinks or snacks are

---

[1]Famous Russian author Fyodor Dostoyevsky once called kissing "a habit of the Russian people when they become famous." Khrushchev was famous for using the socialist fraternal kiss as a greeting of peers and other socialist leaders. The custom was also common during the Brezhnev era but waned during 1980ies. Since then fraternal hug and kisses have more or less died out because neither Yeltsin nor Putin have rarely been photographed kissing anyone.

greatly appreciated. It shows Russians that one's interests exceed the usual polite chitchat.

As in any culture, body language is an important element. When sitting one should try not to sit with their legs apart or with their ankle on their knee as this reveals the dirty soles of their shoes. Also, one should not rest one's shoes on the seat in public (i.e., the Metro). Unwelcome behavior includes standing around with one's hands in their pockets or pointing at someone with their finger. While making and holding eye contact is seen as intimidating or flirtatious with strangers in public, it is important in a business setting. Therefore, one should try to maintain eye contact while having a conversation.

After the Business Meeting: Conversation and Rules of Hospitality

One would not insist on paying for their own meal or to split the bill. It is common in the Russian culture that whoever invites pays the entire bill. This means that if one is invited to a restaurant, all expenses involved will be taken care of for them. As the host, one will be expected to pay. One should keep in mind that it is customary to leave a tip in a restaurant (Regardless of whether service is included in the bill or not). Standard tips are 10–15% of the total price.

One will notice that their business partners will loosen up out of their serious business attitude in the "after hours." Russians then are very talkative and direct. One should be prepared to answer personal questions but should not reciprocate.

Russians will tell long stories and one should not hesitate to share stories of their own although is more important to be a good listener. Russians love intimate conversations: about themselves, their families, and the latest news. They see discussing personal matters as easing for the soul. Additionally, it is seen as beneficial to hear the hardships of others in order to empathize and strengthen social ties.

Talks about politics or international affairs are seen as not that interesting unless it pertains to the individual directly. The reasoning is simple: The origin of these problems is far beyond the control of the average citizen, the truth around political reality is almost completely subjective, and often one has too many personal problems to be concerned about what happens overseas.

Besides intimate conversations, Russians love to sing as it gives them feelings of unity and helps to alleviate the awkwardness that sometimes accompanies inebriated discussions.

Do's and Don'ts in a Nutshell

Do's

- Give out handshakes when greeting someone
- Keep eye contact while talking
- Appreciate hospitality

- Be patient
- Accept lunch and dinner invitations
- Involve yourself in conversations and show interest
- Bring a gift out of politeness
- Make sure to toast
- Always laugh at the jokes being made even if you do not find them amusing
- Show interest in the Russian language and culture

Don'ts

- Be late. Punctuality is important.
- Use first names
- Decline drinks without having an excuse
- Avoid business topics in the after hours.
- Avoid topics that are related to World War II, monarchy or conflicts, and complaints about Russia in general.

> **Tips, Opportunities, and Warnings**
> **Offers for Food**
> Refusal of food, whatever the reason given–being full, dieting, being unaccustomed to eating at that hour of day–is taken as a slight. The only exception made is for illness. Here one will always find understanding. However, they should be ready for a host of questions and advice, for there is nothing the Russians like better than to discuss medically related topics.

Drinking and Toasting

Drinking (usually shots of vodka or a glass of wine) and toasting are common acts while having a meal. The first toast is generally a thank you from the host to the guest (s). The second toast comes normally from the guest(s) to the host. After this, it can go on for several rounds with different dedications: for the women, (often, as a man, one will be expected to stand up). A toast may also be made to one's host and the meeting of the host and the guest, so one should be prepared and plan their own speech in advance to be ready. If it is a toast that is considered especially valuable, such as for "Friends or Friendship," one should make sure to finish their drink "bottoms up." It signals that they value their friends.

When someone is giving a toast, one should raise their glass and hold it aloft for the duration of the toast and then clink it against someone else's glass (The only time one should not touch glasses in Russia is if they are remembering the dead). Once they have touched glasses, one should not put theirs down until they have drunk from it, as to do otherwise is considered a bad sign. Usually one gulps down the whole shot. It is also acceptable to keep one's glass half-filled when they do not want another drink, as an empty glass will always be met with a refill.

In general, it is tradition to drink shots only after a toast. While eating, people only drink juice or mineral water. So one should make sure to always toast even though they just intend to sip on their drink. Please note also that men customarily pour the drinks for the women sitting beside them.

It is no secret that Russians are hard drinkers, especially when having vodka shots. One may circumvent this tradition if one wishes by stating that they have health concerns that do not permit them to drink.

Gifts and Other Rituals

Bringing gifts is always a nice touch and customary when being invited somewhere. As in many other cultures, what counts is the thought rather than the present. Thus, even a small gift will do. Individual and creative gifts from one's hometown are very welcomed. Vodka is not a good present for a foreigner to give to a Russian because it often is misunderstood and may be seen as an insult. Instead, good quality tea, teapots, original sweets, calendars or pictures, towels, and bottles of alcohol make good gifts and are always appreciated. When giving flowers, it is essential to give an uneven number of flowers because even numbers and yellow flowers are connected to funerals. One should not use the number "13" as it is seen as an unlucky number in the Russian culture. The color red is very popular in Russia because of its cultural and historical background. Red has been and continues to be a symbol of beauty, harmony, goodness, and truth (Лебедева 2011).

One should take care to remember that Russians tend to be very modest when receiving gifts. Therefore, one should not be surprised when the recipient argues about accepting their gift—it is considered an act of politeness and modesty.

Tips, Opportunities, and Warnings
Reciprocity

An immediate reply to the hospitality one has been shown is usually not expected of them. For their Russian partners, a foreigner is a visitor to their country, which means that it is their job is to receive and entertain them. It will be quite a different matter if, in the future, they should go to the country of a foreigner whom they previously hosted. Many Westerners fall into this trap: they simply do not make the same effort and reception as was organized for them when they visited Russia. Russians will expect to be received with the same hospitality they showed their guests. Another mistake is that Westerners tend not to stay in touch after their visit to Russia. It must be emphasized that it is important to maintain this relationship.

INSIGHT: Russian Eating Habits and Traditions of Russian Hospitality
Anna V. Pavlovskaya
Moscow State University, Moscow, Russia
Traditional Russian Cuisine

In general, food traditions are rooted in the deep past. Eating habits tend to change slowly over time as internationalization occurs. Often, dishes that are foreign in origin are altered from their original recipes to fit the tastes of the host country's people.

The Russian diet historically consisted of breads, porridge, fermented foods, vegetables (especially turnips and cabbages), meat, fowl, and mushrooms. Before refrigeration, in order to preserve food through the long winters, Russians used fermentation, often with a minimum amount of salt. This has developed a cultural preference for sourer (fermented) and insipid (cereals) dishes.

Many people in Russia eat a full breakfast (even hefty foods such as soup or salted fish with potatoes are the norm). The main meal is taken at lunchtime, and in the evening tea or a light supper is preferred.

Because of the tradition of hospitality and communality, feasts play an important role in Russian communities. Typically the first course is *zakuskas* (pre-meal snacks) A number of different salads are served as well as cheeses, cold cuts, herring, caviar, and other seafood delicacies, salted mushrooms, cucumbers, tomatoes and other salted and fresh vegetables, cooked potatoes, pies with savory fillings and much more.

After the *zakuskas,* people eat soup. Nowadays, soup is often left out from evening meals, but during the day, it is an integral part of the Russian palate and is considered a first course.

For the hot dish, the "second course," there are a number of things one could be offered: fried meat, chicken, or *pelmeni* (minced meat in pastry pillows). Vegetables are not considered to be a dish in themselves and are only served as a garnish. The cold climate and historic economic difficulties have conditioned people to prefer filling foods, giving them large reserves of energy. People who refuse to eat animal products are often looked upon in Russia as rich eccentrics.

Finally, the meal will conclude with tea. The Russians love tea no less than the English do. Coffee is generally drunk in the mornings. Tea is always accompanied by dessert: cakes, biscuits, sweets, jam, honey, and so on.

Buffets are still not very common in Russia, although some leading companies and organizations are introducing them into Russian life. However, the Russians' favorite way of gathering, including for business purposes, is still to sit down in the traditional way and eat food together where one can relax. It is usual to remain at the table throughout the whole meal. Unless there is space to dance, which is the only good reason for leaving the table. The

(continued)

guests will be expected to sit for a number of hours without moving from their places. The whole time, they eat, drink, converse, and pronounce toasts.

International influence on Russian Cuisine

Despite the lifestyle differences of social classes within Russian society, both on a national and regional level, the eating habits of the country have remained largely uniform throughout history.

Following the Monarchy's efforts to westernize Russia, eighteenth century Russian aristocracy was fascinated by Western European culture, influencing their eating habits. Russian versions of French, English, Italian dishes filled the tables of the aristocracy. Dining rituals and etiquette changed as well to be modeled off the Western style. In Soviet times, a state policy of introducing a more varied diet for citizens to promote public health ensured that these dishes were no longer just a privilege of the rich but could be enjoyed by everyone. In the early nineteenth century, Champagne was introduced to Russia and has since then has become the national drink for special occasions. Especially since Soviet times, when it began to be produced by Russian wineries to localize production.

At the end of twenty-first century, international cuisine saw a rise of popularity in Russia. This is especially true with Italian and Japanese cuisine. Where previously, restaurants of this kind were only found in cities like Moscow or St. Petersburg, they are becoming increasingly more popular.

Russian Tea Culture

The most important function of tea drinking is its social factor. The process of tea drinking with colleagues at work helps to relax, create a positive atmosphere, and allows coworkers to deepen their relationship allowing more effective teamwork. There are a number of traditions linked with tea drinking in Russia that are different from elsewhere in the world. Tea is drunk with various different accompaniments such as rolls, *barankas* (a dry, ring-shaped roll) or *pryaniks* (spice cakes), which are specially produced to be taken with tea. Honey and jam are also served with tea, and they are eaten from little dishes using a small spoon, usually without spreading them on bread.

Feasts

The tradition of Russian feasts is rooted in pagan rites. A feast originally served to appease the gods and nature and at the same time, strengthen the social ties. The ritual meals marked the most important events of life: birth and death, war and peace, the end of summer and the beginning of winter, end of the harvest, or good hunting. Russians kept many of these oldest cultural elements through hundreds of years of Christianity and even through the atheist period of the USSR. Normally foreigners are very surprised by the large feasts held after funerals, which come with traditional dishes and large

(continued)

amount of alcohol. This old tradition helps the bereaved to forget their grief by organizing a feast and preparing food. After, the drinking serves to lighten the soul and encourage more conversation with others. This tradition also encourages the strengthening of the ties between family and friends. Lack of attendance at such an event from a close family member or friend will be viewed as highly unusual. Therefore, the feast in Russia is not just a shared meal, but also a special ritual, where the main role is to foster communication. In this manner, the feast is the easiest way for friends, relatives, or business partners to overcome their differences and bond.

The feasts incorporate the historic Russian tradition of hospitality. For Russians, to entertain someone well means first and foremost to feed them well. Even in the difficult times of the twentieth century, hospitality persisted in Russian life with the host trying their best to make the table so covered with food that even after everybody has eaten their fill, there is still food remaining. Despite the trend in recent times towards a healthier lifestyle, a feast table that is not full with food and snacks would be seen as cheap and disrespectful to the guests.

Suggestion for Further Reading

Anna Pavlovskaya: CultureShock! Russia. A survival guide to customs and Etiquette, Marshal Cavendish, 2011

Mary Murray Bosrock: European Business Customs & Manners: A Country-by-Country Guide to European Customs and Manners, Meadowbrook, 2006.

References

Лебедева, Г. Н. (2011). *Символика цвета в русской традиционной культуре.* Царскосельские чтения, p. 142.

Mary Murray Bosrock. (2006). *European business customs and manners: A country-by-country guide to European customs and manners.* Mary Murray Bosrock.

Pavlovskaya, A. (2011) *CultureShock! Russia. A survival guide to customs and Etiquette* (pp. 249–253). Marshal Cavendish.

Education: Quality and Quantity

Olga Medinskaya and Henk R. Randau

Understanding the education system is of great importance for any manager as it determines recruitment strategies. The quality of institutions in education is also an important economic pillar and has a strong bearing on a country's level of productivity, which in turn determines the nation's competitiveness and growth in the end (Schwab 2019).

Overall, Russia has a talented and well-educated population, which certainly represents a competitive strength. The nation ranks comparably well in *OECD reports* on education. A main driver has been the fact that higher education became state sponsored in Soviet times and has been highly valued in society for many generations. The implementation of a highly centralized system in the Soviet Union helped to pull the country's literacy level up close to 100%[1] and the share of working-age adults having attended tertiary education is also high with more than 60%.[2]

Yet there remain many challenges. One being that many schools lack good school supplies since the system has been essentially remained under-funded since the collapse of the Soviet Union. Another reason would be that the school curriculum has left the system struggling to prepare children for the modern world as it lacks courses that give IT knowledge or literacy in multiple languages. Tertiary education needs to improve as well. Even though Russia ranks as high as fourth in the world in

---

[1] World Bank (https://www.worldbank.org) retrieved on October 23rd, 2020.
[2] OECD: Education at a Glance, www.oecd.org/education/education-at-a-glance 2020, retrieved on October 21st, 2010.

O. Medinskaya (✉)
Cultural Connectors, Mannheim, Germany
e-mail: info@cultural-connectors.com

H. R. Randau
Weinheim, Germany
e-mail: henk.randau@whu.edu

terms of formal education attainment, it comes only 42nd in terms of applied skills.[3] The poor quality of practical application in tertiary education is emphasized by the fact that the country's best university (Lomonosov Moscow State University) is only ranked 174th in the *2021 World University Rankings*.[4] In addition, tertiary education also lags behind other countries in regards to the diversity of foreign exchange students. Russia is ranked eighth in number of total foreign students with more than 250,000 inbound students, with around 80% of them coming from former Soviet republics (mostly from Kazakhstan, Ukraine, Uzbekistan, Turkmenistan, and Belarus).[5]

Taking all of these challenges into account, the question arises, where does Russia's educational future lie? Education has become an ideological battleground with traditionalists who favor teacher-centric direct instruction versus progressives who favor student-centered experimental instruction. It remains uncertain which path Russia will take in the future.

> **Tips, Opportunities, and Warnings**
> Contradictory views on historical events in Russia and in the West
>
> The view on history presented in Soviet and Modern Russia history books (e.g., World War II) and accordingly kept in the mind of people may dramatically differ from the viewpoints of the western counterparts. It is better to avoid being involved in discussion.

The Structure of the Education System

All students have the right to attend public educational institutions free of charge as guaranteed by the Russian constitution. All primary and secondary education falls under this category yet an advantage is given to those students who can afford additional private after-school assistance that is typically offered by the school. However, regarding higher education, many students are expected to pay themselves should they choose to pursue it. The state allocates fully funded slots in universities for certain programs but the quotas and availability for these programs varies depending on the program. Those whose performance is insufficient to earn them a slot are burdened with the full cost of tuition.

The Russian school system is generally structured in a similar manner to European countries. Education begins at the age of three when the children enter

---

[3] Ranked were 130 countries. World Economic Forum. The Global Human Capital Report 2017, p. 157.
[4] The Times Higher Education: World University Rankings 2021, at https://www.timeshighereducation.com retrieved on October 25th, 2020.
[5] UNESCO: Global Flow of Tertiary-Level Students, at http://uis.unesco.org/en/uis-student-flow retrieved on October 25th, 2020.

preschool. Formal education begins at the age of 6 or 7 depending on the development of each individual child. As the Federal Law[6] stipulates, each child must have a minimum of 11 years of formal education[7] (Fig. 31.1)

Since the Soviet era, a well-developed system has existed which offers both general schools and specialty schools. The specialty schools will typically have a deeper focus on a particular subject (e.g., mathematic, physic, arts, foreign languages, sport, etc.) Responding to demand for good quality education because of chronic public underfinancing, new types of paid high schools began to emerge in the 1990s. These are called gymnasiums or lyceums, with the latter typically being attached to certain universities which use their staff and infrastructure to offer secondary education at a cost.[8]

> **Tips, Opportunities, and Warnings**
> Grading in schools
>
> The schools in Russia have a five-point grading scale with 5 as the highest score.

Compulsory education for all students in Russia ends with a successful completion of the unified state exam, which serves as the main form of entrance qualification to universities. For postsecondary education options, Russia has institutions called "colleges" (*kolledg*), "technicums" (*tekhnikum*), or "specialized secondary schools" (*srednee spetsial'noe uchebnoe zavedenie*). They provide the rough equivalent of vocational certificates that can be obtained in American junior colleges. In the realm of higher education, Russia has universities, institutes, or academies (in Russian referred to as *VUZ*)[9] that offer traditional degrees such as bachelors (Russian: *Bakalavr*), masters (Russian: *Magistr*), or the traditional professional diploma. Around 20% of all university graduates partake in "part-time" or "distance learning." A system that, in the Soviet Union era, had already garnered a bad image due to alleged poor quality of instruction and for lacking academic volume. Typically, these students spend only a few hours in class every couple of weeks in preparation for their exams. The "full-time" study is more expensive but is clearly held in higher regard by employers and therefore offers more advantages in terms of earnings and employment opportunities.

---

[6]Federal law of 21 July 2007 No. 194-FZ (http://ivo.garant.ru/#/document/12154779/paragraph/8922:0) retrieved on February 1st, 2020.

[7]Before 2007 the minimum have been only 9 years.

[8]https://www.miloserdie.ru/article/tri-puti-chastnoj-shkoly-v-rossii-podrazhanie-otdushina-roskosh/, retrieved on October 1st, 2020.

[9]Russian acronym VUZ stands for vyshee uchebnoe zavedenie, or higher educational establishments.

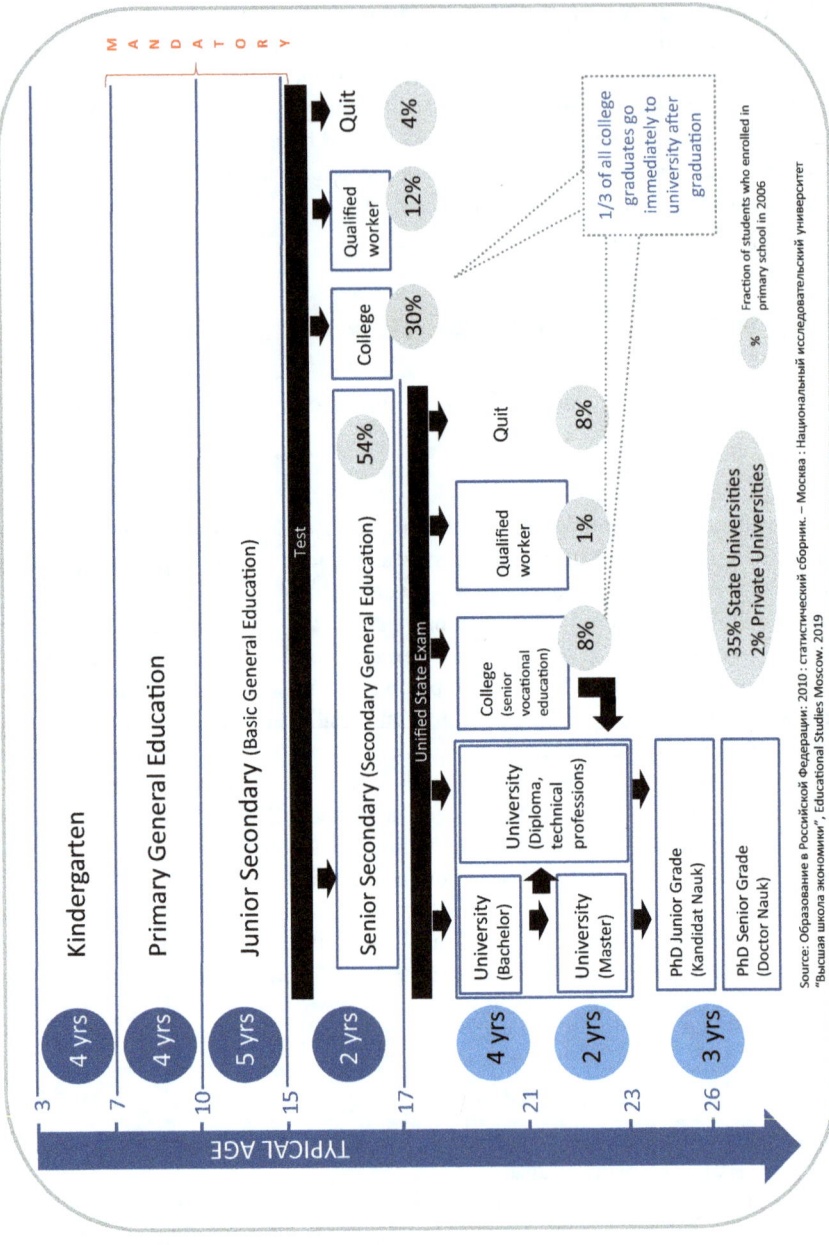

Fig. 31.1 Russian education system

Corruption at all levels of the system; even entrance into kindergarten, still poses a major challenge. This systemic problem makes it all the way to the upper echelons of Russian academia where some students buy fake diplomas and even PhDs.

> **Tips, Opportunities, and Warnings**
> Warning: Fake diplomas
>
> Some sources claim that up to 25 percent of diplomas in Russia are fake. The Higher Attestation Commission of the Ministry of Education and Science and the General Prosecutor's Office of the Russian Federation can check whether diplomas are real.

Reformation of Education and Public Financing

Curriculum and Unified Exam

The goal of education policy in the Soviet Union was to teach the masses how to read and write, and channel talented young people into science and technology. The focus was clearly towards meeting the needs of the state rather than fostering individual development. The end of the communist system has led to extensive curriculum revision in public schools with more attention to the arts, humanities, and social sciences. Even though schools have been allowed to develop their own curricula to a certain extent, the legacy left by the Soviet era has many educators being strongly in favor of standardized instruction and rote memorization rather than encouraging creative thinking or independent research (Dubova 2014).

Another big change was the introduction of a unified state exam in 2009. Traditionally each institution of higher education had its own entrance exam. The entrance to university was solely determined by performance on the exam and not the performance in school although some institutions of higher education kept the right to organize additional examinations and interviews in specialized disciplines. The main purpose of the exam was to standardize the requirements for applicants of tertiary education. The objective was also to make prestigious universities accessible to excellent students from remote areas of the country and to reduce corruption at the university level.

Education System and Financing

Compared to the curriculum, the system of higher education underwent and even stronger transformation. After the collapse of the Soviet Union, it rapidly became decentralized. Courses like "business management" were added while others such as "scientific communism" disappeared from the program. The government no longer determined the number of enrollees in each specialization and private institutions was permitted although enrollments in private universities never exceeded 20% and had fallen to 14% of the total university-level enrollments by 2017.[10] Many private universities do not meet the requirements of federal state educational standards and are not allowed to issue a state-recognized diploma.[11]

Limited financial resources are one of the main reasons for the slowed revitalization of educational reform and development. In former Soviet times, teachers were regarded as advocates of the Communist Party, fairly well paid, and held in high esteem. From the 1990s onward, teachers' salaries had failed to rise in proportion to inflation.[12] This has led to a corresponding loss of qualified and talented teachers. At that time, the main goal in public education was simply to sustain the system. Under Putin in the early 2000s, increases in education spending made it possible to raise teacher salaries, although huge regional disparities still existed between teachers in Moscow and those in rural areas. [13] However, as of today the total education budget still remains slim compared with OECD standards with half of the public spending in Germany and 1/3rd of those in the USA.[14]

Social Concerns Around Education

The high importance of education in Russia makes it a very hot topic connected with various social concerns mainly in regards to quality, access, and corruption.

Access to Education and Corruption

The education system faces problems with corruption. Often this problem becomes apparent as early as when children first enter state kindergarten. Those who make extra payments will quickly get a place for their child while others will need to wait

---

[10] Analytical Center for the Government of the Russian Federation: Development of Private General Education in Russia, 2018, at http://ac.gov.ru/files/publication/a/16496.pdf retrieved on February 1st, 2020.

[11] This is confirmed by the results of audits conducted by Rosobrnadzor in 2014: about 100 universities and branches were excluded from the register of licenses and admission at 66 universities was prohibited.

[12] Especially after the collapse of the ruble in 1998 and the resulting inflation. The average salary for teachers in 2000 was as low as 1240 Rub, only a half of the country's average salary at the time of 2.223 rub. According to Rosstat, at http://www.gks.ru/wps/wcm/connect/rosstat_main/rosstat/ru/statistics/wages/, retrieved on February 1st, 2020.

[13] Teachers' average monthly salaries are not equal throughout the country. In 2018, Moscow city had an average teachers' salary equal to 1440 USD, in North Caucasian federal District it was only 380 USD. In comparison, the average monthly salary of a teacher in the USA amounts to 4.900 USD. According to OECD, at: https://www.oecd-ilibrary.org/education/data/education-at-a-glance/educational-finance-datasets_c4e1b551-en, retrieved on October 1st, 2020.

[14] World Economic Forum. The Global Human Capital Report 2017.

which can take up to several years. Corruption continues by "voluntary" donations into the kindergarten fund after admission, followed by gifts for the staff on holidays, and many other creative and elusive measures intended to cloak the bribery. Some examples include added security fees, laundry detergent, toys, renovation fees, new equipment, and funding for festivals. Since many parents are afraid of unfair treatment towards their child should they not pay, they prefer to do so. To avoid this, parents may consider a private kindergarten or school instead which have substantially higher tuition fees but no additional bribery is needed.

> **Tips, Opportunities, and Warnings**
> **Opportunity: Place in Kindergarten**
> The free places in a state kindergarten are not enough for everyone and long waiting times for many years are not seldom. A letter from employer may help an employee's kid to receive a place more quickly. In the petition, you may give as many reasons as possible, which could affect the positive response in accepting the child.

Commercializing of Public Schools

General public education remains free of charge in Russia. To overcome underfinancing, most public schools have begun to provide additional educational services with out-of-pocket payment for those who want to ensure good academic performance from their child. This has raised concerns in society that higher education is less accessible for poor people. The feeling that the quality of school education is increasingly dependent on the wealth of the parents rather than the child's abilities (Поздняков 1999) is not backed by tangible data. Inequality of education between rich and poor in Russia remains relatively low by international standards. According to OECD data, the impact of social background on education is lower than in Germany, the USA, China, Japan, and the OECD average.[15]

Introduction of Unified State Exam and Rise of Corruption

The unified state exam is heavily criticized in society for its test form, as it is seen as unaccommodating for creativity and originality. The test makes it impossible to differentiate between the students who have deep knowledge and who have just exercised rote learning. Professors at universities have complained about the extremely low general knowledge and worldliness amongst modern high school

---

[15] OECD, PISA 2018 (http://www.oecd.org/pisa/), retrieved on October 1st, 2020.

graduates and the blame is cast on the one-sided training for the state exam.[16] Another point of critique for the exam is that it is not immune to corruption at the secondary education level.[17]

State-Sponsored Higher Education

Responding to the constitution requirement to secure free university education each university is obliged to allocate fully funded slots depending on the student's score on the unified state exam for certain programs (According to the federal standard there should be 800 "budget places" in universities for each 10,000 people aged from 17 to 30 years).[18] Students who do not earn a slot will have to take "commercial" slots, which means they are burdened with the full cost of tuition, which ranges depending on the university and the course from around 1.300 to 9.000 USD per year. Given the limited availability for the full-tuition programs, the competition for these budget places in public universities is tough.

Accordingly, there is much concern about the future of free higher education because the government believes in the necessary to switch to commercial financing for the higher education system and might continue to cut the higher education funding every year. Many parents of schoolchildren are afraid there may be no free higher education in the future at all.

The Cult of Higher Education: Quality and Quantity

The quality of the higher education system is heavily criticized, often compared with "old Soviet times": the universities are not interested in kicking out underperforming students because the higher the number of commercial students the higher the income generated for the university. This induces professors to not challenge students with proper evaluation of knowledge and examination.

Another challenge is that the number of young adults who attain tertiary education remains one of the highest in the world. Though this may seem like a good thing at first glance, the truth is that this figure is deceiving. The cult of higher education is thriving. Naturally, parents wish for a bright future and higher status in society for their children. They support their kids in getting a higher education degree although Russians are perfectly aware of the poor quality of education in many higher

---

[16]https://kuban.mk.ru/articles/2016/10/25/v-rossii-chislo-vuzov-i-studentov-v-nikh-katastroficheski-vysokoe.html, retrieved on October 1st, 2020.

[17]http://imrussia.org/media/pdf/Research/Vladimir_Rimsky__Corruption_of_the_Russian_Education_System.pdf retrieved on October 24th, 2020.

[18]The number of the budget places at a particular university is dependent on the kind of course and prestige of the university: the better the university –the more places. For example, economics and management receive funding from the state for only 22% of their costs, medicine around 50%, and 80% in the natural sciences.

31 Education: Quality and Quantity

67 % of working age adults attended **TERTIARY EDUCATION** (OECD Average: 36%)

Three decades of under-financing of public education: **3.1 % of GDP**

 5 %   6 %

Student performance test: **Pisa** scores are around the **average** for OECD countries

The total spent per student from primary to tertriary of approx. **USD 12,000** is about half of what is spent in OECD countries

Ranks **4th** in the world in terms of **formal education attainment,** but only **42nd** in terms of **applied skills** out of 130 countries in the global human capital report

Ranked 16 in the **overall ranking** out of 130 countries in the global human capital report

RANKED 8 for INBOUND foreign students with **80%** of 244,000 foreign students coming from former Soviet Union republics

Around **57,000** Russian students go **abroad** to study, mostly to Czech Republic, USA and UK

LITERACY 99.6%

Sources: World Economic Forum. The Global Human Capital Report 2017; OECD. PISA 2015 key findings for Russian Federation; OECD Education at a glance 2018, UNESCO, Ministry of Education and Science of the Russian Federation

Fig. 31.2 Facts on Russian education system in international comparison

education institutions, which means that such an education has potential to be meaningless and has no guarantee for employment (Fig. 31.2)

> **Tips, Opportunities, and Warnings**
> **Tips for Managers**
> • Since transformative thinking is not taught so much in Russia, one should include this in recruiting tests and be prepared to train new recruits accordingly.
> • The cheating and corruption in the system also make it necessary to question grades and determine skills through individual tests.
> • Brain drain leads to a war for talents and makes it advisable to have employer branding at universities to find talent and present students an alternative pathway before they are going abroad.
> • As in many other countries with demographic shifts, recruiting and retaining talent is getting increasingly competitive.

References

Dubova, M. V. (2014). Problems of primary education today. Primary education in Russia. *Russian Education & Society, 56*.

Поздняков, А. Н. (1999). *Реформирование системы общего образования России в середине 1980-1990-х годах*.

Schwab, K. (2019). *The Global Competitiveness Report 2019*, World Economic Forum.

Working Culture and Effective Management Style

32

Sergey Frank

In international business, there is always potential for miscommunication. This can be particularly true for westerners doing business in Russia. Culture affects both verbal and non-verbal communication. Therefore, improper handling of this can lead to the breaking down of communication and much time wasted.

There are certain Russian characteristics that should not be ignored nor underestimated. Otherwise, the entire project could be jeopardized. Keep in mind: the devil is in the details.

Inadequate gestures or improper non-verbal communication can turn initial conversations into an awkward first encounter that consequently may affect all future business. Different cultural rules of conduct or different concepts of status and hierarchy can easily offset discussions between participants. Even cosmopolitan managers who have lived in a globalized culture can easily get caught in a cultural trap, especially when the business they encounter in Russia does not resemble the business they are familiar with in the US or in Western Europe.

Western managers often think that Russia is not as different from the West as more exotic regions, such as South-East Asia, South America, or the Middle East. Accordingly, intercultural aspects are often underestimated. Something Westerners may fail to anticipate is the lack of a cosmopolitan business environment outside of the dense metropolitan center. Even within these centers, multicultural business culture is the exception more than the rule. Ignoring this reality is a mistake that can be avoided. Such pitfalls often occur when managing Russian employees or conducting negotiations.

The following pages will outline important considerations managers need to make when doing business, running a subsidiary or when managing employees in Russia.

S. Frank (✉)
Sergey Frank International, Leipzig, Germany
e-mail: sergey.frank@sergey-frank.com

© The Author(s), under exclusive license to Springer Nature Switzerland AG 2021
O. Medinskaya et al. (eds.), *Russia Business*,
https://doi.org/10.1007/978-3-030-64613-4_32

Hierarchy

One essential aspect of the Russian business culture is that it still retains a principle hierarchical structure: rooted in the socialist era, it has influenced all the former countries of the Eastern Bloc and is particularly present among the older generation. Although the younger generation (being educated in a more Western style) is less adherent to the principles of hierarchy, this cultural rule should not be underestimated.

Business with Russian associates, employees, or colleagues cannot be one-to-one as with business in Western Europe. This applies especially to managers from the older generation, who are used to the principles of hierarchy, in which all the power is entrusted to the Managing Director (often called the General Director).

As a piece of advice: decision-making authority is not usually delegated to lower hierarchical levels. In addition, leadership responsibilities are frequently defined only roughly. In Russia, one will find (in both politics and business) a pronounced belief in authority. The Managing Director usually prefers not to delegate his decision-making power to his employees; if he cannot attend a meeting, any major decision will simply be postponed.

Micro-Management

Adapting their working style to hierarchical structures means that Western managers in Russia need to understand that the possibilities to work in matrix-organized project teams or to cultivate autonomous employees are limited. Instead, so-called micro-management is needed. The reason is that despite their often profound academic and technical knowledge, Russian employees adhere closely to rules and orders given by their manager. Therefore, micro-management does not insinuate a lack of trust, but rather a small-scale management style to monitor the employees' activities. At the same time, keep in mind that Russian employees need objective feedback and positive comments to be motivated.

Only after a considerable period of continuous training on the job managers can delegate responsibilities to their employees. Before, it is essential to develop an atmosphere of mutual trust. Furthermore, an intensive professional development program (ideally at the company's Western headquarters) should accompany the process.

Focusing on People

Another characteristic behavior in Russia is a people-centric communication style rather than a process-centric one. Accordingly, projects or negotiations usually do not depend on the process itself (Western managers are used to defining milestones) but on individuals that the Russian partner is familiar with. If these "mediators" are not involved, projects or negotiations can be delayed or—in the worst case—come to a standstill. Therefore, it is highly advisable during extensive negotiations or projects to choose a negotiator that will not focus merely on the processes but the communication with the Russian partner as well.

Western companies often tend to integrate their Russian subsidiary into their organizational structure to underline the importance of their commitment. In this case, the Russian General Director is responsible for reporting to headquarters, where, decision-makers often have little time for day-to-day business communication and operations. This can cause frustration and internal struggles in the Russian subsidiary leading to demotivation and turnover amongst key personnel.

Trust Is Good, Control Is Better

This quote by Lenin is still valid today: Russian business partners have a fundamental need for security. Although the political situation has changed significantly since the 1990s, traditional behavioral patterns and paradigms are still present today. Despite the continuing process of deregulation in the former Soviet states, Russian people still consider regulated processes more trustworthy. Therefore, a Russian business partner may respond disapprovingly to a pragmatic proposal, which is not clearly defined in a directive. Under these conditions, a relationship based on trust is essential in order to work co-operatively.

Regarding technologies and science, local partners are often extremely versed; they not only have exceptional mathematic skills but also a strong knowledge of physics or chemistry. On the other hand, in Russia, some additional training is needed in commercial areas such as marketing and sales. The lack of expertise in these areas can have a negative effect on projects or negotiations—the need for explanation can still be surprisingly high. However, many local companies have undergone positive development during the last years and have adapted to the use of Western standards such as IFRS and/or US-GAAP in accounting in conjunction with local standards.

> **Tips, Opportunities, and Warnings**
> Importance of working experience in international companies
>
> As a piece of advice: when recruiting, managers should focus on candidates who have already gathered three to four years of Western Business Standard working experience in local companies or international subsidiaries. Such candidates are usually also experienced in interacting with international headquarters. Ideally, they even know how to operate within a matrix organization.

Communication

At first glance, business communication in Russia resembles its Western counterpart in many aspects: English is often the preferred language and the communication style is rather direct. Generally, Russians communicate indirectly meaning that topics are addressed in a more subtle way and need to be interpreted in context. In this regard, Russians tend to be less direct than US Americans or Germans. Upon closer examination though, one will notice that Russians are capable of being exceptionally frank when giving criticism or communicating dissatisfaction. Such feedback is given in Russia in a very direct way, especially by individuals to others who they view as their equals or subordinates in the workplace hierarchy. This frankness tends to shock Westerners as it is often felt to be rude by their standards. As with other traps, managers easily forget the cultural dimension of communication and should never underestimate the crucial impact it can have on managing people or on a project's success.

Cultural Sensitivity

Foreign managers should take an active interest in the local culture of the region they are assigned to, as well as Russian culture as a whole. Unfortunately, it happens far too often that ex-pat workers are neutral or indifferent in relation to relevant local events. Openness, interest, and cultural sensitivity ensure mutual understanding and increases trust between business partners.

Furthermore, many West European managers should consider carefully how they communicate their progressive labor standards (e.g., 35 working hours per week or 30 holidays per year) in their home countries or working contracts. In Russia, employees often have only a few holidays and no such benefits when starting a new job. Therefore, a cautious attitude seems to be appropriate when dealing with such topics.

Inappropriate People Management

Almost every international business project in Russia requires a more medium to long-term perspective compared to Western countries. Many foreign investors fall into the trap of losing their patience too quickly should their optimistic preconceptions fail to manifest fast enough. To avoid wasting time, considerable amounts of money, and management resources during a project in Russia, one needs to consider realistic time factors. In this context, it is important to apply an adequate time factor: according to this writer, it takes approximately three times the amount of time to accomplish something in Poland and four times in Russia as in the USA or in Germany.

> **Case Study**
>
> **The following example shows some more mistakes that can easily be made when doing business in Eastern Europe:**
> Peter is Head of Department for Central and Eastern Europe in a company working in the automotive supply industry. After graduating as an engineer, he started to work as Head of Projects and widened his responsibilities.
> Today Peter is traveling to Moscow to negotiate an enhanced cooperation contract with a local partner. On his way to the airport, he pays a visit to his office in the morning to give some further directives. His cooperation proposal in English still needs some modifications, which are to be implemented by Peter's assistant while Peter is on his way to Moscow.
> At the Russian subsidiary, Peter immediately starts to talk to the local employees. In the meantime, the corrected version of the document has been sent. In the evening, Peter and the local Managing Director go out for dinner to discuss some more details concerning the negotiations.
> The next day, Peter briefly prepares for the meeting. During the negotiations in English, it becomes clear that the Russian partner is interested in an offer for an enhanced cooperation. However, in comparison to a Korean competitor, the offer is too expensive, and at the same time, technical problems have occurred lately within the existing cooperation. The Russians ask Peter to visit the factory located 500 km from Moscow. Peter knows that he can solve the problem on-site due to his good personal relationship with the local management. However, he had planned to return to Germany that day to prepare for an important trip to Poland with his boss.
> **What should Peter do?**
> First, Peter's scheduling is rather tight. He should have planned the trip to last at least one additional day to be able to react in case of unforeseen events. Second, Peter should have involved his colleagues more efficiently. If employees are already on-site, closer cooperation is possible. Peter could have talked to the local Managing Director about the project in more detail to understand the current situation in Russia – surprising news such as cooperation problems or Korean competitors could have been evaluated before starting negotiations. Peter did not have to agree to travel to the Russian factory outside Moscow. The other party would have understood if he had arranged an appointment with technical experts later.

Missing Process Support

As described above, people in Russia are more person-oriented and rely on principles of trust. On the other hand, Western matrix structures allow people to be rather easily replaced and the focus is more on processes and operations.

> **Case Study**
> **The following example describes potential problems arising from these differences:**
> Tim is a negotiator for a German plant engineering company. Currently, he is negotiating with Russian representatives. The meeting goes quite well and Tim talks in his usual process-oriented manner about the next steps to substantiate the cooperation. The Russian party does not contradict the proposals, so Tim assumes that all necessary steps will be taken in time. However, two months later Tim learns that the Russian party has not implemented the plan as agreed upon. The partner explains the delay due to unforeseen events. Tim's doubts concerning the situation increases, particularly since the problems were only mentioned after enquiries from the German side. The Russian partners would probably not have mentioned the delays.
> What should one do in such a situation?
> "You have to take them along!" advises a successful Western European manager who has implemented a great number of successful projects in Russia. Which means: processes have to be discussed and agreed upon together. It does not help if only one party imposes the next steps–you always need to make sure your partners actively agree upon your proposals and are able to put everything into practice as planned–this can prevent any unpleasant surprises.
> In the above situation, it would have been helpful to install one or more project managers to monitor the process and all the steps on site.

High Turnover Rates

Western companies often complain about high turnover rates in Russia. One reason for this an opportunist mentality, which can still be found particularly among Managers and General Directors. In these positions, people tend to change jobs multiple times and in rapid succession to improve their financial situation as quickly as possible. However, there are a number of aspects that—if taken into account—can significantly reduce the turnover rate (Fig. 32.1)

If one keeps in mind all of the aspects described above, business in Russia will be successful. On a mid-term basis, one can establish a stable business in a market with high potential and skilled employees.

Fig. 32.1 Retaining employees in Russia

Negotiations: How to Deal in Russia

Henk R. Randau and Olga Medinskaya

- Business in Russia is very relationship based. Relationships and connections with friends, partners, and the extended family play a major role in everyday and business life. One should be willing to tear down barriers and be open to negotiate in informal settings e.g., a restaurant or the private Dacha of a business partner.
- It is thus advised to take enough time to build and deepen relationships. Business trips with short windows for meetings are certainly not the right foundation for a trustful relationship. Building trust is crucial for the success of any negotiation. Meetings in Restaurants, joint visits of cultural sites (museum, theater, and concert) even Sauna or Fishing are events to get to know one another better. Once the connection to the contact person in the target company is solid, these personal contacts need to be extended to the decision-makers in that company.
- Gifts should be appropriate within the scope of etiquette and legal framework.
- One should try to develop a sense of how their partner ticks. Is the partner a person of the new generation who displays openness and professionalism, like many sleek Western counterparts? Or are they a person still stuck in the Soviet Union times, used to maneuvering in black markets and a planned economy?
- Be aware that Russians tend to be very patient and usually do not make quick decisions. Negotiations and business meetings are long and seen as a win or lose situation. The longer you can stay focused and targeted the better you are perceived. A lack of patience or endurance or wanting to make compromises are viewed as showing weakness when doing business (Luthans and Doh 2015).

H. R. Randau (✉)
Weinheim, Germany
e-mail: hrandau@whu.edu; henk.randau@whu.edu

O. Medinskaya
Cultural Connectors, Mannheim, Germany

- Have the partner company checked by an independent agency or consultancy. Business and politics are often closely intervened and not all potential partners play with the rules and regulations.
- Seek the advice of well-known international advisers, consultants, and lawyers for all questions on local regulations and law because official data is often unreliable, does not reflect reality and law can change quickly.
- Be careful; because it is not completely ruled out that Russian companies work in several directions (parallel with several partners) in order to mitigate risks or follow completely different projects and tasks. There is always the possibility that they may commit to parallel tasks in order to "keep another iron in the fire" so to speak.
- Focus on negotiating and closing the frame of the contract first and do not get lost in the details. Nevertheless, do include/fix sanctions to secure your position. One should also be aware that oral agreements are not necessarily binding. Nothing is agreed or fixed until a contract has been signed.

Reference

Luthans, F., & Doh, J. (2015). *International management: culture, strategy, and behavior* (9th ed., pp. 163–165). New York, NY: McGraw Hill Education.

Index

A
Acquired immunodeficiency syndrome (AIDS), 189, 192
  safe sex education, 193
Advanced development zones (ADZ), 246
Agriculture, 28, 66, 128–130, 178, 216, 246, 247
  agricultural sector, 28, 66, 160
Alcohol consumption, 190, 191
Anti-Corruption Foundation (FBK), 210
Anti-Corruption Law, 183
Avtodor, 51

B
Baikal, 131
Bolsheviks, 121, 122
Brain drain, 148, 153
Branch, 215
Brazil, Russia, India, China (BRIC), 31, 34, 77
Business communication, 277, 278
Business incubators, 111

C
Central Bank of Russia (CBR), 56, 59, 72, 73, 78, 81, 84–86
Centralization, 43, 157–163
  hyper centralization, 157
Centrally planned economy, 25
Channel One, 207
Civil War, 25, 141
Cluster
  cluster initiative, 38
  Pilot Innovative Cluster (PIC) Program, 40
  Pilot Innovative Clusters, 42
Cold War, 122
Communism, 56, 122, 165
Constitutional Amendments, 22
Cooperative, 216
Copyright protection, 249, 250
Corona, 26, 32, 47, 60, 66, 102, 107, 200, 202
Corporate income tax (CIT), 224–227, 237
Covid-19, 200
Crimean crisis, 21, 61, 62, 86
Customs duties incentives, 244–245

D
Dacha, 256
Depopulation of rural areas, 163
  dying villages, 160
Doing Business Report, 55
Double tax treaties (DTT), 217, 223

E
Economic partnership, 215
Economic sanctions, 62–63, 100, 123
  corporate debt market, 79
  countersanctions, 59, 60, 63
  crisis in Russia, 26, 59
  economic downswing, 63
  economic effects, 64
  energy sector, 63, 100–102
  financial crisis in Russia, 86
  impact, 87, 88
  industrial policy, 60
  international policy, 61
  lift, 68
  sanction related export losses, 64
  trade with China, 68
  winners and losers, 66–67
Education, 55, 60, 136, 145, 147, 148, 168, 246, 255
  compulsory education, 267
  corruption, 270

Education (*cont.*)
  cult of higher education, 272–274
  education system, 265
  general public education, 271
  higher education system, 110
  investments in education, 30
  National Research Universities, 44
  social concerns around education, 270–272
  strength of the Russian educational system, 45
  structure of education system, 266–269
  tertiary education, 265, 272
  universities, 43, 44, 114
Employment, 154
  contract, 217
  illegal employment, 155
  migrant, 155, 157
Energy sector, 95, 96, 100
  collapse of the oil price, 88
  Countering America's Adversaries Through Sanctions Act, 67
  decline of global oil prices, 26
  dependent on the revenues from oil and gas exports, 64
  economic sanctions, 63, 102
  era of gas, 103
  GDP development and oil price, 27
  influence of oil and gas on the economy, 88
  natural gas and oil, 22
  natural gas production, 103
  natural gas resources, 127
  natural gas transportation pipelines, 97
  oil and gas export, 87, 88, 95
  oil and gas industry, 28, 78
  oil and gas kickbacks, 181
  oil and gas sectoral indices, 80
  oil price, 87, 88
  oil price impact, 88–89
  Russian stock market and the oil price, 77
  transportation of oil and gas, 52
  upward trend in oil prices, 26

F
Feasts, 262
Federal Obligatory Medical Insurance Fund (FOMIF), 197
Federation Council, 11, 14, 15, 17, 20, 132
Fund for the Assistance to Small Innovative Enterprises (FASIE), 112

G
Gazprom, 52, 68, 73, 100, 103, 209
Global Competitiveness Report, 47–49
Global financial crisis, 26, 58, 71

H
Hierarchy, 276
High speed rails (HSR), 50
History of the Ruble, 90

I
Illegal residents, 157
Immigration
  illegal migrants, 155
  inflows, 148
Individual entrepreneur, 216
Industrial policy, 37, 38, 41, 45, 59, 60
Infrastructure quality, 49
Intelligentsia, 255
International Women's Day, 174
Internet Initiatives Development Fund (IIDF), 111, 112, 115
Investment partnership, 215
Isolation policy, 147

J
Joint stock company, 215

K
Kievan Rus, 119

L
Labor productivity, 28, 58
Lenin, 25, 121, 165, 169
Life expectancy at birth (LEB), 136, 187
Limited liability company, 215

M
Marxist philosophy, 169
Minsk agreements, 100
Moscow aviation hubs (MAH's), 51
Moscow Exchange (MOEX), 77–81
MTS Start-up Hub, 111

N
National Association of Stock Market Participants, 78, 81
National Wealth Fund (RNWF), 52
Negotiations, 275–277
  relationship based, 283
New Russians, 256
New-style entrepreneur, 255, 283
New year celebration, 171
North Stream II, 67, 99

Index

O
Obesity, 192
Old-school soviet bureaucrat, 255, 283
Orthodox Church, 165, 167, 174, 194
   Christianity, 119
   Christmas, 174

P
Partnership, 215
Patent
   patent office, 252
   protection, 250
   Rospatent the Russian Intellectual Property Court, 249
   trolls, 252
   work permit, 155
Patronymic (father's) name, 257
Peasant farming, 216
Pelmeni, 261
People-centric communication style, 276
Perestroika, 71, 122, 183
Permanent establishment (PE), 224
Personal income tax (PIT), 224, 228–230
Peter the Great, 147, 158
   Peter I (the Great), 120
Premature mortality, 189
Press freedom, 208
Propaganda, 207, 210–211
Propiska, 154
Putin, v, 12, 13, 17, 19–21, 64, 89, 97, 123, 124, 167, 173, 183, 194, 257, 270

R
Regional disparities, 190, 270
   inequality in regional GDP, 29
Representative office, 215
Residence permit, 154
   permanent, 154
   temporary, 154
Retaining employees, 281
Retirement age, 136
Revolution of 1917, 158
Roskomnadzor, 207
Rospatent, 249, 252
Russian Cross, 134, 135
Russian-German Chamber of Commerce, 114
Russian-related risks, 222
Russian tax code, 223
Russian Venture Company (RVC), 111, 112, 115

S
Sexual minorities, 168
Skolkovo, 38–39, 112, 115, 247
Slavic languages, 145
Slavophiles, 168
Social security contributions, 228, 234
Soviet Union, v, 10, 25
   banking system, 71
   collapse, 136
   collapse of the Soviet Union, 56
   currency, 90
   diet, 262
   education, 265, 267
   education policy, 269
   end of the soviet era, 123–124
   infrastructure after collapse, 47, 49
   philosophy, 169
   religion, 165
   residence permit, 154
   soviet era, 121–122
   students exchanges, 148
   voluntary migration, 151
   world's leading exporter of wheat, 28
Special economic zones (SEZ), 233–243
Special investment contract (SPIC), 243
Stalin, 25, 47, 122, 123, 144, 183
State duma, 11, 13–16, 19
State enterprise, 216
State-owned
   banks, 72, 74
   companies, 59, 111
   enterprises, 13, 74
   holdings, 113
   media, 209
   Osobye Ekonomičeskie Zony (*OEZ*), 234
Subdivision, 215

T
Tax returns, 225
Tea culture, 260–262
Toasting, 259
Trade Marks, 250
Transfer pricing, 230
Transneft, 52
Troll army, 207
Trust, 255, 256, 276–279, 283

U
Unified state exam, 267, 269, 271, 272
Unique Number of Contract (UNC), 85
United Russia (UR), 11, 17

V
Value added tax (VAT), 224, 225, 228, 236, 244, 247
Victory Day, 173
Visa-free travel agreement, 148

W
Wealth disparities, 26, 31
Westernizers, 168
Wheat production, 130
Window to Europe, 120
Withholding tax (WHT), 227

Work permits, 155
World War I, 121
World War II, 25, 122, 173, 259

Y
Yakutia–Khabarovsk–Vladivostok pipeline, 68

Z
Zakuskas, 261

GPSR Compliance

The European Union's (EU) General Product Safety Regulation (GPSR) is a set of rules that requires consumer products to be safe and our obligations to ensure this.

If you have any concerns about our products, you can contact us on

ProductSafety@springernature.com

In case Publisher is established outside the EU, the EU authorized representative is:

Springer Nature Customer Service Center GmbH
Europaplatz 3
69115 Heidelberg, Germany

www.ingramcontent.com/pod-product-compliance
Lightning Source LLC
LaVergne TN
LVHW010337260326
834688LV00036B/755